Truth-Telling and Other Ecclesial Practices of Resistance

Truth-Telling and Other Ecclesial Practices of Resistance

Edited by
Christine Helmer

LEXINGTON BOOKS/FORTRESS ACADEMIC
Lanham • Boulder • New York • London

Published by Lexington Books/Fortress Academic
Lexington Books is an imprint of The Rowman & Littlefield Publishing Group, Inc.
4501 Forbes Boulevard, Suite 200, Lanham, Maryland 20706
www.rowman.com

6 Tinworth Street, London SE11 5AL, United Kingdom

Copyright © 2021 The Rowman & Littlefield Publishing Group, Inc.

All rights reserved. No part of this book may be reproduced in any form or by any electronic or mechanical means, including information storage and retrieval systems, without written permission from the publisher, except by a reviewer who may quote passages in a review.

British Library Cataloguing in Publication Information Available

Library of Congress Control Number: 2020951966
ISBN 9781978712096 (cloth)
ISBN 9781978712119 (pbk)
ISBN 9781978712102 (electronic)

Contents

Acknowledgments		vii
1	Ecclesial Practices of Resistance *Christine Helmer*	1
2	Taking Responsibility for Truth: Ecclesial Practices in an Age of Hypocrisy *Jan-Olav Henriksen*	11
3	Embodying Truth in Ecclesial Practices *Allen G. Jorgenson*	21
4	Telling the Truth about Doctrine: Justification and Justice *Christine Helmer*	29
5	Complicity and the Christological Path of Ecclesial Resistance: Summons to a New Catechesis for a Time of Despair *Paul R. Hinlicky*	47
6	Lutheran Ecclesiologies of Resistance: Starting with the Spirit *Cheryl M. Peterson*	63
7	Resisting Tyranny *and* Polarization: An Ecclesiology of Word and Sacrament from the Midwestern Heartland *Amy Carr*	75
8	Creation Piety and Spiritual Formation *Gordon J. Straw*	97

9	Remembering the Immigrant Experience: The Body of Christ as a Borderless Space to Embrace Our Shared Humanity in the Face of Rising Xenophobia *Man Hei Yip*	111
10	Practicing Jesus Christ in Public, Embodying Resistance *Craig L. Nessan*	127
11	*Seelsorge* for Those Who Resist *Timothy L. Seals*	143

Select Bibliography	163
Index of Biblical Passages	171
Index of Names	173
Index of Subjects	179
About the Editor and Contributors	191

Acknowledgments

I founded the Lutheran Scholars of Religion network in 2016 for the purpose of bringing together scholars working broadly in relation to Lutheran theological traditions. Our group is dedicated to addressing questions of theological, ethical, and political exigency. This volume emerges from the discussion that took place on the topic of "Ecclesiologies of Resistance" at the 2017 annual meeting of the American Academy of Religion held in Boston, Massachusetts. We were concerned with how theologians understood the church's mission in relation to contemporary social and political urgencies, namely immigration, racism, and sexism. Since then, these topics have become even more pressing, particularly in view of the international protests arising in the summer of 2020 against police brutality in Black, Brown, and Indigenous communities. My hope is that this volume's readers continue to explore the church's unique role in more clearly understanding the promise of divine presence in the body of Christ, and how theology can be intimately connected to ecclesial practices of resistance and reformation.

I thank Evelyn Soto Straw for kind permission to publish Gordon J. Straw's article "Creation Piety and Spiritual Formation" as chapter 8 in this volume. Gordon died on January 5, 2019, after a brief illness. He inspired many with his call for justice from his Native American heritage, his commitment to spiritual healing, and his intellectual leadership in seminary and church. My gratitude goes to the scholars who contributed essays to this volume, to my colleague Amy Carr, and to Neil Elliott, editor at Lexington Press/Fortress Academic, for including this volume in the press's offerings.

Chapter 1

Ecclesial Practices of Resistance

Christine Helmer

Our contemporary times demand new theologies, theological practices, and epistemologies.[1] Models of theology that aim to produce knowledge about the past and about normative doctrine in the past have their place in the theological repertoire. In fact, many theologians working in some relation to Martin Luther, the Lutheran tradition, and the churches shaped by Lutheranism, have specialized in methods of historical theology. The Lutheran tradition represents a robust intellectual heritage that has had profound implications for developments in the history of ideas. Yet the world in which we live today has shifted dramatically over the course of the intensifying polycrisis of pandemic, racial injustice, and economic inequality. If theologians are to provide a moral compass for living in an "upside-down" world, if they are to apply their learning to create new possibilities for thinking critically and constructively about the world today, then they must now act, write, and speak.

Lutheran theologians know, perhaps more than those in other Christian denominations, the danger of not speaking out when injustice carries the news of the day. When the Nazis came to power in Germany in the 1930s, only a few took responsibility to protest the authoritarian and anti-Semitic policies of the regime. While some Lutherans joined with the Reformed theologian Karl Barth to draft a theological statement to confess God's truth in resistance to Nazi terror, many others turned away to support the regime, assimilating theological claims to the political culture, becoming silent when Jews, political dissidents, queer people, communists, Roma, and the disabled were marched in full sight to trains destined for concentration camps. Contemporary Lutheran theologians who know this history and seek to prevent an analogous assimilation of their beliefs to unjust economic and political ideologies must articulate positions of moral decency and theological accountability. How adaptable the intellectual strengths of the Lutheran tradition can be to address contemporary urgent questions is the challenge of this volume. How contemporary theologians working in the broad Lutheran tradition may articulate claims that call out falsity and imagine theological, ethical, and political possibilities for being truly human in Christ's image is the task of this volume. This volume's aim is to promote ecclesiologies that speak truth, resist injustice, promote moral courage, and edify the world. Martin Luther spoke truth to power in the sixteenth century; these years of the early twenty-first century demand this and more.

The Lutheran global community of researchers is diverse. Theologians have different ideas about theology's tasks, methods, positions, and cultural attitudes. Some are committed to historical methods, others think that the theological task should include constructive aims. Some Lutherans are averse to connecting theology and ethics; others are aware that cultural values are inevitably expressed in theological reflection. Luther scholars too, like Lutheran theologians, represent a diversity of opinions on Luther's own contributions to the history of the west. Some see Luther in continuity with late medieval thought; others situate him as a visionary herald of modern thought.[2] Luther is either the "last Catholic" or the "first Protestant." Luther's use of philosophy is appreciated by some scholars, while others view it as mainly polemic. Luther's God is either divided between wrath and love, or conceptualized as a metaphysical unity, or contrasted with the God above God. Luther is sometimes viewed as an advocate for progressive politics, sometimes as an ally of conservatism. These debates in theology, intellectual history, and Luther studies are important, and have their own rationales and histories.

With this book, Lutheran theologians intend something quite different from the usual internecine controversies. The name of the group from which this volume has emerged signals this different direction. The group is called "Lutheran Scholars of Religion." Its aim is to inspire discussions between various constituencies in theology, ethics, culture, and the study of religion on how to do theology today in ways that are theologically, morally, socially, and epistemologically adequate to contemporary challenges. The decisive mandate of the group is to "do theology" with a distinctive focus on today's urgent questions. Different methods, some perhaps unusual, are invoked to suit the task; different articulations are dared; fields are approached that might not fit into the traditional ways of doing Lutheran theology. Yet the mandate of these times can be met by the theological rigor and creativity for which Lutheran theology has historically been known. Challenge can be inspiring, pressing demand met with joy for the task at hand.

This volume involves a critical dimension. Analysis of the current context is part of the theologian's task. Jesus' charge to his disciples to know the signs of the times (Matt 16:3) has its theological corollaries in Luther's sixteenth century critiques of ecclesial, political, and economic abuses and in Friedrich Schleiermacher's critical questioning of emerging historical methods and political encroachments into ecclesiastical affairs. Theology includes critique, and fitting critique presupposes meaningful and accurate analysis. In this volume, critical analysis is articulated from a theological perspective, yet it also involves ethnographic, social, ethical, and political aspects in order better to determine the worldly powers to which theologians are called to speak. Different perspectives are included in theological analysis in order to call reality what it is and to determine the questions and issues emerging from perceptions of this reality.

Hope is also a theme in this volume. The gospel of Christ is the truth of God's hope for the world. Christ's incarnation in this world is fundamentally and decisively redemptive. Christ heals its tragedies, forgives sins, restructures evil, and reconciles the world to God. In the midst of plague and death, Christ's presence recreates marred brokenness into objects of beauty. Theologians of the cross, according to Luther's description in his Heidelberg Disputation from 1518, acknowledge the significance of Christ's cross for knowledge of truth, God, and reality, and are courageous in formulating this knowledge for today. This way of knowing calls the realities of climate catastrophe, fascism, racism, and sexism by their names. The hopelessness of escape or extrication from these man-made realities is also named. Yet the theologians of the cross see in Christ the hope for the world. It is this reality that inspires resistance and truth-telling, even if these practices do not yield intended results.

The volume's theological terminology of "ecclesial practices" is owed to recent Scandinavian approaches to constructive Lutheran theologies.[3] This development has its theological foundation in acknowledging that creation is God's good gift. Doctrines, such as hamartiology and justification, are articulated on the basis of recognizing that grace is just as significant, if not more so, for theological construction, as sin and evil; that the gospel is just as important, if not exceedingly more so, for theological analysis as critique. The theological aim of this volume is to remind Christians of the fundamental gift of created existence. Hope and love are already inscribed into creation. From this perspective, critical analysis of the contemporary world becomes sharper and more urgent; the theological articulation of grace becomes clearer and more pressing.

The volume calls for resistance to dehumanizing structures on the grounds of Lutheran theologies invested with commitments to created goodness. Luther's own claims about God's creation are generative for the working out of these commitments. Yet their generativity in view of the questions of what it means to be human in community has been distinctly appreciated by the Scandinavian Lutheran theological tradition. This tradition of thinking, shaped by Scandinavian cultural and political institutions, offers generative possibilities for constructing theologies in relation to culture and politics in ways that perhaps have not been taken as seriously by other Lutheran traditions. With this approach in view, we note the significance of constructing doctrine as particularly motivated by Christological and anthropological topics. This perspective offers possibilities of seeing theology as engaged practices, thereby dissolving the usual binary between theoretical and practical theology. Theological articulation obliges theologians to commit themselves to distinctive practices of truth-telling, resistance, activism, and spirituality. Furthermore, theological activity is necessarily communal. Resistance and vision-making require that theologians come together in distinctive communities. Through dialogue and activism, writing and speaking, calling people and structures to accountability, and offering new patterns for thinking and being, theologians together—even Lutheran theologians accustomed to working in isolation from each other!—can create a community. "Here we stand" is a communal appropriation of Luther's reformation posture. We stand together before the divine judge who condemns all that is nihilistic and the divine Redeemer who sees abundant life as integral to the divine design. This volume is a collection of essays. The communal form attests to the commitment regarding theology as a project of imaginative resistance and vision-making. Ecclesiologies of resistance begin with us.

The approach of this volume represents a shift in Lutheran theologies, primarily as they have emerged from the German context over the past half century. This theological tradition, fixed on a law/gospel binary, has proved powerful in terms of its capacity for identifying the truth of reality. "Law" is this tradition's theological tool for critical analysis of experience in the world. The term identifies the destructive forces that inhibit and prevent Christian freedom; it points out the harmful and evil forces that dehumanize persons. The critical impulse of this aspect of the Lutheran tradition is clear: it pins down with words what the destructive forces are. Luther's terminology about sin, death, hell, and devil capture the devastating effects and results of humans under "law," both their responsibility and their incapacity for escape. As such, the iconoclasm represented by this critical discourse is useful today, not only in theology, but also for its social, political, economic, and cultural purchase.

Gospel, on the other hand, is that which law prepares for but cannot attain. Law judges but cannot forgive. The gospel is God's work without human intervention or sacrifice. God heals what sin has sickened, forgives what law condemns, and restores what evil has destroyed. Experience of gospel is distinguished from experience of the world. Its source is divine, hence it enters into worldly experience as a possibility not available within the world. Yet its mediation into the world is through tangible realities, like words, materials, gestures, and sensations. Gospel brings the way things ought to be into the present, yet in such a way that the present is referred to a divine cause.

The law/gospel binary has been represented as the center of Luther's reformation thought in its German inheritances. Yet it has its limitations, as Finnish and Scandinavian scholars have pointed out. The law/gospel model tends toward a metaphysical dualism between the God of wrath and the God of love that violates the axiom of the unity of the divine essence. It focuses with one-sided emphasis on the divine agency in salvation that neglects the complexities of human existence. It also precludes any connection with sanctification on the polemical grounds of "works righteousness," without considering that Luther himself advocated such a connection, particularly in his later work against the antinomians. As the proponents of Scandinavian creation theology insist, theology's starting point must be created goodness. Only when this point is secured can sin and law be invoked as creation's current condition. A theological treatment of a sinful world that presupposes the divine good will advances the claim that it is precisely this created world that is to be saved. God's aim is to create the new from the old, from alpha to its glorious conclusion.

This volume critically addresses the law/gospel binary and its theological inheritances. The question of resistance is posed to this binary that has contributed to dehumanizing mechanisms in Lutheran theologies. In a recent article, Lutheran theologian Marit Trelstad points out the similarities between the homiletical discourse of law and the abusive rhetoric against women by their male abusers.[4] Phrases about law that "humiliates," that brings a person "to her knees," are also actions inflicted by an abuser onto his domestic partner. For survivors these phrases re-inflict trauma.

A capacious theological framework, one founded on creation and grace, can help to overcome Lutheran ways of thinking that have become frustrated by responsibilities to the past and constrained by their normative pressures. The gospel is free to address contemporary concerns in creative ways. The good news resists the cynicism of the whole that law encompasses. Life-affirming words must be spoken into the abyss. This volume welcomes theologians to remain committed to traditional themes. It also asks that they take up new responsibility for addressing the present. The gospel's transformation of today's indecency and chaos is urgently needed.

Significant for a theological account of resistance is central to becoming human in community. Ecclesiologies are sites in which these commitments are embodied, ritualized, practiced, and imagined. Humans become humane in life-affirming relationships with others. The creation of society is fundamental to human existence; the church is the human society founded on

Christ. This foundation is the unique intersubjective constitution of the new person in Christ. One is knit together with others, as persons develop in being made more cruciform. The theological question as to what it means to be a church is the constructive question endeavored in this volume. Renewing Lutheran thinking about the church, specifically its practices of communal truth-telling, is an important aim here. The exploration of ecclesiologies is inspired by interdisciplinary contributions from psychology, sociology, anthropology, and religious studies. What is envisioned is a doctrine that in the Lutheran tradition has tended to be neglected in favor of what is considered to be the primary doctrine of justification. Yet justification is integrally bound together with community. Lutheranism is essentially based on the materiality of relationships that facilitate the gospel's communication. The theological task of reflecting on what it means to be human in community is the constructive challenge of ecclesiology.

Ritual is important to this constructive understanding. A classic Lutheran understanding of church regards baptism as central. For Luther, baptism is the ritual that brings the individual into Christ's death. The person rising from the waters embodies a resurrection into the new reality of Christian society. An infant or adult is given over to the ritual to be "born" again. One is given over from one biological family into a family constituted by Christ. The infant or adult is given as a gift of incalculable worth to be welcomed and formed. Such an environment is integral to forming a sense of self-worth, growth in spiritual maturity, and development in understanding deep reciprocal connections between individuals within the group. It takes a Christian village to shape souls. The theological significance of the church is much greater and more transhistorical than individual membership. A constructive understanding of church thus begins with new doctrinal readings of ritual, and then integrates interdisciplinary insights on human development from psychologies of recognition and pedagogies of formation. An ecclesiology of resistance must interrogate the link between becoming a Christian and being made human again—in its fullest and truest sense.

A developmental understanding of church has come a long way since the idea of the "invisible church" (Karl Holl) set the parameter for the prevailing Lutheran ecclesiology in the early twentieth century. The church is visible as an embodied community. Bodies are integral to church. Truth is visible. Feminist scholarship has underlined the significance of the body in trauma and ritual studies; human bodies have come to be central to theological analysis. Theologians articulating ecclesiologies today need to take these insights into account. They are asked to see bodies as sites where power is contested and negotiated. People bear the scars and traumas of each other's work in diminishing each other. They are also the sites where grace is glimpsed.

Different Lutheran traditions have various resources in articulating what it means to become a Christian in the church. From a developmental perspective, the church's nature is to become what it is, namely church. The Scandinavian tradition presents a perspective on church as an ongoing renewal event and re-creation. When individuals come together, they create community. The creative dimension is constituted by the participation of those gathered and the individuals contributing to and being changed by their participation. These insights are relevant to the Scandinavian context in which social and political communities are relatively strong. In Nordic countries, the church is seen more in terms of communities that renew for daily life, rather than as independently existing institutions. As a social expression of this context, church is seen to be remade every time individuals gather to share the word. The American context in which social and political structures are much more fragile perceives church in different ways. Churches are regarded as communities of faith, with sustaining and supporting functions for individuals. In this context, churches have lasting institutional strengths. The Scandinavian focus on constant renewal is replaced with an enduring model of a sustaining community. By comparing two different social and political contexts, we can see how culture is shaped by different ecclesiologies. Churches play different roles vis-à-vis the social and political institutions to which they are related. When theologians articulate understandings of church from different contexts, their distinctive challenges for resistance and reformation can be regarded as particular to those contexts. Yet when taken together, different ecclesiologies can represent a diversity of ways in which communities remain committed to renewal in the process of facilitating human becoming. With different perspectives in conversation with each other, theologians can stand to gain a more robust sense of how churches can articulate truth, communicate grace, and resist dehumanizing mechanisms.

When ecclesial renewal and reform are called for, theologians must take up the challenge. Trained theologians are responsible for defining sound doctrine with the aim of enlivening the church's intellectual commitments. The mind is one aspect of the church's life. Mind, however, is in unity with body. Thus theologians must seek ways to renew and reform practices in which the church creates community through its actions. When memory is placed in relation to ritual, when the historical past is critically related to present repetition and remembering, church practices require theological discernment. Church as practice is promoted by theologians who know that humans cannot exist without social structures and memory. These theologians also know that competence and celebratory excellence require rehearsal that takes time. In negotiating memory and present celebration, theologians discern past structures that have encroached on the present life of the church in ways that deaden it. Ecclesial iconoclasm was part of Luther's message.

Like Luther, ecclesially responsible theologians must resist the self-contented fiction of normativity from the past that twists divine gift into unfreedom. Responsibility for the church means freeing Christ's presence for the community that lives in the present tense.

Theological work is also responsible for the world in which theologians live. Theological expression must address the contemporary context in which the church exists. Christianity has a distinctive message of becoming human in different cruciform shapes. When theologians articulate this message in a particular society, they offer something unique. The church's distinctive analysis can boldly articulate resistance to social, cultural, and political demons bent on destroying humanity. The church's constructive project can result in imagining new ways to create community in the memory of and presence with the one who created the church in the first place. Responsibility for the world thus can be taken as a challenge by theologians to be even more serious about their own theological practices.

The world is created by God. However, the church (its theologians, leaders, and community) is born of God. God is actively initiating and sustaining the church, leading it in truth, and gracing it with the divine presence in and among people gathered in worship and song, prayer and adoration. Being part of the church community is participation in a way of becoming human that derives its life from God. As theologians who are part of the church, their ecclesiologies of resistance are ultimately witnesses to God's concern for the church and the world, a concern that includes human development and participation.

The chapters in this volume address various ways of conceptualizing and explaining practices of resistance in the church today. The first section focuses specifically on truth-telling as an ecclesial practice. Luther's commitment to truth as a divine prerogative, with human falsity as its opposite, is well known. The chapters in this section make the case as to why divine truth must be represented in the church's witness, and how truth-telling is both critically necessary and constructively transformative. If resistance is to serve both critique and reform, then it must be oriented to truth. The second section offers imaginative explorations of how the ecclesial context can be constituted as new space for practices of resistance. Word and ritual, piety and pastoral care are invoked as spaces identifying the new creation in the midst of the old. These practices inscribe memory into living experiences and orient embodied minds to new possibilities. In their repetition, practices embody the "mystical" body of Christ in concrete ways of being together in community.

NOTES

1. My gratitude goes to Jone Salomonsen who discussed some of the ideas in this chapter with me.

2. Two recent edited volumes display these two perspectives: Christine Helmer (ed.), *The Medieval Luther*, Spätmittelalter, Humanismus, Reformation 117 (Tübingen: Mohr Siebeck, 2020); Marius Timmann Mjaaland (ed.), *The Reformation of Philosophy: The Philosophical Legacy of the Reformation Reconsidered*, Religion in Philosophy and Theology 102 (Tübingen: Mohr Siebeck, 2020).

3. For a recent example of this approach, see Jan-Olav Henriksen, *Christianity as Distinct Practices: A Complicated Relationship* (New York: T&T Clark, 2019). Reviewed by Paul R. Hinlicky, *Modern Theology* (forthcoming).

4. Marit Trelstad, "Charity Terror Begins at Home: Luther and the 'Terrifying and Killing' Law," in *Lutherrenaissance: Past and Present*, ed. Christine Helmer and Bo Kristian Holm, Forschungen zur Kirchen- und Dogmengeschichte 106 (Göttingen: Vandenhoeck & Ruprecht, 2015), 209–23.

Chapter 2

Taking Responsibility for Truth

Ecclesial Practices in an Age of Hypocrisy

Jan-Olav Henriksen

I start with a slightly edited quote from Wendy Farley:

> Political regimes are committed to shaping our interpretation of events to obfuscate some of the hidden ways policies benefit those behind the scenes. [...] The effect of this control of ideology is difficult to overestimate. It does not control but deeply shapes the symbols and information through which Americans decide the fate of their nation and, to some extent, the world. The interpretation of corporations as primary participants in political decisions comes close to trading democracy [...] for oligarchy. These are political questions, of course; but they are also spiritual ones. Christians, in their devotion to truth, are invited to care about factual truth and to acquire intellectual and spiritual disciplines that would enable them to be more suspicious of ideologically manufactured worldviews.[1]

Over the past few years, we have seen the development of a public display about the need for truth that I guess only a few, if any of us, can remember having seen before in our own lifetime. Some of us will perhaps remember how there were alternative facts about the world when the iron curtain was still in existence—on the other side of the fence, so to say. But we can shrug off these versions of history, now more or less dated, from our shoulders, knowing that they belonged to the world of "the others," those we considered to be set apart from the community of the truthful and reliable. We, on the other hand, were in our own eyes those who were free to discuss and question the truth, and we could assume that we basically shared the same basis for understanding the world, as well as what it meant to be accountable. Not so anymore. "Alternative facts" is, no longer, a notion we learn about in Orwell's *1984*, but is a notion presently pronounced from the podiums of power, together with the concomitant "fake news." The severity of this situation, in which those in power no longer seem to care about being accountable to the public for speaking the truth and for safeguarding those who are in search of it,[2] has significantly changed the Western world and continues to do so at a rapid pace. Somehow, truth does not seem to count.[3]

Moreover, many of us who are not American citizens have previously considered the United States as a place where one could rely on those in power to have some (albeit not always as much as we would want) concern for others, for democracy, and for justice. Of course, this was never unequivocally the case. We had the Iraq War, and there have always been signs of what colleagues called corporate despotism, even before the previousadministration took office. What has changed over the past few years, however, is that there has been a significant drop in the trust many feel they can put in those who are in charge of American politics when it comes to securing the truth and the well-being of those who are not affluent or have access to means of power. In the spring of 2017, a few months after Trump's inauguration, I asked a colleague at Vanderbilt if she considered it to be the case that most Americans were aware of how the rest of the world looked upon the present administration with a combination of disbelief, shock, and lack of confidence. Her answer was a plain, No! The situation has not changed significantly since then.

The Christian church finds its identity and develops its practices by searching for roots in the biblical message about Jesus Christ. It is the reference to and the connection with his specific history that gives the Christian church its distinctive identity and shapes its unique character. I argue, however, that this does not imply that Christians are alone in being called out for stewarding the truth or for holding those in power accountable.[4] That is the task of all humans of good will. But when Christians do this, they do it because they see that this is part of what it means to belong to the community of Jesus Christ. It is the common cause of all who believe in Jesus and in what he called the reign of God, to take responsibility for truth and make sure that *truth is practiced*.

How can the churches respond to the current situation? How can we develop ecclesial practices that provide opportunities for a society in which those in power can be trusted, and where those who are at the margins of society are offered a chance to be empowered and are not left to themselves? There is one story in the New Testament that offers a clue to this situation, one that I think can shed more light on the situation than what one would initially assume.

In John 18:37, when Jesus is asked by the man of supreme power, Pilate, who he is and if he is a king, Jesus answers, "You say that I am a king. In fact, the reason I was born and came into the world is to testify to the truth. Everyone on the side of truth listens to me." It is notable that Pilate responds by replying "What is truth?"—and then leaves him. Pilate does not care about the truth; he has no need for it because he is in power. But he nevertheless finds no basis for a charge against Jesus. This point notwithstanding, he hands Jesus over to others who eventually crucify him. As Pilate turns his back on the question of truth, he also rejects being held accountable for his own actions and thereby opens the door to injustice. However, it is only when we are willing to be held accountable for our actions and opinions that we indeed take responsibility for truth—no matter how hard that may be, at times. *To practice the truth is to provide opportunities for justice.*

This story, therefore, contains several elements that I hold essential for developing ecclesial practices that can deliver resistance to a situation in which truth does not seem to matter anymore. First of all, one should speak truth to power—even when those in power do not care about it. Second, this implies that the calling to speak the truth is not only a calling to follow Jesus, but is the responsibility of all his followers. Third, truth can be recognized by all who are on the side of truth, because truth creates community and shapes commitment to it through practice—a point I will return to. Fourth, to take responsibility for truth implies holding oneself and others accountable. And finally, there is no guarantee that our commitment to practicing the truth will protect us from the injustices of those who are in power. To speak the truth and witness to the truth is a risk for all who take responsibility for it—and it is a risk because the truth is always a threat to those who abuse power for their own good.

TRUTH AS A LIBERATING PRACTICE

When you do not care about being responsible for, or accountable to the truth, you are, in fact, allowing for division, separation, and fear. The church's calling is to create conditions for the opposite qualities. Wendy Farley has poignantly made this point when she speaks of "Devotion to truth as spiritual practice."[5]

A central New Testament passage says that "The truth shall set you free" (John 8:32). In this verse, Jesus refers to his own teaching as that which allows his disciples to know the truth. This is a very interesting claim and one that can be seen as closely tied to both the Jewish and the Greek understandings of truth. In Jewish thinking, the truth is that which is reliable, trustworthy, that upon which one can depend and rely. The Greek understanding of truth sees it as that which is universally the case, that which goes for all, that which does not allow for any alternatives.

To take up responsibility for truth in a way that is liberating for society means, against this backdrop, that there cannot be any alternative facts, and that those who are witness to truth are called to make sure that what they testify to is reliable and something that all members of society can relate to and be accountable in relation to. A biblical understanding of the responsibility for truth means that there can be no truth which is only pertinent to some elect, or that there are different versions of the truth regarding the reliable basis on which society and community can be built. Society and community build on and presuppose that which is common—if not, there is no real and shared world for which to take responsibility.

For the Christian church, this means that the truth this church stewards is not something set apart from the truth of other beliefs or other facts. The only alternative to the unity of truth is different versions of falsehood. The truth of the Church's message is that Jesus came to call everyone into a community in which God cares for the other through the caring and loving practices of the members of this community. It is the actual care for others that is the sign of the reign of God as present in this world. Truth constitutes community, shapes links between humans, and allows for trust and human flourishing. A church that cares about a universal and reliable truth can be recognized by the ways in which such community is flourishing. The truth is also, therefore, in such a context, something that is contrary to fear-mongering and rejection and neglect of the other. Because we have truth together, no one can be separated from the community of truth. Thus, stewardship of truth is, in principle, empowering and liberating.

Consider the alternative: if you hold onto your version of the "facts" and do not want to be held accountable to a universal, reliable, and shared understanding of what is true, you separate yourself from others. What you stand for may then be considered a result of lies and deception, perhaps even self-deception. The path is then not very long to strategies of cover-up and withdrawal from the public eye. Such a practice, guided by alternative facts and one's own version of reality creates not only a lack of trust, but also a deeply divided society.

Such divisions have serious consequences: they easily lead to a preference for some groups on behalf of others. In the present context, the combination of growing nationalism, xenophobia, racism, and general fear about what goes on and what one can rely on, can only be countered by speaking the truth about the humanity of the other, the commitment to human values that apply to all, and information that is well-grounded and can be considered reliable because of its quality and because its witnesses are committed to truth and not to their own agenda separated from that of others. The insecurity created by the fact (sic!) that those in power do not seem to care about the truth contributes further to fear and to divisiveness and discord. Under such conditions, it is impossible to create a society in which every member takes responsibility for a common cause: to create a just, peaceful, and caring society for all. Merely the fact that the American president rejected the idea that someone not wealthy could be part of his cabinet suggests that there are new standards for who counts in politics and not, and whose voices will be heard as speaking about what matters.

Viewed from the outside, the development in American politics over the past few years has been unsettling. With some regularity, we have heard intellectuals like Jeffrey Stout speak about the corporate despotism that shapes American politics and thereby the conditions for creating a just society. But we have over the past years had more examples of this than ever before, and in the most disturbing ways.[6] The appointments to cabinet and to central positions in the administration have shown that what matters most is not the commitment to truth. What matters is a combination of personal support and admiration, possession of wealth, and the willingness to put corporate interests before health care for all, measures to stop the already existing climate crisis, and personal integrity.

In the summer of 2017, a report indicated that more than twenty million Americans would lose their health insurance if the Republican proposal to repeal Obamacare passed legislation. Simultaneously, only a few weeks earlier, the American president announced that he would pull American support for the Paris Agreement on climate—and did so with arguments and information that were so biased or false that one had to stop and wonder if these arguments were not just added *post hoc* in order to legitimize a decision that cannot be considered as anything but determined by short-term corporate goals. They had nothing to do with the truth. Furthermore, the legislation proposed to repeal Obamacare seems to care nothing for low-income people or those who are already on benefits due to permanent conditions or illnesses.

In such a situation, the church cannot hold on to some version of the truth that it thinks is exclusively its own. The church needs to contribute to the nourishing of a social and political culture in which truth is something that matters for all, be it on its own premises or outside of it. The truth afflicts the life conditions of Muslims, Christians, and secular humanists alike. Theological institutions must acknowledge that the biblical understanding of truth means that truth is a gift that is given to all, and that taking responsibility for truth needs to be done by witnessing to both the truth and what is reliable in all segments of society, and not only within secure ecclesial boundaries. Wendy Farley writes, aptly:

Love of truth as a spiritual practice should attempt to overcome hostility to other people, though it is admittedly an advanced spiritual practice to resist frustration with people whose point of view seems to us very destructive. But even in these cases, we need not hate people who oppose us, even as we work with energy and passion in the opposite direction. The desire for truth is a practice, not an accomplishment.[7]

Pilate's question to Jesus was, "What is truth?" Then he turned away. The church cannot turn away from this question. If the truth is universal, it has to be based on the experiences of those without a voice, those who are marginalized from the spheres of power and political influence, and those who do not seem to count in the public eye. Liberation theology taught us decades ago that there is something called the "preferential option for the poor." If this is an insight that still matters, and I argue that it is, it means that there can be no truth unless the reality of those who suffer, who are homeless or sick, or those who speak the truth but are silenced, is brought back and allowed a place among the rest. There is no truth unless those in power listen to the disenfranchised. To speak the truth cannot only be a privilege for those who belong to the recognized faith, but must also be acknowledged as something Muslims and illegal immigrants may have something important to talk about. As long as this is not the case, to take responsibility for the truth means that the church must continue to expose the fact that there are unbearable human costs for a society founded on corporate despotism and fueled by fear and the desire for wealth in a deadly combination.

HYPOCRISY: KEEP UP THE APPEARANCES

To take up responsibility for truth means *not* to take for granted that things always are what they seem. What may look good at first glance may not be so upon a closer look.

Why do appearances matter? Because they are perceived as signs of success, conformity with that which can be idealized or is a cause for admiration. When someone sits in a cabinet meeting and receives praise from the members, one gets the impression that this is a person for whom it matters more than anything to be successful, in power, accomplished, and celebrated. The main thing is not what this person can achieve for those less privileged than himself. And the success of the one in power also rubs off on those who join with him. But how does one measure success, power, or accomplishment? By attendance at the inauguration or by how well one is able to make life better for those who are among the poorest and least privileged?

To speak the truth in times of hypocrisy means that any kind of hijacking of religious symbols or religion in general for the sake of keeping up appearances needs to be called out as deceit. There is no success for any religion, including Christianity, as long as fundamental human rights are neglected, as long as fear-mongering is on the everyday agenda, and as long as those who are sick, poor, or incarcerated are not embraced with care, positive concern, and measures in order to make their lives better. To use religion in order to secure one's political position instead of securing the life-conditions for those who are powerless and not part of the celebrated middle-class is not only profoundly problematic from a political and theological point of view. It is also a vivid sign that the gospel of the reign of God for all is not one among the determining factors of the church's own practice. As long as Christian churches allow politicians to use their podiums and pulpits for political gains, they show themselves to be unreliable witnesses to the truth and they thereby contribute to hypocrisy in ways that put the liberating power of the gospel in the shadows.

I am not arguing for the churches to stay out of politics. What churches do (and not do) has political consequences. Hence it matters if one listens to the truth or if one is on the side of truth (or not). In the current situation, the churches need to witness to the truth by speaking up for those who are not Christians and who are not middle-class; in short, for those who do not seem to matter, those paid no attention by those in power.

The ecclesial practices I am promoting in this article have been beautifully formulated by the group of constructive theologians that recently published the book, *Awake to the Moment.* I quote:

> We believe that the Christian story must be grounded in the radical egalitarian love disclosed in the life and work of Jesus and his community of followers—love for neighbor, stranger, the poor, the dispossessed, and even the enemy. We pray for the courage and power to resist the forces of violence, racism, terror, and oppression—even unto the cross. We are claimed by an erotic love for the world as God's beautiful creation and so yearn to save it from ecological degradation. These are norms of love, justice, and flourishing.[8]

Those who speak in the name of God and Jesus, but are not committed to those values, but strive first and foremost for their own position and wealth, need to be called out as hypocrites. Not so in order to shame them, but in order to make room for a liberating truth that allows for the empowerment of the powerless. Such a speech opens up the new possibility that the world will not be ruled by fear, destitution, and hate, but by faith, hope, and love. To steward and witness to the truth is to take on responsibility for a society that is for all—and not only for the so-called successful, viewed by the standards of this world.

CONCLUSION

No church is exempt from the responsibility for truth. The truth creates community instead of division and fear. The truth enables justice to flourish. The only ones who need to be afraid of truth are those who are not in favor of justice and equality—the two values that can create reliable and trustworthy conditions for society. *Thus truth exists primarily as a practice that shows what true humanity is*; it is to take on responsibility for those at the margins, those who suffer, are incarcerated, and suffering from illness and disabilities. Truth is liberated by being practiced. As long as the gifts of creation and redemption are not offered to all and are not distributed to every human being—and recall that every human person is created in the image of God—there is still something wrong with the human condition, something still to come, outstanding and unresolved. It is the task for all of us to give power to those who can make sure that this is done in the best way possible. To give power only to those who act on behalf of the few is to open the world to the rule of those who do not care about the truth, and to neglect the liberating power of truth.

NOTES

1. Wendy Farley, *Gathering Those Driven Away: A Theology of Incarnation* (Louisville, KY: Westminster John Knox Press, 2011), 209–10. Farley already discussed the problems of truth in a theological context shaped by postmodernity in her *Eros for the Other: Retaining Truth in a Pluralistic World* (University Park, PA: Pennsylvania State University Press, 1996).

2. Including the working conditions and resources for scientists who are concerned with the future of the planet.

3. I have written this article with an eye to Harry Frankfurt's thorough discussion in "On Bullshit," which I think sheds a lot of light on contemporary circumstances, but which I cannot go into in detail in the following, despite the temptation to do so. However, there is one point Frankfurt makes in order to distinguish the bullshitter from the liar that is worth pointing out: whereas a liar says something that he knows is false and is therefore in one way responding to the truth, this case does not apply to a bullshitter: "He is neither on the side of the true nor of the false. His eye is not on the facts at all, as the eyes of the honest man and of the liar are, except insofar as they may be pertinent to his interest in getting away with what he says. He does not care whether the things he says describe reality correctly. He just picks them up, or makes them up, to serve his purpose" (14). Later on, and equally apt: "Bullshit

is unavoidable whenever circumstances require someone to talk without knowing what he is talking about. Thus the production of bullshit is stimulated whenever a person's obligations or opportunities to speak about some topic is more excessive than his knowledge of the facts that are relevant to that topic" (14). Harry Frankfurt, *On Bullshit*; online at http://www2.csudh.edu/ccauthen/576f12/frankfurt__harry_-_on_bullshit.pdf (accessed Feb. 6, 2020).

4. An important contribution to the understanding of the ecclesiological understanding of accountability is offered in Olav Fykse Tveit, *Truth We Owe Each Other* (Geneva: World Council of Churches, 2016).

5. See Farley, *Gathering Those Driven Away*, 206–207.

6. See Jeffrey Stout, *Democracy and Tradition*, New Forum Books (Princeton, NJ: Princeton University Press, 2004), 23, who points out the need for a *common* discourse that is necessary for the improvement of society: "We should also recognize, however, how disastrous it would be—in an era of global capitalism, corporate corruption, identity politics, religious resentment against secular society, and theocratic terrorism—if most citizens stopped identifying with the people as a whole and gave up on our democratic practices of accountability altogether." However, Stout is also addressing critically how the "corporate influence over the electoral and legislative processes now threatens to circumvent a politically effective and open public exchange of reasons on issues of concern to the citizenry. One cannot honestly call our mode of government democratic if corporate influence on it is so strong that the reasons offered by the public against its decisions have little bearing on legislative outcomes" (317).

7. Farley, *Gathering those Driven Away*, 207.

8. Laurel C. Schneider and Stephen G. Ray Jr. (eds.), *Awake to the Moment: An Introduction to Theology* (Louisville, KY: Westminster John Knox Press, 2016), 81.

Chapter 3

Embodying Truth in Ecclesial Practices

Allen G. Jorgenson

CONTEXT

In response to Jan-Olav Henriksen's stirring call to "Take Responsibility for Truth," I advance that truth-telling needs to be communally embodied in ecclesial practices for the good of the cosmos.

I begin by acknowledging that our colloquium on truth-telling took place on the traditional territories of the Pawtucket, Massachusett, and Pokantoket peoples.[1] Context matters, and wherever we dwell, wherever we meet—in a city, a state, a country, and a continent—the spaces we inhabit simultaneously occupy histories that are still unfolding. As a Canadian, I am acutely aware of American developments. Being a Canadian in North America is to live in the shadow of all things American: with a population one-tenth of that of the U.S., Canadians—the majority of whom live within two hundred miles from the border—have to shuffle when Americans cross the socio-political floor. Our economies and socio-cultural realities are thoroughly intertwined, but yet with a kind of asymmetry. Our long-standing lop-sided relationship results in a kind of curious way of being for Canadians: "carefully patriotic" might name it, a way of being that has analogues across the globe. But despite this important difference, still more important similarities obtain. Here I attend to one in particular as I consider the ecclesial practices for faith communities.

The United States of America and Canada are both political constructs as instantiations of colonial designs. And while the word construct might suggest some kind of arbitrary character, it really finds its footing in the Doctrine of Discovery.[2] Jennifer Reid notes that it is "the legal means by which Europeans claimed rights of sovereignty, property, and trade in regions they allegedly discovered during the age of expansion."[3] This Doctrine of Discovery is grounded in papal bulls published in the fifteenth century in response to the "discovery" of previously unknown lands, including those now identified as the Americas.[4] These bulls are also the foundation for the concept of *Terra Nullius*, presuming that lands not settled by Christians are, in fact, politically void and so subject to Christian rule, which may well include enslaving and executing those not inclined to the Christian faith.[5] It should be noted that the Doctrine of Discovery has been used in a court ruling regarding traditional territories as recently as 2005.[6]

Behind the Doctrine of Discovery and its nefarious implementation was the presumption that the peoples indigenous to the Americas were spiritually, intellectually, and culturally inferior. At its best, colonialism was a parochial effort to form native children into good citizens of empire; at its worst it was a demonic design intended to enslave or slaughter sub-humans in expanding the insatiable reach of empire. As one might well imagine, this *was* not well received by those subject to such machinations; and indeed it *is* not well received because the patterns of empire in both its parochial and genocidal modalities is perdurable. The natives are becoming increasingly restless, and so we have Standing Rock and Oka and Caledonia and more as instances of resistance. A small but very vocal and growing minority in North America is using such events to remind settler North Americans that the historic treaties—many being broken in many ways—were established on the basis of a nation to nation basis. For this reason, a significant number of Indigenous people in both Canada and the United States do not identify themselves as Canadians or Americans and so some refuse to carry the passports, and to identify as Canadian or American. Audra Simpson writes, "Refusal comes with the requirement of having one's *political* sovereignty acknowledged and upheld, and raises the question of legitimacy for those who are usually in the position of recognizing."[7]

A passport is a tool of recognition: the citizen is recognized as such and given rights concomitant to citizenship. Simpson, and others, see passports as a metaphoric Trojan horse. They have come to this realization in a hard way. And so their refusal to be Canadian, or American, gives them a unique vantage point that differs from mine in ascertaining the present context: their assessment is that the current solipsistic tenor of political insularity and colonial design that Americans and others are experiencing anew across borders has been happening for years *within* the borders of Canada and the U.S.A.—those borders of the primordial nation to nation relationships: between Canada or the United States of America and the nations of the Haudenosaunee, the Navajo, the Inuit, the Osage, etc. Their assessment is that empires establish borders for the sake of extraction and expansion. Their experience, in short, is that empires ensconce borders in establishing reservations in order to keep the natives in while taking out timber, minerals, and more. Empires extract resources and more across borders for resources for their insatiable appetite. Empires, then, expand by establishing borders that do not limit their influence but multiply it by way of the calculus of divide and conquer.[8] We are seeing more and more of this on the world stage, but our indigenous neighbors have been living this in our contexts since contact. This, then, is the context out from which we must begin to envision ecclesiologies of resistance. This brings me to Henriksen's very helpful list of ecclesial practices. In what follows, I will consider these in turn.

ECCLESIAL PRACTICES

Henriksen helpfully points us to protocols for ecclesial practices of resistance in a time of fake news by turning us to truth. He reminds us of the following: truth speaks to power; truth's concern is the province of the followers of Jesus; truth creates community and has a universal reach; truth calls forth a self-critical moment; and truth may very well suffer the injustice it reveals. In sum, we might say that the ecclesial practice of truth will of necessity be public, expansive, and expensive. What might this mean for faith communities in a North American context that is coming to see that an America-first *modus operandi* of expansion and extraction has been a perdurable colonial characteristic experienced on both sides of the border for far too long?[9] What might this mean for faith communities and more specifically for that community we call the church?

The church, clearly, has been a co-opted partner in the project of colonization. Canada has been working this truth through in its recently completed Truth and Reconciliation Commission.[10] Herein the Canadian public has heard something of the experience of Indigenous students in residential schools run by churches at the behest of the government. The abuses resulting from this are demonically legion, and only now is the Indigenous community beginning to work through the collective trauma of this attempt at cultural genocide. A few years ago I had the Indigenous curriculum specialist at my university speak to my Christianity and Global Citizenship class. At one point she turned to me and asked: "Allen, all of the churches were involved in this, right?" I responded "Yes and No." No, because the project of colonialism, which aimed to homogenize the Canadian public under the paradigm of British sensibilities—outside of Quebec—meant that immigrant churches were not asked to run these schools since, I suspect, it would do damage to the Dominion of Canada if brown children started speaking the Queen's English with Northern and Eastern European accents. But I quickly added yes because the theological truth by which the Christian church exists is that there is one Lord, one faith, one baptism (Eph 4:4–6), and no church is exempt from identifying with this sinful church. Beyond this, all non-Indigenous Canadians—and their churches and synagogues, their mosques and temples—enjoy luxuries afforded by the expropriation of Indigenous lands.[11] Churches have been party to this abuse and faith communities have benefited.

If truth speaks to power about the dangers of extraction and expropriation then the fact that the very school where I teach sits on land once deeded to the Six Nation of the Grand River Nation means that not only will my faith community speak but my church must first be spoken to.[12] This latter stings and makes for some uncomfortable moments since this truth demands that we begin with repentance rather than resistance. Christians in our pews will squirm. Pastors in our pulpits will sweat. Naysayers to things religious will rub their hands in gleeful expectation of the demise of the church, a demise that may well be the very thing needed. The condition for the possibility of an ecclesiology of resistance most certainly is repentance, a repentance resisting an ecclesiology of entitlement; an ecclesiology in the lap of empire and content in the confines of colonialism. In North America, things will most certainly get worse for the church before they get better. Indigenous people have reminded me that there is no reconciliation without truth, and in North America, at least, this truth is hard, and it will be hard for a time. Moreover, this truth needs to be understood communally and first told from perspectives that have been marginalized. This brings me to some reflections on the relationship between truth and freedom.

TRUTH AND FREEDOM

Under the heading "Truth as a Liberating Practice" Henriksen helpfully explicates the nature of truth in the gospel of John, referencing John 8:31–32:

> Then Jesus said to the Jews who had believed in him, "If you continue in my word, you are truly my disciples; and you will know the truth, and the truth will make you free." (NRSV)

Jesus says: "If you remain in my word you will know the truth and the truth will make you free." But that isn't quite right. In Greek the word free is a verb, not an adjective. Jesus actually says "If you remain in my word, the truth will free you." Free is a verb here. And the interlocutors in the text, who serve as a kind of teaching foil here, respond "We are children of Abraham, we have never been in bondage. How can you say that 'We will be made free?'" But they do not actually respond with that: the Greek text has "How can you say that 'We will become *the free*?'" Here the verb free is made into a noun by Jesus' interlocutors. Jesus replies that "If the Son makes you free, you will be free indeed!" However, we have another translation issue here. In Greek we read "If the Son frees you will really be free." Jesus insists on the verb and invites us to ponder the difference between nouns and verbs. You can *have* that which a noun references. In many cases you can actually have it in your hands; you can hold it; you can keep it; you can parcel it out; you can sell it; you can buy it. When freedom is a noun it becomes a thing, some*thing*, something *valuable*. This notion of freedom as *something* was on display in sixteenth century debates about freedom, in the slave trade, and in the logic of a wall stretching across the U.S. and Mexico. Such a notion suggests that freedom can be commodified. But freedom isn't a thing for Jesus, who insists on identifying freedom as a verb. Jesus frees, truth frees. Freedom isn't something you have. Freedom is something Jesus does, and the above text identifies freedom as a verb.

Of course the same obtains with truth. When truth is a noun—a thing—then I can have it and you can't. Truth that is a noun is subject to the calculus of colonial lack and an economy of scarcity. There is only so much truth. Some have it; some don't. Some people are truth rich and some are truth poor when truth is a thing. But truth isn't a thing. Jesus proclaims "I am the way, and the truth and the life" (John 14:6). Truth is identified with a person here. But it isn't only Jesus who is connected to truth. In John 3:21 Jesus says that the person who does the truth comes to the light. Truth here is something that we do: just like freedom. Truth, too, is a verb it seems. When you do truth you come to the light. Doing truth reveals. Heidegger explored the idea that the Greek word for truth derives from the verb *alanthano*: a privative of "I cover" and so to do truth is to un-cover, or dis-cover.[13] Truth is about uncovering. Freedom is about letting go. The praxis of Jesus, then, is to uncover and release; to free and enlighten. Jesus' preference for verbs here reflects his identity as an itinerant preacher, a man with no place to call home, no place to lay his head, and no pension plan. Jesus' very name instantiates the identity of God (*Ja*) as the one who saves (*shua*). Indeed, God's very name in the Hebrew Scriptures is a verb: "I am who I am." (Ex 3:14) God is identified with a verb, and so are we as human *beings* who are called to be by being free and by doing truth. To live in the *imago Christi* then is to free and to true, in the old English sense of that rarely used verb, which is to set aright. But what does truing look like when it is done freely in the church in resistance to the machinations of empire? What does truth look like when it is embodied?

EMBODIED TRUTH

As Henriksen thinks through the task of discipleship in a time such as ours, he notes that part of what it means to be disciples is to be about the business of "stewarding the truth." I quite like this emphasis for two reasons: first, he notes that it is not the business of the church alone to do this, but that the church does truth with "all humans of good will." In a fashion he hereby invites us to imagine the church in community: first with itself and second with all humans who will the well-being of the cosmos. The communal character of this church is explicated in Paul's powerful image of the church as a body—the body of Christ. Motifs of coordination, and physicality, and interrelationship attend such a vision, to great effect. Communally, as a body, the church does the truth which sets free, which sets free even the church bound at times in the lies of empire. But especially helpful, I think, is Henriksen's assertion that this truth is not limited to the province of the church but embraces the broad sweep of God's good creation. The church's appeal to the truth is not incommensurable with that of other publics. Or to put it more pointedly: the body of Christ and the body politic are answerable to the same activity of truth. This is incredibly helpful but by framing it with respect to the body, I intend to gesture toward the carnal character of this truth. Truth-telling is always embodied truth.

As of late I have been reading *Carnal Hermeneutics* by Richard Kearney, and I suspect that some of his thought may well be germane to the present theme. Kearney notes that "the work of Hermes goes all the way down."[14] This messenger bridging heaven and earth knew them both intimately, and yet Kearney notes that the linguistic turn of the modern era came with the unhappy correlate of the erasure of the importance of the carnal for the human.[15] But Kearney fears that identifying the task of interpretation in linguistic terms alone is dangerously restrictive in being dismissive of the body. This is a truth told well by feminists, womanists, mujerista theologians, and more, those whose commitment to the material has spared them from the illusion that the body is not a reliable source for discerning the pathway of truth. Indeed, Kearney asserts that

> Existence comes into its own in the body and finds there its originary sense. Expression does not exist apart from the body and the body does not exist apart from expression.[16]

And yet it might be worth noting that the body is not only indispensable in its role of expression, but in the play of impression as well. The body both expresses the truth discerned by the mind, but also discerns truths sometimes blind to the mind. The body, it seems, knows and so the ancients were able to assert that all knowing is foundationally and fundamentally phantasmal in character.[17]

Every instance of our knowing has its roots in the apprehension that accompanies our bodily being in the world. And that apprehension has both a recollective and a prospective character. It is not unimportant that Aristotle considered the faculty of memory to be a part of the lower faculties of the person: memory was a part of the life of the body, not the mind.[18] Certainly Proust knew this to be true, and yet perhaps we might imagine that this ability of the body to re-mind us of the past and to sense, or anticipate, a future is not lower in the way of being lesser, but lower in the way of being nearer the ground: grounded as it were. The body is grounded, and no part of the body is as close to the ground and the air that wraps it round as the skin. The skin is the pinnacle of corporeal existence.

Luther spoke of the skin in its nakedness as the "unique adornment" of being human.[19] Skin is especially apt at the task of disclosing our vulnerability: our need for the other is ever in the flesh and so a church that lives the authenticity of its identity as a body will be of necessity in the flesh, living liminally at the edges of its existence, where alone it is able to re-member its past and anticipate its future. A church that lives an embodied existence is attentive to its edges, and the same is true of our body politic. Both church and society live authentic embodied experiences by attending to those on the edge, the porous edge where hard truths seep in and strange graces call us to new possibilities. Church and society live well by willing their way to the edge, by feeling their way around their limits. Or, to quote Henriksen: "there can be no truth unless the reality of those who suffer, who are homeless or sick, or those who speak the truth are heard."[20] To be a body, either of Christ or of the politic, is to listen, to see, to touch and be touched by those who suffer colonial insolence. In North America, we simply must begin with those whose beginning is here; with those who made space for a new beginning for my ancestors and yours. We need to begin with the people of the land, which brings me to my final point, made in a very brief conclusion.

COSMOLOGICAL CONCLUSIONS

An ecclesiology of resistance in a time of ecological crisis will of necessity also be an ecclesiology of subsistence in the most fundamental ways possible. The church must become green. I have no idea how this will look *in situ*. I suspect it will be radically different across the globe. But the fact of the matter is that empire erodes the earth, and our Indigenous neighbors remind us that the earth is our mother. The earth, then, is not for sale. The earth is not a commodity, nor a resource, nor a backdrop for any drama, whether it be the drama of salvation or colonialism. Indeed, to imagine the earth as a backdrop is already an act of colonialism. A church resisting the lies of empirical bravado, then, will have to learn how to say no to easy ways of being human; we may well have to spend some time on the land, as our Indigenous neighbors have done, to learn again how to live with a modicum of humility and appreciation. Perhaps the land will teach us a truth anew that Luther alluded to in his lectures on Genesis: to be human in the image of God is to be content with God's favor and without fear of death, because die we must—in so very many ways—if we want to be raised into an ecclesiology of resistance.[21]

NOTES

1. The colloquium, hosted by Lutheran Scholars of Religion during the 2017 meeting of the American Academy of Religion, was held in Boston on November 19, 2017.
2. Jennifer Reid, "The Doctrine of Discovery and Canadian Law," *The Canadian Journal of Native Studies* 30, no. 2 (2010): 335–59.
3. Reid, "The Doctrine of Discovery," 336.
4. Reid, "The Doctrine of Discovery," 339.
5. Reid, "The Doctrine of Discovery," 340.
6. "CITY OF SHERRILL V. ONEIDA INDIAN NATION OF N. Y. (03-855) 544 U.S. 197 (2005) 337 F.3d 139, reversed and remanded," Legal Information Institute; online at https://www.law.cornell.edu/supct/html/03-855.ZO.html (accessed September 26, 2019).
7. Audra Simpson, *Mohawk Interruptus: Political Life across the Borders of Settler States* (Durham, NC: Duke University Press, 2014), 11.
8. The colonial designs of England in India are a very fine example.
9. See James Daschuck, *Clearing the Plains: Disease, Politics of Starvation, and the Loss of Aboriginal Life* (Regina, Sask.: University of Regina Press, 2014) for a historical treatment of strategies used by both Americans and Canadians intent on removing Indigenous peoples from the Great Plains.
10. For a list of resources see Truth and Reconciliation Commission of Canada; online at http://www.trc.ca/websites/trcinstitution/index.php?p=905 (accessed March 19, 2018).
11. Allen G. Jorgenson, "Empire, Eschatology and Stolen Land," *Dialogue: A Journal of Theology* 49, no. 2 (Summer 2010): 115–22.
12. "The Haldimand Treaty of 1784," Six Nations Land and Resources; online at http://www.sixnations.ca/LandsResources/HaldProc.htm (accessed March 19, 2018).
13. Martin Heidegger, *Being and Time*, trans. John Macquarrie and Edward Robinson (San Francisco, CA: Harper & Row, 1962), 57 n1.
14. Richard Kearney, "The Wager of Carnal Hermeneutics," in *Carnal Hermeneutics*, ed. Richard Kearney and Brian Treanor (New York: Fordham University Press, 2015), 1.
15. Kearney, "The Wager," 17.
16. Kearney, "The Wager," 41.
17. Aristotle, *On the Soul*, trans. W. S. Hett (Cambridge, MA: Harvard University Press, 1995), 177.
18. Aristotle, *On Memory*, trans. Richard Sorabji (Chicago: The University of Chicago Press, 2004), 48, 49: "Any connexion between memory and the intellect is merely incidental. [...] So memory will belong to thought in virtue of an incidental association, but in its own right to the primary perceptive part."
19. Martin Luther, *Luther's Works*, vol. 1: *Lectures on Genesis Chapters 1–5*, ed. Jaroslav Pelikan, trans. George V. Schick (Saint Louis, MO: Concordia Publishing House, 1958), 176.
20. Cf. Henriksen's article in ch. 2 of this volume.
21. Luther, *Genesis Chapters 1–5*, 63.

Chapter 4

Telling the Truth about Doctrine

Justification and Justice

Christine Helmer

I recently read Carol P. Christ's personal account of her time in the Yale graduate program in theology. In the book *Goddess and God in the World: Conversations in Embodied Theology* that Christ co-wrote with Jewish feminist theologian, Judith Plaskow, Christ compared notes on their experiences in the graduate program in Religious Studies at Yale University.[1] Christ recalled that she had wanted to work on women in the history of Christianity for the church history comprehensive exam. Christ and Plaskow proposed a reading list for the exam. This custom beloved by Yale students allowed them to explore their research interests. Christ notes that the professor of church history, whom she describes as an arrogant and self-absorbed church historian, banged his first on the table and said, "Not for me, you're not!"[2] My hunch regarding the identity of the historian was confirmed in Plaskow's account of the same incident. The professor's name was Jaroslav Pelikan, Sterling Professor of History at Yale University, one of the most famous church historians in the world during the second half of the twentieth century, speaker of nineteen languages (as he told me on our first encounter), Lutheran Church Missouri Synod trained theologian, chief editor of the American edition of *Luther's Works*, and author of countless volumes, including the five-volume *History of Christian Doctrine* that is on every single library reference shelf if not in every theologian's personal library.[3] Christ and Plaskow continued to recount their experiences as women in Yale's graduate program in theology. Their concerns were silenced, their identities diminished, their research questions unrecognized in a program presided over by some of the most prestigious theology professors in the country. Doctrine not experience, Aquinas not Adrienne Rich, ecumenism not feminism—the lines of acceptable research were clearly drawn, and disciplined by the professors who considered it their vocation to train the next generation of scholars.

I immediately wrote an email to Carol Christ, letting her know that I cried while reading her story. I too had experienced my male colleagues and professors as pipe-smoking, beard-stroking interlocutors who dictated the theological agenda and determined which questions were relevant. Not much had changed in the twenty years between Christ's time at Yale and mine. I had a suspicion about the professors she hinted at in her book. I asked: "Were some of those professors by any chance Lutheran?" The Lutheran presence in the last third of the twentieth century in American divinity schools was strong. After World War I, the Lutheran denominations in America were caught up in a moment of academic ambition. Church historians, biblical scholars, and systematic theologians received their degrees from top American universities and some went to Germany to study with Werner Elert in Erlangen, Karl Barth in Basel, and Edmund Schlink in Heidelberg. They brought form criticism to America, taught the history of doctrine from a German-theological perspective, and brought Americans into conversation with Wolfhart Pannenberg. The doctrine that had been excavated from the sixteenth century by early twentieth-century German theologians as *the* center of Luther's reformation theology was taught to American students as the article by which the church stands or falls.[4] Justification by faith without human merit or works became the Lutheran mantra, disseminated in seminaries and divinity schools where Lutheran professors taught, also at Yale.

The women educated by this older generation of Lutheran male theologians commiserate about a common theme. We have all experienced the theological policing that dictated the terms of our scholarship. We have all encountered arrogant men who erase women's contributions and silence them in public. A hostile voice who addressed me during a conference, a fist slamming on a table, deliberate avoidance but all smiles for my male interlocutor, explicit put downs, all reflect a regime that Lutheran men apply to discipline their female students and colleagues. To put it bluntly: Every female Lutheran theologian has an unwritten curriculum vitae of experiences that they can list under the hashtag #toxicLutheranmasculinity.

The question is: why is Lutheran theology permeated with this harmful presentation of masculinity? Is there a connection between the doctrine of justification as represented by the male theological elite and the deficit of justice for female theologians? In this chapter I explore this connection, specifically the way in which justification has been communicated as the truth of Lutheran theology, yet in such a way as to abdicate responsibility for embodied justice. I first diagnose the distinctive theology inherited from German Lutheranism that has shaped fundamental behaviors, specifically how the doctrine of justification developed during the second half of the twentieth century is integrally bound together with a type of masculinity that reinforces male power in theology. I underscore that the sickness of misogyny is contagious and has affected an entire theological culture. After diagnosis I turn to prescription. For the health of body and soul, church and theology, I reflect on how the doctrine of justification requires an account of embodiment that entails justice. A resistance to the sort of toxic ecclesiology entailed by the traditional Lutheran doctrine of justification requires thinking in new ways about the body of Christ. The object of justification is an embodied soul, as I argue, that becomes the subject of justice.

DISEMBODIED JUSTIFICATION

The doctrine that has most clearly identified Lutheran theological and ecclesial identity is the doctrine of justification by grace without human works or merits. This doctrine—identified by proponents of the Luther Renaissance at the turn of the twentieth century in Germany—is proudly the prerogative of Lutherans.[5] Luther, so the familiar story goes, pounded the nails into the door of the Wittenberg Castle Church, advertising ninety-five propositions that combatted papal indulgences by insisting that God alone justifies human sinners. Sinners are incapable of obeying one jot or tittle of the law. The law, cognizant of human incapacity, shifts from prescription to accusation. The law according to its "second function" accuses humans of their sin—all sins, great or small, are equally flattened and all meriting of eternal punishment. The law drives the old Adam to acknowledge his impotence for any good work. Yet where there is human impossibility, there God reveals the power of the gospel, the divine work that alone is potent to absolve sin, to restore right relationship between sinner and God, and to open the gates of paradise. Justification identifies the work of God to save. It is thus known as the article by which the church stands or falls.

Carol Christ, however, draws attention to a different aspect of justification. She observed among her male professors at Yale that they were intellectually committed to doctrine yet were not interested in questions of how doctrine is related to gender. The question of gender concerns how doctrine is embodied in the history of the church. Doctrine is commonly understood as a linguistically articulated proposition. Its truth (or falsity) is determined by its correspondence to reality or how it coheres with other propositions. Even a theory about the social verification of doctrine, or how doctrinal propositions cohere with behaviors of Christians, has been advanced in this theological discussion.[6] Yet doctrine as embodied in gendered relationships was not part of the theological equation. Embodiment within the body of Christ as ethical conformity with doctrine, yes, but not conceptualized in embodied relationships of persons within the mystical body.

The challenge is the following: Feminist scholars have advanced the claim that the rationality in the west is imagined as disembodied and universal. This legacy goes back to Plato who defined knowledge as the eternal contemplation of the forms that transcends the embodied world of temporalized particulars. Feminist philosopher Pamela Sue Anderson explains how the western tradition lauds "pure reason" that is abstracted from empirical content as the way in which knowledge of objects of experience is made possible.[7] This type of reason is deployed to make claims whose truth can be tested according to criteria of knowledge. Furthermore, this rationality aims to articulate claims that do not take into consideration variations due to embodied, linguistic, and cultural factors. Feminist philosophers and theologians have proposed corrections to this restriction of knowledge to these conditions that have historically been prescribed by a white male intellectual elite. They have expanded restrictive epistemologies to non-cognitive, experiential, and mystical ways of knowing. They have moved past essentialist descriptions of "nature" by explaining how constructions of gender shape feminist perspectives on the world. The body, particularly its cultural constructions, is significant for revising the traditional mind-body dualism that has funded limited notions of a universal rationality. An expansive and multiperspectival imaginary challenges the one-sided elevation of one kind of rationality to a universal place of privilege.

A version of the Lutheran doctrine of justification that has been prevalent on both sides of the Atlantic since the 1960s plays precisely into the epistemological bias presupposed by western rationality. The specific issue has to do with empirical concretion. The doctrine according to this version prohibits the actualization of justification, namely human works, in space and time. In fact, it forbids works in any direction—as a precursor to the gospel and as consequence of the gospel. As a precursor to the gospel, works serve solely to expose the human failure to achieve justification. Works are judged by the law to be entirely deficient in merit; even the best works of the saints are deemed worthless in God's sight. Works after justification are also deemed insufficient in terms of their salvific merit. Yet even works done out of love as a consequence of the gospel do not serve any habitual technology of the self. Rather their status as works of love elevates them to a status of exceptional ethics. Works of love do not obey any laws because love knows no laws. Works of love spring forth spontaneously from the justified self and are directed wholeheartedly to the indiscriminate neighbor with a selflessness that indicates the freedom of a Christian. Both the works condemned as deficient prior to the gospel and those works springing forth from love that knows no laws are works that fall outside the bounds of concrete interpersonal relations[8]—embodied relations that would be the realm of concrete ethical action. Works are characterized as either accused or as the generic love of neighbor on both sides of justification's equation. The doctrine of justification by faith alone falls if works are somehow integrated into its inner systematics. The doctrines stand in the abstract yet fall when applied to concrete life.

This particular version of the doctrine of justification is an inheritance of a particular moment in German theological and cultural history. Justification did not always entail a prohibition against works. Some versions of German Lutheranism, specifically those inflected by Pietism and neo-Kantian philosophy, stipulated an ethical dimension to the doctrine. According to a version appropriated by Pietist theologians in the seventeenth century, life lived after justification turned the soul toward the good. Faith is expressed in works of love (cf. Gal 5:6). Lutheran Orthodox theologians of the eighteenth century conceptualized justification in terms of trinitarian indwelling in the soul. When the Trinity takes up its abode in the soul, an "essential righteousness" is created with an openness to concretizing justice in works. Albrecht Ritschl inherited these Lutheran traditions and oriented justification to reconciliation in his own construction of the doctrine. Justification is concretized when the believer works the good in the community.[9] The communities of church and world are the places in which justification is actualized as reconciliation.

A distinctive conceptualization of justification apart from works only emerged after World War II. It is this version articulated by particular German Lutheran theologians that was inherited by North American Lutherans and thus became dominant on this side of the Atlantic. Werner Elert is the representative voice of this theology of justification in antithesis to works. He deployed the Kantian distinction between the transcendental and the empirical in order to map the subjective sites that are the objects of divine justifying activity.[10] The transcendental aspect of the self, the transcendental unity of apperception that structures the faculty of representation as a coherent "I" through time, never however appearing in time as a distinct object of perception, is, according to Elert, the site of justification. Justification of the transcendental I never needs to appear in any distinct works in time—its justification is complete and whole. Empirical works in space and time are works that may exhibit the inner justification. Yet there is no necessary relation between transcendental justification and empirical justice. In his theological appropriation of Kant, Elert distinguishes between two accounts of the self, the transcendental and the empirical. While the justification of the sinner is complete in the transcendental I, the temporal self remains permeated by sin in life, incomplete in view of a final justification. Elert could not determine how the word of grace could take empirical hold in the reality of this world. His Kantian conceptuality made this philosophically impossible. His legacy separated justification from sanctification, gospel and law, in ways unprecedented in earlier Lutheran traditions.

A brief historical reflection on the social-cultural context in which this version of justification was articulated notes a crisis in German masculinity. Both world wars, with Germany the aggressor, ended in devastating loss. Particularly the scores of maimed, crippled, and devasted male bodies who had been conditioned by militarized "hardness" returning from the infamous trenches precipitated a crisis in masculinity.[11] How male theologians articulated the doctrine of justification during these traumatic times is both a social-cultural and a theological question. Elert's example exposes the horror of empirical reality while simultaneously addressing another reality, that of justification without temporal concretion. Justification cannot take hold in a world in which destruction reigns. Justification was to be rescued from horrifying embodiments.

On the terms of how male German Lutherans and their American counterparts formulated the doctrine in the second half of the twentieth century, justification denigrates any technology of the self that might be connected to works in systematic relation. A temporal series of good works does not add up to a technology of the self. The paradox thus reigns supreme in this post-war theological culture—the paradox of justification in the disembodied transcendental I, and the embodied self whose works do not merit anything, are permeated with sin and are not oriented in any way to a unifying good. "Paradox" was the leading term identifying this iteration of justification: the paradox of the *simul iustus et peccator* or, in other words, the division between disembodied doctrine and embodied sin under the law.[12]

Justification by divine fiat is the toxic version of the doctrine. Unmoored from any ethical concerns, it leads to an exclusive preoccupation with divine agency. This focus on divine agency as the power of the divine fiat becomes the model for human male power. When this power is related to the disregard for concrete ethical relations, one that has been justified theologically at the outset, it is rife for raw abuse.[13]

When I got to Yale the Lutheran professoriate had not really changed since Carol Christ and Judith Plaskow's days. The Lutheran theologian Søren Kierkegaard was still read, even though his ethic of universal neighborly love evaded the concrete love of the real neighbor. Postliberal theology was still dominant, even though it presupposed an anti-realist notion of truth as coherence.[14] An orthodox doctrinal system without consideration of epistemological issues had been constructed as the "grammar" of a Christian worldview. The disembodied doctrine of justification appeared in new postliberal form.

DOCTRINE AND BODIES

Lutheran churches in America have preached this toxic doctrine of justification for decades. In seminary, Lutheran students are taught to correctly distinguish between law and gospel so that they can teach and preach both terms of justification: the sinful human and the justifying God. Yet as feminist Lutheran theologian Marit Trelstad has aptly diagnosed, the language in which this homiletical recommendation is couched is disconcertingly similar to the language of sexual violence. She refers to the text published by C. F. W. Walther and popular in seminary instruction. Walther advocates preaching the law in "full sternness" and states that "if you do this, you will be handling a sharp knife that cuts into the life of people.... From the effects of your preaching they will go down on their knees at home" and "see how awfully contaminated with sins they were and how sorely they needed the Gospel."[15] The aim of Lutheran preaching was to "[d]rive people to their knees and make them need the gospel."[16] On their knees, begging for mercy, sinners confessed their incapacity for any good. Only at that point of no escape could the divine gospel do its work.

The preaching of the law is the sole precursor to the gospel. The accusing law is one "word" that brings people to their knees. Yet the second word of justification is no less part of an abusive structure. Its effect is in the transcendental "I," achieving so to speak the revolution in the hidden reaches of the heart to which self-consciousness has neither reflective nor empirical access. As transcendental, justification grounds an exceptional ethic of generic love of neighbor that cannot be regulated by any laws of duty because love knows no laws. Love arises spontaneously from the forgiven heart in ways that can even result in a teleological suspension of the ethical. Such an exceptional ethic was central to the modern ethos that bore the seeds of fascism in the 1920s.[17] As we now know, many German Lutheran theologians became supporters of the Aryan Paragraph from 1933 and other racist policies of National Socialism. Elert was one such theologian who supported this paragraph that forbade people identified as "non-Aryan" to work in the state as civil servants, a category which included pastors and professors. After the war, American Lutherans came to Erlangen to study with Elert. American theologians like Gerhard Forde and Robert Bertram insisted, like Elert did, on the centrality of the law/gospel dialectic in the doctrine of justification. Law is accusatory, while love has the potential of amplifying abuse in the state of exception.

This version of the disembodied doctrine of justification, however, is not truly an abstract formulation. Doctrine is articulated by persons who embody distinctive cultural expressions. The German men whose politics were associated with National Socialism and the Americans who learned from them communicated this version of the doctrine into the Lutheran churches. They embodied justification as an abstract doctrine in the mystical body of Christ. Yet although allegedly disembodied in order to preserve the right distinction between law and gospel, justification in this sense expressed the cultural values associated with the doctrine's production from the 1930s through to the 1990s. Particular features of this doctrine convey its resistance to concretion, namely the capacity to correctly distinguish between law and gospel, the justification of the transcendental I, and the abusive rhetoric that communicates divine judgment as prelude to gospel. As such, the disembodied doctrine embodies a toxic theological perspective articulated by male Lutheran theologians. The article by which the church stands is permeated with a toxic form of masculinity.

DISGUST

How are doctrines embodied in personal bodies and institutional bodies, even when the message they communicate is devoid of concrete experience? The truth of doctrine does not only exist in the mind; ideas shape and are shaped by their concrete embodiments. Ideas have real effects on the bodies that perpetuate them. New research in psychology and neuroscience shows toxic effects of injustice on bodies. Abuse changes cellular, neurochemical, and hormonal pathways. Bodies traumatized in early childhood continue to struggle throughout their personal lives. Trauma is a life sentence. Physiological trauma shapes ways of relating that express foundational events, and minds rehearse, sublimate, and perennially interpret scarring experiences. The effects of a doctrine that presumes a disembodied subject has tangible and real effects.

Contemporary feminist philosopher Kate Manne considers how patriarchal values are communicated and absorbed at the level of physiological reactions. She writes about misogyny in her book *Down Girl* as practices of enforcing patriarchal norms.[18] Practices like mansplaining are designed to exert a power dynamic that is skewed in favor of male knowers and grateful female recipients of that knowledge. Women are punished who transgress the female roles associated with caregiving that society assigns to them. Manne also attends to the particular challenges women in leadership positions face. Female politicians, business leaders, and professors are particularly prone to the enforcing of cultural norms because their job descriptions are perceived as antithetical to maternal caregiving.[19] Manne analyzes the social dynamics that punish these women in different and unconscious ways. The punitive regime is, in short, embodied as it enforces social hierarchies.

The common perception of the patriarchy is that women, since Aristotle, have been viewed as deficient men in terms of rationality. Sexism, however, is not a matter of rationality. Women have proven time and time again that their rational functions are at least equal to those of men. In running for office, in job applications, in prizes awarded to outstanding undergraduates, women have superb credentials. Yet they still do not get the jobs for which they are immensely qualified; they continue to be valued as less than men in terms of pay equity; they continue to be scrutinized by the media in distinctively punitive terms; their contributions are blatantly erased from the record. The meritocracy cannot account for the persistence of glass ceilings. There are deeper mechanisms at stake.

Manne details these mechanisms in her book. One of her case studies is the female politician, Hillary Clinton.[20] Clinton is an example of a woman who dared to run for the highest political office in the U.S. Manne carefully surveys the specific judgments she received at the hands of journalists, politicians, the public, and especially the 53 percent of white women who did not vote for her in the presidential election. Reasons were given for votes against Clinton. Her voice was too shrill. Her hands were always hiding something. Her rapid disappearance from a meeting coupled with the diagnosis of pneumonia made her too fragile for the presidential office. Her emails—even after nine hours of interrogation by Congress—were blanketed by the suspicion that marked her entire candidacy. She was judged to be crooked, dishonest, and corrupt. Manne's analysis of these damning epithets—damning when compared with her adversary who had a documented history of groping women and bankrupting his businesses—is that they expressed bodily discomforts conditioned by a sexist culture.

Manne focuses on disgust as the feeling that elicits expressions of suspicion.[21] Disgust is an embodied reaction that is first directed to poisonous food. A physical aversion is conditioned by encounter with this food so as to protect the person from harm. Manne explains how this feeling is extended from the physical into the socio-cultural realm that is characterized by distinct practices habituated over time. Through habituation, experience becomes predictable reality. Disgust is physically experienced as a reaction to toxic foods. When transposed into the social register, persons too can be perceived as "disgusting." Disgust is elicited by a person perceived as transgressive. The question concerns why specific persons are deemed repulsive. Manne explains that this aversion has to do with persons who trespass the cultural norms for their gender (and/or race). Some women, specifically women in leadership positions have trespassed the cultural identification of what it means to be a "woman." While "man" signifies human personhood on its own terms, "woman" signifies giver. A woman is identified with her roles of giving, as mother, partner, caretaker, and teacher to the extent that teaching is a caring role. Her role is determined as caretaker in relation to others. Cultural norms enforce and reward this behavior, while punishing those who transgress it. In the case of professions in which the circle of influence is not directly associated with degrees of care—for example, teaching large lectures or political influence in which interpersonal care is suppressed in favor of universal policy, judgments about a woman's lack of care are much more pervasive. A woman in a position of leadership has trespassed the very definition of her role as a giver of care. Her presence is experienced as disgusting. Disgust, an emotional response originally felt in the presence of poisonous food, is displaced as the disgust of transgressive women.

An encounter with a transgressive woman elicits disgust. Yet this physical sensation has been conditioned through socio-cultural habituation. What an individual experiences as disgust is actually a feeling constructed through and infused with cultural values, in this case the patriarchy. The mechanism, however, is unconscious. The feeling of disgust is uncomfortable. The individual who experiences disgust reacts to the presence of this bodily feeling and seeks to blame the cause of this discomfort. The cause is sought outside the self. Blame is attributed of the cause; the transgressive woman is blamed as cause of the feeling of disgust. She is disgusting. Epithets of "crooked" and "suspicious" identify the reasons in the cause for the elicited feeling. Hillary is crooked, her hands look suspicious, she is hiding something. The reasons for disgust are invented *ex post facto*. Her person is blamed as the external cause for bodily discomfort. In this way the body's emotions are moral signifiers. Disgust assigns moral deficiency to its cause. Women are the immoral causes of emotions and as such, their disgusting presence becomes the rational justification for discrediting their leadership.

Manne's research on the moral signifiers of embodied feelings is pertinent to the Lutheran discussion of justification. This doctrine has been the prerogative of the male theological elite. The theological theorizing of this doctrine assigns its workings to the abstract. The gospel is God's word that communicates the divine work to effect forgiveness of sins in the transcendental I. How God's word is embodied in intersubjective communication is not the issue at stake; that God's word has these effects is the key element of this "pure" doctrine. Furthermore, it is this version of doctrine that is embodied by its representing theologians. While the doctrine is articulated as an abstract mechanism, its proponents are not. They are theologians inhabiting flesh and blood, gendered predominantly male.

The mystical body of Christ is a physical society. Christians experience, feel, and project bodily discomfort onto causes. Feelings of disgust are felt to be triggered by the presence of female and queer clergy. Words discipline these purveyors of the gospel—their voices are too shrill, suspicious hands hide something, the gifts they offer are suspect of not being the reality that they liturgically identify as body and blood of Christ. The embodied effects of this circulation of misogyny in the body of Christ are deleterious. Trauma compromises a body's immune system, bends and constricts a body's postures, represses natural cortisol levels, and increases risks of cancer and heart disease. This disembodied doctrine makes people sick, physically, emotionally, and intersubjectively. The abstraction from the body distorts doctrine and the ways in which its reality is circulated in the body of Christ. A patriarchal church has pernicious effects on the women that its word of law strikes down or the word of gospel that is divorced from the ethical mandate, "Go and sin no more" (John 8:11). The sickened recipients of this doctrine of justification cry out for justice.

THEOLOGICAL REPARATIONS

How can theologians repair a doctrine that has pernicious effects on women's bodies, the church body, and the body politic? How can theologians rewrite the doctrine of justification so that the injustice of misogyny be transformed to justice for each one of God's creatures? Theologians need to be doctrinal surgeons. They must diagnose the illness and prescribe healing. They must recover the truth of justification by identifying how the divine attribute of righteousness transforms bodies according to relations of justice. If theologians truly believe that the gospel brings abundant life for all, then they must reconceptualize justification as a doctrine that embodies justice. Justification is God's communication of Christ's benefits, yet its effects must free minds from the sins of false thinking about gender, free hearts from desires to hierarchize bodies according to gender values, and heal bodies from the pernicious psychological and physiological effects of sexism. This is a tall order for the doctrine of justification. Are theologians up to the task of doing right by God's righteousness?

The divine attribute of righteousness is central to the doctrine of justification. The connection between righteousness and justice has been severed in English because a single term—righteousness—is the common English translation of the Latin *iustitia dei*. Luther anxiously obsessed about the phrase in Romans 1:17: "For in the gospel the righteousness of God is revealed...." When Luther recounts his reformation experience in the 1545 preface to his Latin writings, he writes that he had misunderstood *iustitia dei* according to the inherited philosophical understanding that the divine attribute identifies God's unchanging essence.[22] Luther's theological reparation consisted of reconceptualizing the philosophical predication to a theological predicate of action: God is righteous by actively making sinners righteous, in effect, giving them this attribute so that it identifies the person as free from sin. God's essence is to give what characterizes divinity, such as righteousness, life, and salvation, to humanity. God gives to sinners what belongs to God.

The terminology that Lutherans deploy to talk about the way in which God's gift of righteousness is attributed to humans is "justification." Yet the usage connotes a "coram deo" (before God) relation. Justification is exclusively preoccupied with divine agency. A qualitatively different meaning is assigned to interpersonal justice that is "coram hominibus." Justification connotes a distinctive relation between God and the human that has little to do with concrete relations that embody justice or injustice.

A reorienting of justification to justice requires connecting both together as constitutive of the doctrine of justification. It is a recovery of a metaphysic of the soul and a mysticism of the body of Christ that is at stake. The explicit turn away from metaphysics and mysticism in Lutheran theology was prioritized by Albrecht Ritschl at the end of the nineteenth century. He appropriated a neo-Kantian philosophy in order to articulate the doctrine of justification in terms of its effects in an individual's thinking, willing, and feeling. The turn away from the discourse of the soul had the consequence of orienting justification to the forensic—its declarative—connotation that it now has. In order to connect justification to justice, the discourse of metaphysics and mysticism must be recovered from the Lutheran Orthodox theologians who Ritschl rejected. Such a discourse is, as I claim, better suited to conceptualizing justification and justice with embodiment as central.

Lutheran theologians in the seventeenth and eighteenth centuries worked out an understanding of justification from the perspective of a metaphysic of the soul.[23] Aristotelian philosophy had been integrated into academic discussions of doctrine, particularly because the discourse of the soul dovetailed with the Johannine accounts of the Spirit's indwelling in persons and community. At this time, Pietists, confessional Lutherans, and Enlightenment philosophers were coming to terms with new accounts of subjectivity. While Enlightenment philosophers contributed the notion of universal reason to the discussion, and Pietists a notion of the subject's responsibility for deepening personal spirituality in order to reinvigorate the church with spiritual life, Protestant Orthodoxy offered an understanding of the effects of divine righteousness in the soul as one of trinitarian indwelling. Justification, communicated by the word of preaching that set people free from sin, was the beginning of the soul's conversion to a new way of being. Justification was the beginning of an essential righteousness, the presence of the Trinity in the soul, that oriented its substance, namely will and reason to abundant life.

Protestant Orthodox theologians wished to preserve the Reformation's commitment to justification as communicated by the preaching of the word and the distribution of the sacraments. The liturgical proclamation required an ecclesial context. The gospel was to be communicated to anxious souls and their faith strengthened by being in communion with Christ in the church. Essential righteousness has two dimensions. Trinitarian indwelling honors the individual soul by endowing it with the gift of righteousness. Individuals are joined together in the community through their common grounding in the Trinity and the concrete ways in which Christ's gospel is circulated.

The Reformed theologian Friedrich Schleiermacher inherited Protestant Orthodoxy's link between justification and church. He deliberately connected individual and community in his understanding of how Jesus mystically communicates his perfect God-consciousness to individuals. This action orients individuals to each other, facilitating communal flourishing.[24] While rejecting a metaphysical concept of nature in order to reconceptualize the soul in terms of the relations between immediate and sensible consciousness, Schleiermacher made productive use of the Johannine notion of indwelling in order to explain how it is that Jesus has transformative effects in the soul. Schleiermacher's reformulation of justification as "person-forming" is exemplary here. The effects of Jesus are the contagion of his God-consciousness, mediated through his person to those who come into contact with him. Jesus' words bring life and his deeds redirect a body to health. They do this, Schleiermacher explains, by rearranging the relation between immediate and sensible self-consciousness in a person's soul. Immediate consciousness is raised from its suppression by sensible self-consciousness, and is elicited by Jesus' action in such a way as to begin permeating sensible self-consciousness with its orientation. Justification begins a process by which the person is formed in ways that correct delusional thinking, heal the emotions, and recreate a person who is capable of living in relation to others. A person is formed for flourishing in community. The justification that Jesus initiates in individuals is immediately related to their capacity for life with others. The justification of the sinner creates the church.

The notion of soul—whether metaphysical as in Lutheran Orthodoxy or transcendental as in Schleiermacher—is crucial to a theological reparation of a disembodied doctrine of justification. Both Lutheran Orthodox theologians and Schleiermacher intended to express the idea that the soul is God's area of justifying activity. The inner recesses of the soul, its opacity, its hiddenness, is the place of God's indwelling. It is the site of new subjectivity. It is, as Paul exclaims, "not I but Christ who lives in me" (Gal 2:20). Here is personal substance that is itself constituted and held in existence by the presence of another, a person whose ground of being is informed and created by another. Justification is the entry into the explication of this ground of being as external to the self, yet interior in its recesses. Or in other words, the invocation of the soul has to do with a notion of divine omnipresence that is particularized as salvific, working in the recesses of the soul to give abundant life. Christian theology particularizes that presence in trinitarian terms. Divine presence justifies, and thereby constitutes subjectivity.

The recovery of the soul as site of God's justification is generative for an embodied notion of justification. A person is formed by the Trinity's presence to the soul. The person-forming effects include the constitution of subjectivity through intersubjectivity, the initiation of the soul into an explicit awareness of this indwelling through reception of preaching and the sacraments, and a development of the person under the influence of the real presence of Christ in the soul. Justification is explicated by a doctrine of how Christ is present to the soul in order to transform it, and how this presence is particularized and rendered explicit through verbal and sacramental cues.

The important question is how justification addresses the injustices of bodies traumatized by original sins that are both pervasively pernicious in our culture and socially constructed in our society in which original sins are deployed, reenacted, and reinscripted onto bodies. The soul in the classic Christian theological tradition is the reality with which Christ is concerned. Christ is the *Christus medicus*, the carer for and healer of souls permeating bodies. A theology that underscores Christ's real presence in the world begins with an understanding of justification in which Christ is present to the human subject as soul-forming reality. Christ's presence in the soul infuses the soul with healing effects that orient the body/soul unity to coherent meaning, to healing from suffering, and release from the effects of sadistic structures that diminish the I as appendage of sado-masochistic relations. Christ works in the hidden recesses of subjectivity in order to coax a traumatized soul/body into a new creation. The Spirit's presence reconstitutes the soul's emotional makeup—the gifts of kindness, joy, peace, love, and self-control are infused into the soul's inner ground so that the Spirit forms the person in new ways. The triune God constitutes subjectivity in its person-forming activity of extending the effects of justification into justice—for the embodied soul that bears the trauma of evils. The God of justification is the God of justice—the divine righteousness makes good on every soul that is judged by God to have infinite value in the divine presence. Justification effects the constitution of new subjectivity according to the work of the divine justice.

The body of Christ, designated "mystical," is a gathering of embodied persons. Justified persons embody a new kind of community that is grounded in trinitarian presence. The divine presence justifies by communicating the divine justice to persons. Justice takes hold in the community as the reality in which it is grounded.

The term "justice" in the sense I am advocating has to do with theological content. Theologians must recover and construct a distinctive theological perspective on justice. The term has in recent years been coopted by a political semantics. Culture wars have been played out in the churches, positioning political issues on either side of the pew. Homosexuality, women's reproductive rights, and critical race theory are issues that rally church politics. Progressive churches have taken up the struggle for political equality. Conservative churches make a case for the opposite by arguing that the gospel is antithetical to culture. Politics has monopolized justice discourse in the churches. Christianity, especially in America, is divided by litmus tests determining appropriate political positioning.

Embodied justice is the issue. Critical theory provides the categories to analyze constructions of reality and to highlight how these constructions express contingent socio-cultural values that have serious political implications. Critical theory is a tool that raises awareness of injustice, its causes and effects, and prescribes justice-making action. A theological account of justice can add its distinctive perspective on a critical theory of embodiment and its social signifiers. Theologians have long recognized the pervasiveness of the will to corruption, power, and pettiness. The biblical prophetic tradition from which they draw is clear that the fight for justice is a divine work. A theological reparation of the doctrine of justification imagines the body of Christ as a justice-making community.

Here justice is reclaimed not merely as political progress, but as justice conceived in alignment with justification. How might this be conceived? The Lutheran tradition notes vocation as a significant theological concept with socio-political implications. If this concept is reconceptualized explicity in terms of reciprocity, then it conveys the intersubjective understanding of justification I have noted above. If Christ dwells in the soul, thereby creating a new person, then justice enacts intersubjectively constituted existence in the community. Vocations serve the neighbor. Rather than merely expressing individual talents and skills, vocations are exercised for the purpose of neighborly flourishing. Justice means taking on someone else's struggles as one's own, and then working to acknowledge, alleviate, and transform struggle into joy.

A theological reparation of justification takes seriously the justice issues implied by an embodied construction of the doctrine. Justification is a person-constituting divine activity. The triune presence in the soul informs the soul's substance. Sometimes its effects are hidden as Christ cares for the soul in its deep recesses, possibly hidden even from the individual's view. But this embodied notion of justification orients justice in embodied community, where persons continue to be formed in reciprocal relations with each other. Reciprocity takes place when trauma is recognized and rendered in the story of the community. Injustices are taken up into the body of Christ; reparations imagined and created so that the new creation becomes a reality.

As theologians, we bear and convey the culture in our articulations of doctrine. Yet as theologians we can also be therapeutic in our production of doctrine. The tools we work with are designed to perceive the reality of God, the God who created embodiment for good reasons and who will make good on the divine promises to the material world. A theological reparation that tells the truth about justification does justice to this God.

NOTES

1. Carol P. Christ and Judith Plaskow, *Goddess and God in the World: Conversations in Embodied Theology* (Minneapolis, MN: Fortress Press, 2016).

2. Christ and Plaskow, *Goddess and God*, 28.

3. Jaroslav Pelikan, *The Christian Tradition: A History of the Development of Doctrine*, 5 vols. (Chicago, IL: The University of Chicago Press, 1973–1990).

4. See my *How Luther Became the Reformer* (Louisville, KY: Westminster John Knox Press, 2019) for a detailed account of the Luther Renaissance and its creation of a particular image of Luther as modern Protestant reformer.

5. See ch. 3 of my *How Luther Became the Reformer*.

6. George A. Lindbeck, "Atonement and the Hermeneutics of Social Embodiment," *Pro Ecclesia* 5, no. 2 (1996): 144–60.

7. Pamela Sue Anderson, "Feminist Theology as Philosophy of Religion," in *The Cambridge Companion to Feminist Theology*, ed. Susan Frank Parsons (Cambridge: Cambridge University Press, 2002), 40–59.

8. For example, see M. Jaime Ferreira, *Love's Grateful Striving: A Commentary on Kierkegaard's Works of Love* (Oxford: Oxford University Press, 2001).

9. Albrecht Ritschl, *The Christian Doctrine of Justification and Reconciliation: The Positive Development of the Doctrine*, trans. H. R. Mackintosh and A. B. Macaulay (Edinburgh: T&T Clark, 1902).

10. See his account in Werner Elert, *The Structure of Lutheranism: The Theology and Philosophy of Life of Lutheranism Especially in the Sixteenth and Seventeenth Centuries*, trans. Walter A. Hanson, Concordia Classics (Saint Louis, MO: Concordia, 1962), 141.

11. Ute Scheub, *Heldendämmerung: Die Krise der Männer und warum sie auch für Frauen gefährlich ist* (New York: Pantheon Verlag, 2010); see also Thomas Kühne, *The Rise and Fall of Comradeship: Hitler's Soldiers, Male Bonding and Mass Violence in the Twentieth Century* (Cambridge: Cambridge University Press, 2017).

12. The German theologian Rudolf Hermann proves the exception. He situates the paradox of the *simul* in a temporal horizon that is framed by prayer. See Christine Svinth-Værge Põder, "Die Römerbriefvorlesung bei Karl Holl und Rudolf Hermann," in *Lutherrenaissance: Past and Present*, ed. Christine Helmer and Bo Kristian Holm, Forschungen zur Kirchen- und Dogmengeschichte 106 (Göttingen: Vandenhoeck & Ruprecht, 2015), 64–65.

13. I thank Jacqueline Mariña for helping me to think through the toxic implications of the divine fiat of forensic justification.

14. See ch. 3 of my *Theology and the End of Doctrine*.

15. C. F. W. Walther, *The Proper Distinction Between Law and Gospel* (St. Louis, MO: Concordia Publishing House, 1929), 72, 73, 83. Cited in Marit Trelstad, "~~Charity~~ Terror Begins at Home: Luther and the 'Terrifying and Killing' Law," in *Lutherrenaissance: Past and Present*, ed. Christine Helmer and Bo Kristian Holm, Forschungen zur Kirchen- und Dogmengeschichte 106 (Göttingen: Vandenhoeck & Ruprecht, 2015), 220.

16. Trelstad refers this quote to a course she took on Lutheran preaching, "Homiletics," with instructors Gracia Grindal and Cathy Malotky, Lutheran Northwestern Theological Seminary, Saint Paul, Minnesota, spring 1993: lecture by Grindal, April 19, 1993; as cited by Trelstad, "~~Charity~~ Terror Begins at Home," 220.

17. See my *How Luther Became the Reformer*.

18. Kate Manne, *Down Girl: The Logic of Misogyny* (Oxford: Oxford University Press, 2017), esp. ch. 8 (249–78) on women leaders.

19. "I present misogyny as a system of hostile forces that by and large *makes sense* from the perspective of patriarchal ideology, inasmuch as it works to police and enforce patriarchal order." Manne, *Down Girl*, 27 (emphasis K. M.).

20. Content taken from ch. 8 of Manne, *Down Girl*.

21. Disgust thematized in Manne, *Down Girl*, 256–63.

22. Martin Luther, "Preface to the Latin Writings (1545)," in *Luther's Works*, vol. 34 (Philadelphia, PA: Fortress Press, 1960), 336–37.

23. Heinrich Schmid (ed.), *The Doctrinal Theology of the Evangelical Lutheran Church*, trans. of 6th German edn. Charles A. Hay and Henry E. Jacobs, 2nd edn. (Philadelphia, PA: Lutheran Publication Society, 1889).

24. Friedrich Schleiermacher, *The Christian Faith*, ed. H. R. Mackintosh and J. S. Stewart, trans. D. M. Bailey et al. (Edinburgh: T&T Clark, 1999), §§100–101 (425–38).

Chapter 5

Complicity and the Christological Path of Ecclesial Resistance

Summons to a New Catechesis for a Time of Despair

Paul R. Hinlicky

OVERTURE

An acute problem of Christian conscience today is that of complicity in structures of malice and injustice. If all are entangled in webs of racism, sexism, and classism (the unholy trinity opposite the Apostle's assertion of the Beloved Community in Christ, Gal 3:26–28), there is accordingly no simple exit, neither individualist nor collectivist. There is, however, a way through the sinful web of complicity by the incision of the Christ-event. Just so, the plight of unwilling guilt, which accompanies this path and afflicts the conscientious believer as in Romans 7, cries out for illumination.

Such illumination would distinguish between universal sinfulness and relative guilt as between relations *coram deo* and *coram mundo,* respectively; this illumination is brought by the gospel which breaks in like a thief into a strong man's house. The distinction points those thus set free from captivity away from moralistic or utopian posturing for the re-engineering of individual or society. It points them instead to the struggling life of the ecclesia as the form of Christological resistance given here and now under prevailing structures, provided only that redemption is taken to affirm the goodness of the oppressed creation by way of new creative work for the vindication of the suffering (as per Romans 8's "redemption of our bodies").

If cooptation of this resistance by the dynamic "governmentality" (i.e., "governing rationality," Foucault) of contemporary neoliberal[1] structuring of malice in injustice is to be averted, the theological need is for a new catechesis in congregational life. This new catechesis would teach the "power of the powerless" (Havel)—"living in the truth" within a "system" of mendacity—and this "upward calling" (Solzhenitsyn) as the redemptive path of holy resistance through the tangle of complicity and despair.

COMPLICITY AND DESPAIR

One leg pushes to free the other from the morass, but in the process sinks itself more deeply into it. A foot pushes free only to land anew in mire. Resistance thus seems futile; reaction only makes one complicit in new ways. In this counsel of despair, activism at length turns to resignation. The defeated individual finds serenity in his Epicurean garden or her Buddhist-mystical *Gelassenheit*.

The foregoing paragraph is a reflection to be made as recently as the transformation of 1960s protest into the 1970s Me Generation's culture of narcissism; yet it is as old as Paul the Apostle and Luther his interpreter: knowledge of sinfulness leads to despair of self. Such is our contemporary plight. So Wendy Brown concludes her exemplary analysis of neoliberalism as the "governing rationality" spreading across the globe today: "we know what is wrong with this world, but cannot articulate a road out or a viable global alternative ... we are reduced to reform and resistance ... action as reaction.... [But] the Left's predicament refracts a ubiquitous, if unavowed, exhaustion and despair in Western civilization ... Neoliberalism's perverse theology of markets rests on this land of the scorched belief in the modern."[2]

Brown's precisely articulated despair fairly begs for a renewed theological grounding of the human subject with attendant illumination of the modern self's ironic denouement today in paralysis. In an important study that aims to liberate Luther's Paulinism for new appropriations in the Global South, Vítor Westhelle shrewdly observes, "If the heirs of the Reformation paid more attention to the fact that the reformers eliminated the difference between sinful acts and concupiscence, they might acknowledge the immense difficulties twentieth-century European theology had in explaining *theologically* how citizens who abide by the law can still connive in systems that standardize evil. One is a sinner and a murderer not only by pulling the trigger, but already by being part of the system that condones and promotes it."[3]

This rebuke contains a bold claim for the Christian doctrine of human sinfulness. Complicity is, by this reading, a socially "objective" state in which desire is captured and, being captive, takes the collaborative form of malicious envy—even in would-be "resistance." In a feedback loop, the malice of envy becomes in turn the energy which powers the social system that standardizes evil, configuring also its supposed dissidents. Exposition of these dense claims will be provided in what follows as we turn to Havel and Solzhenitsyn.

Westhelle in any case goes on immediately to discuss the systemic blindness of complicity to its own captivation by way of Hannah Arendt's notion of the "banality of evil." Analyzing the testimony of Adolf Eichmann, Arendt came to the daunting realization of Eichmann's "sincere"[4] struggle against personal inclinations to save some Jews as a "temptation" contrary to his Kantian sense of duty as configured within the National Socialist regime.[5] Because of this insight, both the judges at Eichmann's trial and Arendt herself struggled to articulate precisely the special criminal responsibility of Eichmann for obeying orders and doing his duty by masterminding the sprawling logistics of the Holocaust. "If everyone is guilty," Arendt finally expressed the conundrum, "then no one is guilty."[6] Christian insight into universal sinfulness cannot descend into a fog in which the difference between victim and perpetrator is no longer discerned or prosecuted.

Westhelle parses this conundrum with the Lutheran-Pauline distinction that, while spiritual sinfulness *coram deo* is universal, criminal guilt *coram hominibus* is particular and relative. He concludes that one's position in the power hierarchy determines the degree of responsibility and guilt, while giving no one unlimited responsibility and guilt, nor completely absolving anyone. The crucial insight here, if also offensive to modern sensibilities, is that everyone who participates in the system is passively, if not actively, guilty of the system's sinfulness. Also the one who actively resists its criminality remains passively guilty by sheer dint of participating in the system, which as master configures its own resistance. Note well, however: the "alien," as identified by the system of malice and injustice, is as such hapless, a *non-participant* yet present within it. It is "mere life" and thus rather purely its pitiful *victim*.[7]

One can evade this troubling insight into the tangles of complicity, paradoxically, by consigning it to the exceptional case of Nazism as some kind of aberration over against the historical march of progress. But the insight applies broadly to modern social systems, liberal democracy under today's regime of neoliberalism included. In my 2013 study, *Before Auschwitz*, I accordingly warned that fascism is neither a reversion from modern progress to medieval barbarism (the usual liberal interpretation of Nazism as a special relapse), nor is it the logic of capitalism driven to an extreme by internal contradictions (the Marxist interpretation). Fascism is rather an endemic *modern* possibility, where "modern" indicates the rival possibilities of realizing the Cartesian-Kantian sovereign self, whether in fascism, in Marxism-Leninism, or in (today) neoliberalism,[8] even though all these end ironically in bondage and thus at length in despair.

Václav Havel saw *precisely this* about *us* in the West and made a point of it in his magnificent essay, "The Power of the Powerless," to which we shall carefully attend as our catechetical primer on authentic resistance under conditions of intractable complicity. The web of complicity through which human beings sacrifice their integrity through ideological rationalization to the "system" is not, he wrote, "the result of some incomprehensible misunderstanding of history, nor is it history somehow gone off its rails."⁹ Rather, as Havel detected from within the Brezhnev-"normalized" Czechoslovakia of the 1970s, there is "in modern humanity a certain tendency towards the creation, or at least the toleration, of such a system. There is obviously something in human beings which responds to this system, something they reflect and accommodate, something within them which paralyzes every other effort of their better selves to revolt … alienated humanity supports this system as its own involuntary master plan, as a degenerate image of its own degeneration, as a record of people's own failure as individuals."¹⁰

Havel here presumes, as one must in an analysis of "alienation," that there is underlying the modern social systems some "proper" humanity. He writes that the essential aims of life are present "naturally" in every person, and he specifies these aims as longing for dignity, for moral integrity, for the free expression of oneself, and a sense of transcendence. Havel in this way seeks a different source for human agency than those provided by the materialist Marx's *homo faber* or the idealist Kant's ethical subject. The source is, I daresay, the "theological subject." Readers may recognize in his list fragments (vestiges) of the biblical doctrine of humanity as made in the image of God for likeness to God.¹¹ This calling designates the theological subject.¹² As we shall see, this notion of human calling *by God*, of the human *vocation*, is integral to Havel's crypto-*theological* analysis of alienation.

Because of our thorough-going historicism, a muted appeal to the theological tradition such as Havel made seemed to be the only, lonely recourse from within the immanent plane of complicity-cum-mendacity. There is for us at the end of modernity no *philosophical* foundation available anymore to identify an underlying human "nature" or "essence" which, on account of its timeless substantiality, naturally resists its own supposed "alienation" and thus is always there to awaken, to activate, to arise in revolt as the "political" or "revolutionary" subject, agent of its own liberation. All that remains is theology's witness to God who calls and humanity as called; yet, in Havel's Euro-America, such witness is but the muted resonance of a fading memory.

In just this *desperate* way, however, Havel's crypto-theology is relevant for us in the United States today as we endure the demoralizing catastrophe of the Trump presidency, including a merely political "resistance" which increasingly apes precisely what it otherwise rightly despises in the scoundrel-president. While the "post-totalitarian system" of communist Czechoslovakia which Havel described had evolved, as he acknowledged, from the historical encounter between communist dictatorship and capitalist consumer society, Havel's analysis of "living a lie" bore a deep connection with the sibling unwillingness of Western consumers to sacrifice material blessings for the sake of their own spiritual and moral integrity. Thus his reflection on living in truth in a system of mendacity issues, as he explicitly notes, in "a kind of warning to the West, revealing to it its own latent tendencies."

For in truth we were in the 1970s but *sibling* rivals! "The post-totalitarian system is only one aspect ... of the general inability of *modern* humanity to be the master of its own situation...." (emphasis added). Note the irony of Havel's analysis of the paradoxical powerlessness to which the modern dream of sovereignty comes. The sovereign self of modernity becomes enslaved by the pursuit of mastery, though in varying ways. "The deep crisis shared with Western consumerism drags humanity helplessly along by the automatism of global technological civilization" while "there is no real evidence that Western democracy can offer solutions that are any more profound."[13] Indeed, in the West "people are manipulated in ways that are infinitely more subtle and refined than the brutal methods used in the post-totalitarian societies, as Solzhenitsyn pointed out in his 1978 Harvard lecture."[14] We will capitalize on Havel's allusion here to an exemplary resister, Alexandr Solzhenitsyn, in the conclusion to this chapter.

The conundrum—that even the awoken who would resist remains entangled in the system's sinfulness, that rebuke of another for complicity rebounds like a boomerang on the one who hurls it—gives rise to a desperate search for the missing "political" or "revolutionary" subject as may be seen in Alain Badiou's[15] (or Wendy Brown's) neo-Marxist quests for alternatives to neoliberalism's purchase of the human self, or in Edward Nik-Khah's similar nostalgia for the Kantian subject in his exposé of the idolatry of treating the unfettered market as an "omniscient" information processor.[16] If all we have as an alternative is such philosophical wishful thinking and/or nostalgia for a modern subject who can both see through the fog of systemic mendacity and act against natural inclinations to choose rewardless duty to universal values for their own sake, our plight is beyond redemption.[17] But in truth, not only is this lost Kantianism fatally predicated on an invidious anthropological dualism,[18] it arose in tandem with modern Europe's post-Christendom project of global colonialism and constitutes its deep rationalization. Not accidentally, Kant pit his "Tribunal of Reason" precisely against the theological subject.[19] Just so, the utopian dream of the modern subject in due course comes to grief in either the Marxist "god that failed"[20] or the liberal Mark Lilla's "stillborn God."[21]

Still confident modern philosophers, like Lewis White Beck, opine that the Kantian subject was justified as a rebuke to Lutheran pessimism and quietism,[22] as grounded in its doctrine of inherited sinfulness, descended from Augustine's doctrine of the sin of origin. Indeed, as Luther himself put it, "original sin is so deep a corruption of nature that reason cannot fathom it. It must be believed on the basis of the revelation in the Scripture."²³ Yet pessimism and quietism in face of this *revelation* of bondage would follow only from a Christological amnesia of which Luther is professedly not guilty. Despair of self is rather the gateway to a revolutionary reorganization of the self, its "new creation." For discovery of this plight and the strength to persevere in the struggle it denotes depend on a break-in from outside of the system, by one who will bind up the strong man to plunder his goods (Mark 3:27). One comes to know this bondage truly only in the event of being liberated from it. "God's mighty claim on upon our whole life," as the Barmen Declaration put it, brings "a joyful deliverance from the godless fetters of this world for a free, grateful service to [God's] creatures." Such deliverance provides the missing Christological link in Havel's paradoxical case for the "power of the powerless."

HAVEL'S CRYPTO-THEOLOGY

Groaning under the shroud of moral catastrophe in our time, it is worth time to recall carefully, and in some detail, the crypto-theology of Havel's essay. Havel argued that the Western press's identification of himself and other signatories to Charter 77 as "dissidents" within a "dictatorship" was quite misleading, projecting as it did a Western construal of the East's predicament, as if all that freedom required was the procedural justice of liberal democracy, as opposed to communist dictatorship. He detected in this projection of the Western press a definite blind spot to the web of mendacity engulfing communist and capitalist regimes alike, which he identified as but rival pursuits of the good life, taken as materialist "consumption." In reality, however, the "system" in communist Czechoslovakia was *not* that of a "dictatorship" any longer but had become "post-totalitarian." He meant by this a system had emerged such as what Foucault later called "governmentality."

So Havel:

> an incomparably more precise, logically structured, generally comprehensible and, in essence, extremely flexible ideology that, in its elaborateness and completeness, is almost a secularized religion. It offers a ready answer to any question whatsoever: it can scarcely be accepted only in part, and accepting it has profound implications for human life. In an era when metaphysical and existential certainties are in a state of crisis, when people are being uprooted and alienated and are losing their sense of what this world means, this ideology inevitably has a certain hypnotic charm ... of course, one pays dearly for this low-rent home: the price is abdication of one's own reason, conscience, and

responsibility, for an essential aspect of this ideology is the consignment of reason and conscience to a higher authority."[24]

—the Party in the East, the Market in the West.

To illustrate the penetration this "secularized religion" into the human interior, Havel took up a slice of ordinary life: the greengrocer who thoughtlessly puts up at his market stall the sign provided by the local Party boss, bearing the slogan from the Communist Manifesto: "Workers Of The World, Unite!" He comments that the greengrocer does this thoughtlessly with regard to the meaning of the slogan, which is but empty words to him. His conformity, or shall we say "complicity," consists in his reflection that this is the way things are, that he knows what is expected of him, that he is dependable and beyond reproach, obedient and therefore has the right to be left in peace. But the entire reflection is in reality rooted in the greengrocer's fear. Honesty would acknowledge "I am afraid, and therefore unquestionably obedient."

But displaying the sign allows the greengrocer to evade this painful introspection. After all, the defense springs up, what's wrong with workers of the world uniting? "Thus the sign helps the greengrocer to conceal from himself the low foundations of his obedience, at the same time concealing the low foundations of power. It hides them behind the façade of something high. And that something is *ideology*. Ideology is a specious way of relating to the world."[25] Havel in this way turns an original insight of Marx into ideology as "false consciousness" against the "real, existing socialism" of Marxism-Leninism.

The system's hold is not then by overt dictatorship, but rather "the post-totalitarian system touches people at every step, but it does so with its ideological gloves on. This is why life in the system is so thoroughly permeated with hypocrisy and lies ... because the regime is captive to its own lies, it must falsify everything. It falsifies the past." Havel continues: "It falsifies the present, and it falsifies the future. It falsifies statistics. It pretends not to possess an omnipotent and unprincipled police apparatus. It pretends to respect human rights. It pretends to persecute no one. It pretends to fear nothing. It pretends to pretend nothing. Individuals need not believe all these mystifications, but they must behave as though they did ... for this reason, however, they must *live within a lie* ... by this very fact individuals confirm the system, fulfill the system, make the system, *are* the system."[26]

The post-totalitarian system transcends the physical aspects of coercive power and establishes itself, then, as the pervasive way of living in the lie. What else, he asks, is "the greengrocer's slogan, but a small component in that huge backdrop to daily life?"[27] This makes the greengrocer both the victim of the system and its instrument, surrendering "human identity in favour of the identity of the system, that is, so that they may become agents of the system's general automatism and servants of its self-determined goals...." How do these passive victims become active, if unwitting collaborators with their victimizers? "[U]ltimately, and with no external urging, they come to treat any non-involvement as an abnormality, as arrogance, as an attack on themselves ... the post-totalitarian system makes everyone instruments of a mutual totality, the auto-totality of society."[28] In this way, Havel likens the profile of a genuine resistance to the member of a dysfunctional family who ceases any longer to enable the cover-up of the family secret. Thus this very "pillar"—of living in an ideology which systematically deceives—provides a very unstable foundation for the system. "It works only as long as people are willing to live within the lie."[29]

So precisely in his powerlessness, as both victim and unwitting agent of the lie, the greengrocer possesses a latent power: simply to tell the truth. Havel "imagines" that one day the greengrocer just "snaps" and stops displaying the party platitudes merely in order to ingratiate himself within the system which despises him and which he in truth despises in turn. Havel calls this imagined revolt "an attempt to *live within the truth*."[30] The Johannine echoes are palpable. This breach of truth-telling seems an "arrogant abnormality," as the snapped greengrocer now appears as an impolitic disruptor in the eyes of peers. Nonetheless he exposes, as Havel writes referring to the well-known fable, the "nakedness of the emperor." Truth-telling breaks the spell of the systemic lie in principle and thus threatens it entirely. Truth-telling ignites and spreads like a contagion because "under the orderly surface of the life of lies ... there slumbers the hidden sphere of life in its real aims of its hidden openness to truth"[31]—a crypto-theological reference once again to the *imago Dei*. Truth-telling finds an ally here in the invisible but omnipresent sphere of authentic humanity.

From this, however, Havel draws a perhaps surprising implication: living in the truth does not, and need not, "participate in any direct struggle for power."[32] Attestation of truth within systemic mendacity is a politically vulnerable witness in terms of what the system regards as power. The revolt against manipulation made by truth-telling manifests merely "a free expression of life" to which no one would attribute "any potential political significance, not to mention explosive power."[33] The martyr-testimony—recall the Johannine scene of Christ before Pilate—is made by someone "who is unwilling to sacrifice his or her human identity to politics, or rather who does not believe in a politics that requires such a sacrifice."[34]

By contrast, a "person who has been seduced by the consumer value system, whose identity is dissolved in an amalgam of the accoutrements of mass civilization, and who has no roots in the order of being, no sense of responsibility for anything higher than his or her personal survival, is a *demoralized* person. The system depends on this demoralization, deepens it, is in fact a projection of it into society."³⁵ Echoing down into the spiritually exhausted "post-humans" of Euro-America today, the demoralized person asks with Pilate, "What is truth?"

Pilate, captain of the demoralized and guardian of their order, is in charge. Steel upon steel, Pilate prevails, and if not, those who would prevail against him become themselves new captains of the newly demoralized. Accordingly, movements for living in the truth, Havel avers, "for the most part originate elsewhere, in the far broader area of the 'pre-political,' where living within a lie confronts living within the truth, that is, where the demands of the system conflict with the real aims of life."³⁶ The system generally fails to appreciate the significance of such "pre-political events and processes" that provide the living humus from which genuine change may sprout and spring into a new humanity.³⁷ Indeed, more than ever before such authentic "change will have to derive from human existence, from the fundamental reconstitution of the position of people in the world, their relationships to themselves and to each other, and to the universe … it must derive from profound existential and moral changes in society."³⁸ The evangelical call to conversion thus sounds from Havel's crypto-theology.

Havel accordingly called for the cultivation of "independent life" within the system which would be marked by "a relatively high degree of inner emancipation." He envisioned everything from philosophizing to artistic activity to free civic associations as arenas in which "living within the truth becomes articulate and materializes in a visible way."³⁹ The truthful life includes such pre-political *action* to make room for the genuine aims of life. By the same token, this program of living within the truth must be "fundamentally hostile towards the notion of violent change—simply because it places its faith in violence."⁴⁰ Faith in violence, beneath the veneer, is politics as usual. Zealot proponents of violent change are not "radical enough."⁴¹ What would be?

Citing the philosopher Jan Potočka, Havel argues that radical change, change which goes to the root, change which converts captivated desire is the *responsibility* that we carry with us everywhere (*imago Dei*, again); as such, "we must accept it and grasp it *here*, *now*, in this place and time where the Lord has set us down, and that we cannot lie our way out of it by moving somewhere else … Christianity is an example of an opposite way out: it is a point of departure for me here and now—but only because anyone, anywhere, at any time, may avail themselves of it."⁴²

So the Christian doctrine of vocation as "pre-political" conscience, "responsible to God for the world,"⁴³ does not offer an alternative program within "the spirit and methods of traditional politics." Its dissent is instead organic to "real, everyday struggle for a better life here and now … the everyday, thankless and never ending struggle of human beings to live more freely, truthfully, and in quiet dignity."⁴⁴ This is true because "the most intrinsic and fundamental confrontation between human beings and the system takes place at a level incomparably more profound than that of traditional politics."[45]

Havel, whose covert theological inspiration only thus slightly surfaces in the end, takes us no further. Indeed, we do not know how to proceed out of the morass, he confesses in conclusion, foreshadowing Wendy Brown's *political* despair. In sad fact the post-1989 transition to liberal democracy in Czechoslovakia, and Havel's own journey "to the Castle and back" as a democratic politician cannot be said to have brought about the profound remoralization to which his essay summoned. On reflection, however, to affirm responsibility apart from the Word that calls and thus empowers its own response is utopian; needed is news of One who has broken into the system of complicity-cum-mendacity to recapture its prisoners. The space taken up by this news in pre-political culture is the life of the congregation of Christ.

Christian theology in Luther's tradition that recovers its nerve in our time of moral catastrophe would see in congregational life the matrix of an organic and principled resistance to the commoditization of all things which is capturing desire under the regime of neoliberal governmentality. This would mean, of course, re-orienting the line of battle to the pre-political level of culture, as Havel diagnosed, in the place of the clumsy political interventions, both left and right, at the level of church bureaucracy lobbying that are commonplace in American Christianity. Such interventions presume politics as usual. But we are in much greater danger than business as usual allows.

Recall here the "state of exception" (Agamben) which scapegoats aliens. Refocusing to a new catechesis for congregational life neither declines nor minimizes the sacred duty always to bear a true witness in public against victimization at the hands of power, especially for the alien in one's midst, as the Law of Moses frequently reminds liberated Hebrews to bear in mind that they were once aliens as well. The Christian is under the divine imperative to bear true witness on behalf of the defenseless before the court of public opinion. Yet true witness is precisely not an alternative political program, and indeed witness in its integrity is jeopardized when it becomes instrumentalized by the competing partisanships for political power, also in liberal democracy.

So what would instruct an authentic resistance, to be forged as congregational life under our present circumstances? In conclusion, we take up Havel's hint by turning to Solzhenitsyn's Harvard Address to probe the more specifically and explicitly theological contours of authentic resistance, not in normalized Czechoslovakia or the U.S.S.R., but today.

SOLZHENITSYN'S SUMMONS TO THEOSIS[46]

Solzhenitsyn's 1978 Harvard Address was years ahead of its time. In its own time it was notorious for offending the neoliberal sensibilities of the elite American audience gathered at a Harvard commencement, even though at the outset Solzhenitsyn alluded to the commandment in Ephesians about speaking the truth in love; he intended to speak as "a friend, not as an adversary." But truth-telling in contemporaneous America, no less than within Havel's communist Czechoslovakia, offends, in so far as it exposes systemic lies which darkness's denizens prefer to light (John 3:19–21). In any case, one hardly need agree with every characterization Solzhenitsyn made of the Western world to appreciate today the *prescience* of his analysis from thirty years ago—the very time, according to scholars, of the ascendancy of neoliberalism.

Already in 1978 Solzhenitsyn foresaw the decline of the superpower rivalry of the U.S. and the U.S.S.R. and the emergence of a multipolar world. He traced the present decline of the West to modern Europe's "easy" colonization of the globe in the nineteenth century, "not only without anticipating any real resistance, but usually with contempt for any possible values in the conquered people's approach to life." This "blindness of superiority" is still operative today, however, in "the assumption that the rest of the world should be pursuing Western pluralistic democracy and adopting the Western way of life." In this latter assumption, the colonialist sense of superiority only twists and turns in order to endure; under the banner of economic "development,"[47] the nineteenth century white man's burden to lift up little brown brothers by teaching an honest day's labor is not abandoned, but merely modernized by dint of economic rationality. Critical awareness of the crimes of colonialism and the dim awareness that these crimes continue in "globalization" and "development" work a paralyzing guilt. This guilt manifests as a loss of "civic courage" which is "particularly noticeable among the ruling and intellectual elites."

Needless to say, Solzhenitsyn was hardly recommending the kind of machismo recklessness in foreign relations that George W. Bush would consequently pursue. Rather he was criticizing the contemporary West for its root belief that "man lives in order to be free and pursue happiness," a belief that cannot co-exist with conscientious courage, personal or civic, willing to risk or sacrifice for the common good. The fatal error of consumerist materialism consists in one "psychological detail" that has been "overlooked: the constant desire to have still more things and a still better life[;] ... the struggle to this end imprint many Western faces with worry and even depression, though it is customary to carefully conceal such feelings." Envy is insatiable; the solution is not to satisfy it, but to extinguish it.

The 1987 analysis of envy anticipates the frank confession of the neoliberal credo by Gordon Gekko in the 1987 film, *Wall Street*: "The point is, ladies and gentlemen, that greed—for lack of a better word—is good. Greed clarifies, cuts through, and captures the essence of the evolutionary spirit. Greed, in all of its forms—greed for life, for money, for love, knowledge—has marked the upward surge of mankind." A better word would be *envy*[48]—envy as ancient as the serpent's *sicut Deus eritis*—as greed is only the derivative form envy takes among those rich in things.

In this vein, Solzhenitsyn captures the dynamic of nascent neoliberalism: "This active and tense competition comes to dominate all human thought and does not in the least open a way to free spiritual development." Who would ever renounce an almost "unlimited freedom in the choice of pleasures ... to risk one's precious life in defense of the common good?"

Solzhenitsyn next extends his critique to the litigious, as he puts it, "legalistic" Western culture deriving from its sole shared good of protecting the individual's assertion of rights; but this effects a social world where cross-bearing self-restraint or even a renunciation of rights to bear another's burdens would "simply sound absurd." Rather, legalistic adjudication becomes as inevitable as it is protracted, in that the individualistic assertion of rights must come into continual conflict with rights asserted by others, where and when a legal order protecting predatory competition is all that binds these free individuals together through regimes of procedural justice. "Whenever the tissue of life is woven of legalistic relationships, this creates an atmosphere of spiritual mediocrity that paralyzes man's noblest impulses." Not merely mediocrity, but the liberal imperative to maximize personal freedom grants ever-expanding space to destructive and irresponsible impulses. "For example, against the misuse of liberty for moral violence against young people such as motion pictures full of pornography, crime and horror ... life organized legalistically has thus shown its inability to defend itself against the corrosion of evil."

Blind faith in freedom "stems from a humanistic and benevolent concept according to which man—the master of the world—does not bear any evil within himself, and all the defects of life are caused by misguided social systems"—recalling here Havel's point that misguided social systems exist symbiotically with the modern self's craving for autonomy.

The freedom of the press is likewise corrupted by a blind faith in its own innocence. "There is no true moral responsibility for distortion or disproportion. What sort of responsibility does a journalist have to the readership or to history?" In-depth analysis "of a problem is anathema to the press; it is contrary to its nature. The press merely picks out sensational formulas." In spite of the alleged freedom of the press, someone coming from the totalitarian

East is especially surprised at the conformism manifest in the supposedly competing media: this newcomer finds "generally accepted patterns of judgment and maybe common corporate interests, the sum effect being not competition but unification ... in fashionable trends of thought ... hemmed in by the idols of the prevailing fad."

Solzhenitsyn's exercise in prophetic iconoclasm draws to an end with the observation that many in the West who are dissatisfied with their own society (for the very reasons that he has given in this speech) are swaying toward socialism; yet he begs that his criticism of the Western system not be taken to suggest socialism as an alternative.[49] In the same breath, however, he says that he would not recommend Western capitalism as a model or ideal for the transformation of his homeland. For all the reasons he has given he believes that, just as Marxism-Leninism is now bankrupt, "the Western way of life is less and less likely to become the leading model."

With his refusal of these two rival versions of modernity, Solzhenitsyn anticipates the Islamic revolution against what "could be called rationalistic humanism or humanistic autonomy: the proclaimed and practiced autonomy of man from any higher force above him." He calls the shared trajectory of the Renaissance through the Enlightenment onto the contemporary West *and* its sibling rival, the "naturalized humanism" of Marxism-Leninism, historically inevitable because the Middle Ages had become "an intolerable despotic repression of man's physical nature in favor of the spiritual one." But the one-sided over-correction by modernity "did not admit the existence of intrinsic evil in man, nor did it see any task higher than the attainment of happiness on earth." In the decline of the West today, it becomes increasingly visible that "mere freedom per se does not in the least solve all the problems of human life and even adds a number of new ones ... when the individual is granted boundless freedom with no purpose, simply for the satisfaction of his whims."

In sum, the development of modernity represents "a total emancipation from the moral heritage of Christian centuries with their great reserves of mercy and sacrifice ... man's sense of responsibility to God and society has grown dimmer and dimmer ... all the celebrated technological achievements of progress ... do not redeem the twentieth century's moral poverty." What has been lost is the sense "of a permanent, earnest duty so that one's life journey may become, above all, an experience of moral growth: to leave life a better human being than one started it." So Solzhenitsyn concluded by pointing to the way through our morass with the Eastern Orthodox doctrine of theosis: "No one on earth has any other way left but—upward." Or in the words of Michelle Obama, "When they go low, we go high." Does "resistance" today remember this?

Can we imagine a new catechesis along these lines which would nurture the life of our congregations as creative minorities in the darkness of this present culture? We can if we begin with Westhelle's Lutheran insight into the apocalyptic "incision" of the proclamation of the in-breaking Christ who reveals our bondage in the act of delivering from it and re-forming us as theological subjects. We can if we connect this proclamation and new-formation redemptively to Havel's Johannine venture that truth-telling in the world of mendacity finds a hidden ally with the authentic, but alienated human vocation, made in the image of God for likeness to God. We can if with Solzhenitsyn we soberly see from the moral ruins of the twentieth century on which we uneasily stand—Hitler, Hiroshima, and Stalin—that in Christ we have no way through the morass but *upward*.

NOTES

1. For present purposes, let me stipulate without arguing the point: I understand *neoliberalism*, not as classical liberalism's affirmation of the wealth-producing efficiency of free markets exchanging goods and services, but as the generalized paradigm of market exchange as omniscient processor in all domains of life, resulting in the commoditization of all things. See further Paul R. Hinlicky, "Luther in Marx," in *Oxford Encyclopedia of Martin Luther*, 3 vols., ed. Derek R. Nelson and Paul R. Hinlicky (New York: Oxford University Press, 2017), vol. 2:322–41.

2. Wendy Brown, *Undoing the Demos: Neoliberalism's Stealth Revolution* (New York: Zone Books, 2015), 220–21.

3. Vítor Westhelle, *Transfiguring Luther: The Planetary Promise of Luther's Theology*, foreword by David Tracy (Cambridge: James Clark, 2017), 236–337.

4. Hannah Arendt, *Eichmann in Jerusalem: A Report on the Banality of Evil*, revised and enlarged edn. (London: Penguin Books, 1994), 146.

5. Arendt, *Eichmann in Jerusalem*, 277, 135–37.

6. See the discussion in Paul R. Hinlicky, *Before Auschwitz: What Christian Theology Must Learn from the Rise of Nazism* (Eugene, OR: Cascade, 2013), 109–17.

7. Giorgio Agamben, *Homo Sacer: Sovereign Power and Bare Life*, trans. D. Heller-Roazen (Stanford, CA: Stanford University Press, 1998).

8. On the sovereign self of modernity, see Paul R. Hinlicky, "Augustine, Luther and the Critique of the Sovereign Self," ch. 8 in *On the Apocalyptic and Human Agency: Conversations with Augustine of Hippo and Martin Luther*, ed. Kirsi Stjerna and Deanna A. Thompson (Newcastle upon Tyne, UK: Cambridge Scholars, 2014), 81–92.

9. Václav Havel, *Living in Truth*, ed. Jan Vladislav (London and Boston: Faber and Faber, 1990), 53.

10. Havel, *Living in Truth*, 54.

11. On this theological anthropology, see Paul R. Hinlicky, *Beloved Community: Critical Dogmatics after Christendom* (Grand Rapids, MI: Eerdmans, 2015), 281–92, 341–48.

12. Westhelle provides an excellent dissection of Lynn White Jr.'s influential confusion of the image of God anthropology with the sovereign self of modernity in *Transfiguring Luther*, 137–40.

13. Havel, *Living in Truth*, 115.

14. Havel, *Living in Truth*, 116.

15. See the critique in Brent Adkins and Paul R. Hinlicky, *Rethinking Philosophy and Theology with Deleuze: A New Cartography* (London and New York: Bloomsbury Academic, 2013), 193–202.

16. Philip Mirowski and Nik-Khah, *The Knowledge We Have Lost in Information: The History of Information in Modern Economics* (Oxford: Oxford University Press, 2017).

17. Not to mention Marx's hope for the emergence—precisely through the purifying fire of capitalist exploitation—of a revolutionary proletariat, a universal class shorn of particular attachments with nothing to lose but its chains.

18. Adkins and Hinlicky, *Rethinking Philosophy*, 11–36.

19. Immanuel Kant, "The Conflict of the Faculties," in *Religion and Rational Theology*, trans. Allen W. Wood and George Di Giovanni (Cambridge: Cambridge University Press, 2001), 233–328. See Paul R. Hinlicky, *Paths Not Taken: Fates of Theology from Luther through Leibniz* (Grand Rapids, MI: Eerdmans, 2009), 43–87.

20. Arthur Koestler, *The God That Failed*, ed. Richard H. Crossman, foreword by David C. Engerman (New York: Columbia University Press, 2001), 15–75

21. Mark Lilla, *The Stillborn God: Religion, Politics, and The Modern West* (New York: Knopf, 2007).

22. Lewis White Beck holds that Luther's "theodicy" at the conclusion of the *Bondage of the Will* "is the source of the strict Lutheran sense of the helplessness of man, the futility of practice, and the indifference or even evil of works." In contrast, the "modern world, with its emphasis on practice, required Arminianism, a polite Protestant name for the Pelagian heresy; hence Luther's denial of man's freedom did not make fruitful contact with humane activism, while Calvin's did." This modern need for Pelagian activism, Beck generalizes, is the reason why: "the German Enlightenment was secularized Calvinism, not Lutheranism, even though almost every German philosopher from Leibniz to Kant was confessionally Lutheran." Lewis Beck White, *Early German Philosophy: Kant and His Predecessors* (Bristol, UK: Thoemmes Press, 1996), 99. Calvinist friends will be abashed to learn here of their covert Arminianism.

23. *The Book of Concord: The Confessions of the Evangelical Lutheran Church*, ed. Robert Kolb and Timothy J. Wengert (Minneapolis, MN: Fortress Press, 2000), 311.

24. Havel, *Living in Truth*, 38–39.

25. Havel, *Living in Truth*, 42.

26. Havel, *Living in Truth*, 44–45.

27. Havel, *Living in Truth*, 51.

28. Havel, *Living in Truth*, 52.

29. Havel, *Living in Truth*, 50.
30. Havel, *Living in Truth*, 55.
31. Havel, *Living in Truth*, 57.
32. Havel, *Living in Truth*, 58.
33. Havel, *Living in Truth*, 60.
34. Havel, *Living in Truth*, 61.
35. Havel, *Living in Truth*, 62.
36. Havel, *Living in Truth*, 65.
37. Havel, *Living in Truth*, 68.
38. Havel, *Living in Truth*, 70–71.
39. Havel, *Living in Truth*, 85.
40. Havel, *Living in Truth*, 92.
41. Havel, *Living in Truth*, 93.
42. Havel, *Living in Truth*, 104.
43. Hinlicky, *Beloved Community*, 613–21.
44. Havel, *Living in Truth*, 113.
45. Havel, *Living in Truth*, 114.
46. Online at http://www.orthodoxytoday.org/articles/SolzhenitsynHarvard.php (accessed Feb. 10, 2020).
47. See the devastating case study, which is also theoretically rich, of Timothy Mitchell, *Rule of Experts: Egypt, Tecno-Politics, Modernity* (Berkeley, CA: University of California Press, 2002). The period of Soviet development in Egypt proves to be not materially different than that conducted later under USAID.
48. See the discussion of Daniel Bell's Deleuzian analysis of perverted desire in *Beloved Community*, 142–46.
49. Allowing for a certain lack of nuance here from the pen of a refugee from the U.S.S.R.: "The communist regime in the East could endure and grow due to the enthusiastic support from an enormous number of Western intellectuals who (feeling the kinship!) refused to see communism's crimes, and when they no longer could do so, they tried to justify these crimes. The problem persists: in our Eastern countries, communism has suffered a complete ideological defeat; it is zero and less than zero. And yet Western intellectuals still look at it with considerable interest and empathy." For reference, see n. 46.

Chapter 6

Lutheran Ecclesiologies of Resistance

Starting with the Spirit

Cheryl M. Peterson

People typically do not turn to Martin Luther's theology and the Lutheran theological tradition when looking for resources to resist a government that has lost its moral compass and is unashamedly nativistic and bigoted, blind to the ecological crisis facing this planet, and that only seems to be interested in helping those who are already economically powerful and successful. Scholars often note that, with few exceptions such as Dietrich Bonhoeffer, the Lutheran tradition was mostly anemic in the face of the idolatrous Nazi regime.

Many point to the way that the so-called "Zwei-Reiche" or "two kingdoms" doctrine was misused by German theologians in the 1930s who turned it into a dualistic doctrine that posited two separate spheres of God's activity that do not overlap, instead of hewing to its original intent as a dialectical and paradoxical interpretation of God's "two-fold" rule. As Robert Benne states, "Such a dualistic approach was used to argue that Christians as Christians had no grounds for resisting tyrannical governments, be they of Hitler, Joseph Stalin, Auguste Pinochet, or John Vorster. This led to the infamous political quietism that Lutherans have sometimes fostered."[1]

Some, such as Lutheran ethicist William Lazareth, have proposed a reconsideration of the two-fold rule of God that can support a more public role for the church, that is, as a public corollary to the two-fold way that God's word is preached. The church is called to proclaim the whole word of God: law and gospel. Whereas "Luther had to put the church back under the gospel," Lazareth states, "we must put the state back under God's law."[2] When governments are not ruling in accord with God's law, it is the job of the church to call them to back to that task. Through the proclamation of God's prophetic law, the church calls the state to adjudicate the law in ways that promote the common good for all people. What is needed for that task is a "prophetic counterpart to the priesthood of all believers," a social ethic of "love seeking justice," along with a personal ethic of "faith active in love."[3] As Cynthia Moe-Lobeda and others have pointed out, Luther himself did just this, writing more than one thousand letters to princes and other office holders, reminding them of their duty to care for the poor and treat people justly.[4] However, at the same time, Luther famously did not support the overthrow of unjust systems through uprisings and rebellious resistance to political authorities, as seen in his response to the Peasant uprisings of 1525.

How do we do the work of resistance *as church*, and what theological resources, in addition to the two-fold reign of God, might the Lutheran tradition have to offer to Christians today in this work of resistance? In this chapter, I suggest and explore two—1) the theology of the cross, particularly as applied to the North American context by Canadian theologian Douglas John Hall; and 2) Luther's concept of the Holy Spirit in his Sermons on John's Gospel—in sketching out a framework for a Lutheran ecclesiology of resistance in the contemporary era.

At the onset, I need to be clear that resistance for Christians cannot be considered only in terms of external resistance to the injustices perpetuated by our own government. We also need to consider this question of resistance internally, that is, we must also resist the ways that we as Christians and the message of Christianity have been co-opted by interests that oppose God's kingdom rule, whether they be political, economic, racial, gender, or other.

The story of the German Church Struggle during World War II is instructive here, because it was not only a struggle against the National Socialist State, as Arthur Cochrane points out, "but even more a struggle against the heretical 'German Christian' party."[5] The German Christians had "camouflaged" their persecution of the church and Jews, by claiming to represent "positive Christianity" against "godless Bolshevism"[6] combining Christian teachings with the tenets of National Socialism and distorting the gospel into false doctrine.[7] The doctrinal distortion that was the major impulse behind the Confessing Church—which was at the heart of the anti-Christian myth of the neo-pagan Nazi message—was the "Aryan Paragraph." Renunciation of the Aryan paragraph as a violation of the church's confession was central to the pledge of the Pastors' Emergency League founded by Martin Niemöller in 1933 that would become the seedbed from which grew the Confessing Church movement. According to Cochrane, this vow "laid bare the basic issue, namely anti-Semitism, particularly as it related to the nature of the church."[8]

The German Church Struggle shed light on the apostasy of the German Christians, for whom the church had "become more bourgeois than had been realized. God had been thought of as the protector of an ordered family life," and the guarantor of a nation and race.[9] In this way, the German Church Struggle served as a catalyst that awakened the faith of the people and helped to reclaim an understanding of the church that was based on the "power of the Word" alone, and not natural theology or "orders of creation."

While the U.S. context is quite different politically and ecclesiologically, the majority of Lutherans in America are white, economically middle-class, and educated, which is to say that on the whole, they enjoy racial and economic privilege in society. Although founded by immigrants, Lutheran congregations were not immune to becoming captive to forms of U.S. culture-religion, "the American way of life," that minimized the public and prophetic role of the church. As E. Clifford Nelson wrote, "As a matter of fact, Lutheran congregations across the land in the prosperous fifties gave evidence that they were enamored of the desire for popular approval and success. Accepting uncritically the approbation of middle-class America, Lutheranism was in danger of becoming what its theology did not allow, a culture-religion."[10] Further, according to the 2014 "Religious Landscape Study" by Pew Forum, the largest Lutheran denomination in the U.S. today (the Evangelical Lutheran Church in America [ELCA]) is currently also the whitest denomination, at 96%.[11] The question must be asked: How does a church of such privilege engage the question of resistance—not only against external forces of injustice, but also from within, against internal forces of sin—and what theological resources might help us to practice resistance, ecclesiologically?

Douglas John Hall reminds us that resistance is inherent in the confession of faith, especially within Protestantism.[12] He situates the ethic of resistance, which he pairs with the ethic of public responsibility, within his call for an ecclesiology of the cross for the North American context. For too long, the church in North America has adopted the dominant culture which conflates progress with divine providence, resulting in an incapacity to live with unresolved negatives. The church has promoted itself as a place where negatives are turned into positives, where every problem has an answer, and where people can find a sanctuary against the darkness.[13] With irony, he notes that

> the very failure of the New World Dream has in some sense enhanced the public role of religion. For large numbers of our fellow citizens are unable to face the decline of their culture, and many look to the churches to help them repress their social doubt and identity crisis.... Now these churches are expected to reinforce the social vision of success long after it has ceased concretely to inform most other institutions of the society, even government. Now one goes to church in

order to be able to believe in America again.[14]

Or, as some today might say, "to make America great again," which, as many have pointed out, is coded language for retaining white privilege in this country.[15]

Hall employs Luther's *theologia crucis* as a critical tool to engage the dominant culture in North America. The cross is able to reveal "the One who meets us in our darkness and death," that is, in places that theologies of glory (and privilege) consider to be weak and foolish.[16] Such a theology that finds "strength in weakness, significance in littleness, purity in brokenness, and life in the midst of death," Hall posits, just "might have something real to say to our world."[17] If the North American churches will give up their theologies of glory for a theology of the cross, and adopt a stance of humility, they have the opportunity to reclaim their true ecclesial identity and mission in the world, and along with it, the prophetic tradition of resistance.

The theology of the cross calls for a new vision of the church: an "ecclesiology of the cross," which understands the church as "the cruciform body of Jesus Christ, a priestly and prophetic community of The Way."[18] By this phrase, Hall suggests not only a community committed to living out the Way of Jesus as his disciples, but also a people in transit and on the move. Alternatively, Hall speaks of the church as a *diaspora*, a scattered people who are willing to be dispersed as they follow the Lord "on the way."[19] Hall's use of *diaspora* is distinct from the concept of "resident aliens" used by Yale School theologians Stanley Hauerwas and William Willimon.[20] In response to their refusal to let the world "set the agenda," Hall pointedly asks, "But is the agenda that the church is to set, in their view, one that is conscious of the world's needs … if not, then have they not opted for a new kind of ecclesiastical-theological 'imperialism?'"[21] It is also, as Jennifer McBride points out, "disingenuous" for White Protestants (not least of all members of the ELCA, which is 96 percent white in membership) to suppose themselves "aliens" in a culture and society that benefits them, one that in fact, was created to benefit them.[22]

As the church moves "on the way," it heeds the call to be prophetic first by rediscovering "the possibility of littleness."[23] Hall believes that many mainline churches have lost their prophetic voices by becoming part of the dominant culture, with its white, middle-class privileges. Thus, it can only regain its prophetic voice in the world by becoming "little" again in the eyes of the world. This includes not only recognizing and naming the ways that the church belongs "to a system and a world that creates oppressive conditions for many both beyond and within the boundaries of our nations,"[24] but also divesting itself of its social standing, its cultural power (including white privilege), and the dominant worldview in this system. In her book, *The Church for the World: A Theology of Public Witness*, Jennifer McBride makes a similar argument by calling for a non-triumphalistic witness that begins with a posture of humility and repentance.[25]

The prophetic task of this "little flock," Hall says, is announcing that "the day of the Lord is darkness and not light"[26] (cf. Amos 5:18). Although the more common biblical motif is for the church to bear witness to the light, Hall believes that North Americans have used the "light" to ward off the "darkness." Because of this, the church's first task is to bear witness to the darkness, the margins, those places of pain caused by systems of inequality and oppression, by entering into those places in solidarity with others.[27] It is only by entering the experience of negation that the church can bring hope to it.

As a corollary to his emphasis of darkness over light, Hall emphasizes participation in Christ's death more than in Christ's resurrection. It is in this sense that Hall speaks of the *ecclesia crucis* or the "suffering church." For Hall, suffering is "the one indispensable mark of its authenticity—because there is still suffering in God's beloved world and God would be involved in it."[28] For Hall, the church is called to be in solidarity with the suffering and oppressed in the world, and to accept the consequences of that solidarity, knowing that God is at work through all of it. This is not a masochistic suffering for the sake of suffering, but rather "the consequence of our incorporation into the One who through voluntarily assuming the burdensome suffering of the world would transform it for life."[29]

Part of what must be brought into the light, as suggested above, are the ways that the church has been complicit in sinful systems of racial, class, economic, and gender privilege. Along with McBride, Karen Bloomquist and Jason Mahn have pointed to the practice of repentance and truth-telling as central to an ecclesiology of resistance. Jason Mahn develops Hall's thinking in dialogue with feminist Lutheran theologians Mary Solberg and Deanna Thompson, and proposes "relocation to abandoned places of empire" (as is practiced by the "New Monasticism") as the first step in enabling the *metanoia* that is required to be an *ecclesia crucis*.[30] He points to two ecclesial practices to help the church better "see": the Eucharist to see the crucified Christ "hidden" (in, with, and under) the breaking of the bread, and the practice of repentance and confession help the church see its own sinfulness and complicity in structures of oppression.[31] We resist empire by first confessing our participation in it, by resisting idolatry. In his essay in *The Forgotten Luther*, Jon Pahl offers an economic reading of Luther's catechisms, showing how his critique of economic idolatry is "the first and most crucial point." Even so, Luther's ultimate aim is pastoral, Pahl says, because these idolaters are among us—and are us—as well as "them."[32]

Karen Bloomquist further develops these ideas by proposing the ecclesial subversive practices of "seeing, remembering, and connecting" to nurture and organize communities of resistance against the narratives and systems of domination and injustice in which they find themselves today.[33] She says that truth-telling becomes possible through remembering who we are in relation to God, our histories, and the situation of our neighbors. We cannot do this alone; because of "how deeply we are implicated in and complicit in the social structure of sin, we need one another to know truthfully."[34]

Part of this truth-telling involves uncovering what Robert Schreiter has called "narratives of the lie." In his important work on reconciliation, he writes about the way violence not only does harm to people's bodies, but also destroys the narratives that support people's identities and self-worth, substituting its own narratives, which he calls "narratives of the lie." Because humans cannot live without narratives, it is not the purpose of violence to abolish them, but rather to provide alternative narratives that enable people to live under oppression. These "narratives of the lie" will eventually come to be accepted as the truth if the original narrative can be suppressed or co-opted.[35] In an age where lying has become the new normal and "facts" are presented as opinions, especially regarding narratives of violence against African Americans, women, Muslims, and Latin American immigrants and refugees (to name only a few), Schreiter's point is even more important to heed.

The mainline churches need to become bolder truth-tellers by uncovering and exposing the "narratives of the lie" at the heart of the American experience, starting with America's Original Sin of Racism. Jennifer Harvey has called for a paradigm shift from reconciliation to reparations in addressing racial injustices in this country, because the former is often promoted at the expense of the kind of truth-telling required for real healing. She writes, "If we continue to live in an unacknowledged brutal history of injustice, harm done, white hostility to and violence against communities of color—histories with legacies that are alive and well in the present—then speaking of reconciliation may do more harm than good, may cover more than it discloses."[36] Reparations in a Christian context require that repentance precede reconciliation, and for that to happen, the narrative of the lie must first be exposed. Further, as this narrative is resisted, it must also be replaced with the narrative of the cross and resurrection, as that which can speak hope and power to those whose lives and identities have been violated by injustice and oppression.

These are all important elements of a Lutheran ecclesiology of resistance, but what is missing explicitly is a robust pneumatological focus. Without attention to the work of the Spirit, calls to enter into another's suffering, to expose narratives of the lie, and to repent of one's complicity in sinful structures, can easily become a form of liberal or progressive "work-righteousness." While Hall acknowledges the role of the Holy Spirit in conforming believers to the life and suffering of Christ, and thereby the suffering of the world,[37] he does not explicitly connect the Holy Spirit to the work of solidarity and prophetic resistance. The evangelist John's designation for the Holy Spirit as *paraclete* is a helpful resource. To be in solidarity with another means to accompany them in their suffering, in their marginalization. If we think of solidarity as a kind of accompaniment, then drawing on Johannine particular pneumatology, the Holy Spirit becomes the primary "accompanier" for the church (and the world)—the *paraclete*, literally the one who "is alongside of," that is, the one who accompanies. As the *paraclete,* the Spirit not only enters into solidarity with humanity—in joy and sorrow—but even abides, dwells deeply, in our human situation (John 14:17). John also writes of the Spirit's accompanying and abiding in order to bring conviction for sin and truth-telling (John 16:8; 16:13), teaching and guidance of what Jesus said to the disciples in his earthly life (14:26; 16:13), testifying to the power of his love and life for the world (John 15:26–27), and ultimately the power of forgiveness and reconciliation (John 20:22–23).

An underappreciated resource for Luther's own pneumatology is the series of sermons he preached on John's gospel, where he develops these ideas. In his exposition of John 14–16, Luther focuses on two titles for the Spirit: the Comforter and the Spirit of Truth. As our Comforter, the Holy Spirit will "console, strength[en], and preserve" believers in every need, so that they may abide in God's grace and love and have the strength to endure whatever happens. Luther calls the Holy Spirit the "comforter of all the weak, not only for us, but for everyone in the world."[38] But Luther goes on to describe what that comfort consists of; this is not a "shoulder-to-cry-on" kind of comfort, but the kind that makes believers "defiant and courageous in the face of all kinds of terror."[39] While Luther specifies the "assaults" of the devil or afflicted consciences that make believers doubt in their salvation, one might interpret "all kinds of terror" as anything in the personal self or the world that resists or opposes the kingdom of God. Luther assures his hearers that the Holy Spirit "will not stop fortifying our hearts" against such attacks, and further will inspire them with "a courage that will overcome it all."[40]

This courage is also needed for Christian witness in a world that will often hate those who uncover the narrative of the lies and telling the truth, especially those narratives that promote racial and class privilege for some at the expense of others. The Holy Spirit is not only Comforter, but also Spirit of truth, who "will fill us with a courage that is called a divine, holy, and bold defiance."[41] The Spirit of truth not only teaches believers the Truth, who is Christ, but also gives them the courage to stand in it and to oppose all lies and false gospels, impelling them to testify to that truth.[42] The first reference to the "Spirit of truth" appears in John 15:26, in a section about the persecution Christians face as followers of Jesus, after the image of the vine and the branches is used to describe the relationship of Jesus to his disciples (John 15:1–11) and Jesus gives his disciples the love commandment (John 15:12–17). For Luther, Christian witness includes bearing fruit, a sign of rebirth by the Holy Spirit (John 15:5). The fruit of the new birth, Luther writes, is to attend to the welfare and improvement of one's neighbor: when someone is "willing to risk life, goods, and honor for Christ's sake, is eager to bring all to the faith, serves his neighbor faithfully, treats him justly and brotherly."[43] In short, it means to love one another as Christ has loved us (John 15:5).

Cynthia Moe-Lobeda also points to the Holy Spirit as the "power for confessing faith in the midst of empire."[44] She cites a sermon Luther preached on the Sixteenth Sunday after the Trinity in which Luther, in language similar to his Johannine sermons, calls the Spirit "bold, undaunted courage." She then examines the gulf between this powerful description of the Spirit (which she shows is rooted in the scriptural witness as well), as well as the failure of churches in North America to act upon it, and their silent complicity in the face of unjust systems.

An ecclesiology of resistance "starts with the Spirit" because the Spirit keeps the church in that truth and emboldens disciples to stand against all who teach a false gospel, who promote violence through "narratives of the lie." Today the progenitors of false gospels in the U.S. are those Christian preachers and others who forget the theology of the cross and identify the gospel with messages of prosperity and national strength, and who use the symbols of the church to promote racist and nativist ideologies that deny the image of God in all people.[45]

At a special session at the 2016 American Academy of Religion, Michelle Alexander, civil rights activist, legal scholar, and author of *The New Jim Crow*,[46] had a conversation with Kelly Brown Douglas. Alexander reiterated her call for a "spiritual revolution" to address racial violence that continues to plague the U.S., from shootings to the ongoing mass incarceration of people of color. In 2015, Alexander resigned her position as a law professor at the Ohio State University to teach and study at Union Theological Seminary in New York. She explained her decision this way:

> Who am I to teach or study at a seminary? I was not raised in a church. And I have generally found more questions than answers in my own religious or spiritual pursuits. But I also know there is something much greater at stake in justice work than we often acknowledge. Solving the crises we face isn't simply a matter of having the right facts, graphs, policy analyses, or funding. And I no longer believe we can "win" justice simply by filing lawsuits, flexing our political muscles or boosting voter turnout. Yes, we absolutely must do that work, but none of it—not even working for some form of political revolution—will ever be enough on its own. *Without a moral or spiritual awakening, we will*

remain forever trapped in political games fueled by fear, greed and the hunger for power.... At its core, America's journey from slavery to Jim Crow to mass incarceration raises profound moral and spiritual questions about who we are, individually and collectively, who we aim to become, and what we are willing to do now.[47]

The day after Trump's inauguration, more than a half a million people marched on Washington, joined by millions more in other cities. Jennifer Butler dubbed this event an act of spiritual resistance.[48] It was intended to send a bold message to the new president on his first day in office, and to the world, that women's rights are human rights, and to stand in solidarity with all of the marginalized. The resistance to Trump's agenda has continued, in big and small ways. In a 2016 interview, Michelle Alexander said while she understands the call for resistance in the wake of Trump's presidency, "I think we've got to get beyond resistance. Resistance is inherently defensive.... As I see it, Trump is the resistance. There is a revolutionary spirit alive and well that is trying to birth a new America, and Trump and his cronies are resisting, wanting to take America back."[49]

Luther's idea of the Spirit as the courage by which one testifies to the truth of Christ can be a resource to all those seeking "spiritual revolution"—those inside as well as outside of the church. Many described the Women's March the day after Trump's inauguration as more than political activism; instead it was a spiritual step by which "we're choosing the way of Jesus, who taught us about loving our neighbor as our self and dismantling fear with love.... The hypocrisy of Christian right leaders shows how women must march to reclaim our faith from those who use religion to abuse and control others. We march to reclaim the soul of our nation, which must include reclaiming my faith from those who use it to endorse misogyny and bigotry."[50]

For Luther, the Spirit is at work not only "blowing" new birth into believers, but transforming believers to "resemble" the Holy Spirit. The Spirit then "blows" them where the Spirit wills, into the world to stand for the truth. The Spirit empowers us to testify to the gospel and against lies, idolatries, and false gospels, especially narratives of racial and gender privilege, to be defiant in the face of powers that claim to give us what God in Christ alone can, and to live in the power of the Spirit, which means to live for the neighbor, especially those neighbors who are marginalized or oppressed by racial, gender, and other forms of injustice.

NOTES

1. Robert Benne, "The Twofold Rule of God," *Journal of Lutheran Ethics* 2, no. 8 (Aug. 1, 2002), para. 3; online at https://www.elca.org/JLE/Articles/936 (accessed Feb. 10, 2020).

2. William Lazareth, "Luther's 'Two Kingdom' Ethic Reconsidered," in *Marburg Revisited: A Re-examination of Lutheran and Reformed Traditions*, ed. Paul C. Empie and James I. McCord (Minneapolis, MN: Augsburg Publishing House, 1966), 175.

3. William Lazareth, "Political Responsibility as the Obedience of Faith," in *The Gospel and Human Destiny*, ed. Vilmos Vajta (Minneapolis, MN: Augsburg Publishing House, 1971), 261–62.

4. Cynthia D. Moe-Lobeda, *Public Church: For the Life of the World*, Lutheran Voices Series (Minneapolis, MN: Augsburg Fortress, 2004), 42.

5. Arthur C. Cochrane, *The Church's Confession under Hitler,* ed. Dikran Y. Hadidian, Pittsburgh Reprint Series 4 (Pittsburgh, PA: Pickwick Press, 1976), 19.

6. Edmund Schlink, "The Witness of the German Lutheran Church Struggle," in *Man's Disorder and God's Design*, vol. 1, ed. W. A. Visser't Hooft (New York: Harper & Brothers, 1948), 97.

7. Schlink, "The Witness," 98–99.

8. Cochrane, *The Church's Confession*, 109.

9. Kent S. Knutson, *The Community of Faith and the Word: An Inquiry into the Concept of the Church in Contemporary Lutheranism* (PhD. diss., Union Theological Seminary, 1961), 265.

10. E. Clifford Nelson (ed.), *The Lutherans in North America*, rev. edn. (Philadelphia, PA: Fortress Press, 1980), 525–26.

11. "Racial and Ethnic Composition among Mainline Protestants by Religious Denomination," *Pew Forum Religious Landscape Study* (2014); online at https://www.pewforum.org/religious-landscape-study/compare/racial-and-ethnic-composition/by/religious-denomination/among/religious-tradition/mainline-protestant/ (accessed Feb. 10, 2020).

12. Douglas John Hall, *Confessing the Faith: Christian Theology in a North American Context* (Minneapolis, MN: Augsburg Fortress Press, 1996), 333. At the same time, Hall points out that the idea of resistance is one that most Christians find difficult, "if not abhorrent," and one that many Christians will themselves resist. (334–35)

13. Douglas John Hall, *Lighten Our Darkness: Toward an Indigenous Theology of the Cross* (Philadelphia, PA: Westminster Press, 1976), 103–106.

14. Douglas John Hall, "Metamorphosis: From Christendom to Diaspora," in *Confident Witness-Changing World: Rediscovering the Gospel in North America*, ed. Craig Van Gelder (Grand Rapids, MI: Eerdmans, 1999), 77.

15. See for example, the op-ed by Farid Hafez, "Racism and the Privilege to 'Make America Great Again'," *Daily Saba* (Aug. 2, 2019); online at https://www.daily-sabah.com/op-ed/2019/08/02/racism-and-the-privilege-to-make-america-great-again (accessed Feb. 10, 2020).

16. Hall, *Lighten Our Darkness*, 149.

17. Douglas John Hall, "Responses to the Humiliation of the Church," The William Porcher DuBose Lectures (Oct. 21–22, 1992), *Sewanee Theological Review* 36, no. 4 (1993): 479.

18. Douglas John Hall, *The End of Christendom and the Future of Christianity*, Christian Mission and Modern Culture Series (Valley Forge, PA: Trinity Press International, 1997), 49.

19. Douglas John Hall, *Has the Church a Future?* (Philadelphia, PA: Westminster Press, 1980), 54ff.

20. For example, see Stanley Hauerwas and William H. Willimon, *Resident Aliens: A Provocative Christian Assessment of Culture and Ministry for People who Know Something is Wrong* (Nashville, TN: Abingdon, 1989).

21. Douglas John Hall, *Thinking the Faith: Christian Theology in a North American Context* (Minneapolis, MN: Augsburg, 1989), 51n57.

22. Jennifer McBride, "White Protestants aren't Aliens: Resident Aliens at 25," *Christian Century* (Sept. 16, 2016); online at https://www.christiancentury.org/article/2014-09/white-protestants-arent-aliens.

23. Hall, *End of Christendom*, 66.

24. Hall, *Confessing the Faith*, 334.

25. Jennifer McBride, *The Church for the World: A Theology of Public Witness* (Oxford/New York: Oxford University Press, 2012).

26. I put these terms in quotation marks because these are terms Hall uses, but their use can be problematic. Recent voices have raised concerns about "light" always being associated with goodness and "darkness" being associate with evil, and how these images have been racialized in American society. See for example, Lenny Duncan, *Dear Church: A Love Letter from a Black Preacher to the Whitest Denomination in the U.S.* (Minneapolis, MN: Augsburg Books, 2019), 67–68.

27. Hall, *Lighten Our Darkness*, 220–21.

28. Hall, *Lighten Our Darkness*, 140. See also *Confessing the Faith*, 90ff.

29. Hall, *Lighten Our Darkness*, 137–38. Others, however, have pointed out the middle-class bias in the voluntary nature of solidarity, as a choice rather than an inescapable reality (as it is for the poor, for example). For example, Gordon Jensen agrees that while such an emphasis on solidarity is important for those in the middle-class who tend to avoid suffering, "what about those who are too familiar with suffering and struggle—the 'victims' in our society as Hall calls them in *Thinking the Faith?* The stress for them must be on hope, rather than entering into darkness." Gordon Jensen, "Hall's Use of Theologia Crucis," *Toronto Journal of Theology* 7, no. 2 (1990): 205.

30. Jason A. Mahn, "What are Churches for? Toward an Ecclesiology of the Cross after Christendom," *Dialog: A Journal of Theology* 51, no. 1 (2012): 20.

31. Mahn, "Churches," 21–22.

32. Jon Pahl, "An Economic Reading of Martin Luther's Catechisms in the Long Context," in *The Forgotten Luther: Reclaiming the Social-Economic Dimension of the Reformation*, vol. 1, ed. Carter Lindberg and Paul Wee (Minneapolis, MN: Lutheran University Press, 2016), 61.

33. Karen L. Bloomquist, "Transforming Domination Then and Now," in *Lutheran Identity and Political Theology*, ed. Carl-Henric Grenholm and Göran Gunnar, Church of Sweden Research Series 9 (Eugene, OR: Pickwick, 2014), 216.

34. Bloomquist, "Transforming Domination," 216.

35. Robert J. Schreiter, *Reconciliation: Mission and Ministry in a Changing Social Order*, The Boston Theological Institute Series 3 (Maryknoll, NY: Orbis, 1992), 34–36.

36. Jennifer Harvey, *Dear White Christians: For Those Still Longing for Racial Reconciliation* (Grand Rapids, MI: Eerdmans, 2014), 5.

37. Hall, *Confessing the Faith*, 92.

38. Martin Luther, *Luther's Works*, vol. 24: *Sermons on the Gospel of St. John, Chapters 14-16*, ed. Jaroslav Pelikan (St. Louis, MO: Concordia Publishing House, 1961), 116 (hereafter LW); *D. Martin Luthers Werke, Kritische Gesamtausgabe*, 73 vols., ed. J. K. F. Knaake et al. (Weimar: Böhlau, 1883–2009), vol. 46, 566–67 (hereafter WA).

39. LW 24, 117; WA 46, 567, 568.

40. LW 24, 116; WA 46, 566, 567.

41. LW 24, 118; WA 46, 568, 569.

42. LW 24, 357, 292; WA, 46, 52, 53; WA 45, 727, 728.

43. LW 24, 263.

44. Cynthia Moe-Lobeda, "The Holy Spirit: Power for Confessing Faith in the Midst of Empire," in *Being the Church in the Midst of Empire—Trinitarian Reflections*, ed. Karen L. Bloomquist, Theology in the Life of the Church Series (Minneapolis, MN: Lutheran University Press, 2010), 125–46.

45. For example, see Lawrence W. Rogers, "White Supremacy in American Christianity," *Christian Century* (Aug. 16, 2016); online at https://www.christiancentury.org/blogs/archive/2016-08/white-supremacy-american-christianity; and Jack Downey, "Hard Truths about White Supremacy," *America: The Jesuit Review* (March 8, 2018); online at https://www.americamagazine.org/arts-culture/2018/03/08/hard-truths-about-white-supremacy-america (accessed Feb. 10, 2020).

46. Michelle Alexander, *The New Jim Crow: Mass Incarceration in the Age of Colorblindness* (New York: The New Press, 2010).

47. Michelle Alexander made this announcement on social media on September 14, 2016 (emphasis mine). The full text can be found online at https://www.facebook.com/permalink.php?story_fbid=1090233291064627&id=168304409924191.

48. Jennifer Butler, "Why the Women's March is a Spiritual Act" (Jan. 19, 2017); online at https://medium.com/@JenButlerFPL/why-the-womens-march-is-a-spiritual-act-3a285387a778#.oq4j0arqs (accessed Feb. 10, 2020). Marches were held in five hundred cities across the U.S., and the total estimated attendance was between 3.3 and 4 million people.

49. Michelle Alexander, Naomi Klein, and Keeanga-Yamahtta Taylor in Conversation, "People Were Resisting Before Trump," *Truthout* (June 18, 2017); online at http://www.truth-out.org/opinion/item/40969-people-were-resisting-before-trump-michelle-alexander-naomi-klein-and-keeanga-yamahtta-taylor-in-conversation (accessed Feb. 10, 2020).

50. Butler, "Women's March" (see n. 48).

Chapter 7

Resisting Tyranny *and* Polarization

An Ecclesiology of Word and Sacrament from the Midwestern Heartland

Amy Carr

Ecclesiology draws from a gradual coming to awareness about what is and what will be within the corporate body of Christ—historically and eschatologically—as refracted through the local liturgies we live, as well as the scriptural, doctrinal, and Spirit-driven voices that inform our perception of church and world in God. My own ecclesiological sensibilities have been shaped by a lifetime of worship in mostly U.S. Midwestern LCA and ELCA[1] congregations, as well as by attention to an ever-reforming Lutheran theology which nevertheless remains steeped within its Catholic and monastic lineage. As I see it, a Lutheran ecclesiology houses all of life within a proleptic vision— one that perceives the historical *now* as already caught up in eschatological redemption. We glimpse the union among sacred past ("Christ has died"), present ("Christ is risen"), and future ("Christ will come again") whenever we share bread and wine during communion, proclaiming a "foretaste of the feast to come" in the reign of God. Our embrace of infant baptism reflects the centrality of grace—the gift of divine initiative—in drawing us into a beloved community. We are able to risk a weekly confession of our wrestling with the power of sin, death, and the demonic precisely because we frame our lives within a baptismal identity of belonging always to the body of Christ—aware that our current sin- and suffering-saturated lives are united with the life of Christ, who bears our wounding and our woundedness and shares with us the power of becoming a new creation in an exchange that Luther models on marital sharing.[2] To be sure, this recognition that we are simultaneously sinners and saints in Christ may tempt us to be at ease with the present world as it is, but only insofar as we lack the ears to hear the demanding yet promising word of God, lack eyes to see the sacramental vision of future redemption shining insistently within our gathering to share bread and wine.

It is this proleptic ecclesiological vision—disciplined by the word, sacramentally beheld—that I want to meditate upon here, discerning its potential contributions to a way of perceiving identity and conflict in our broader public life together. Certainly the twentieth century history of the complicity of German Lutheran churches in Nazi atrocities leaves Lutherans with no room for an "ecclesiology of glory" that asserts the inherent superiority of a Lutheran expression of church (especially when we settle for what Bonhoeffer called "cheap grace"[3]). At the same time, in the United States a Lutheran ecclesiology that is fed by European state church assumptions, yet unmoored from a state church context, generates sensibilities that Lutheran Christians can bring to bear fruitfully in a time of national political polarization.

In a country shaped heavily by evangelical word-centered ecclesiologies that condition belonging on being born-again, a Lutheran emphasis on word and sacrament nourishes a kind of Protestant Christian witness that notices the ways we always already belong to one another. This is so even as Lutheran churches have grappled with how to move beyond their roots in immigrant communities that only slowly adopted English as the language of worship—churches shaped by a long transition from ethnically-hyphenated American identities (German-American, Swedish-American, Finnish-American, etc.) to mainstream and often "white" North American identities, to a sense of being Lutheran that is increasingly shaped by interactions with southern-hemisphere Lutherans and by the hope and challenge of becoming a more multicultural church domestically. Across these transitions, a Lutheran Protestant emphasis on word *and* sacrament provides a rich theological resource for expressing anew in each generation how we do and how we can belong to one another, ever reforming as we stay attuned to the Spirit's nudging to hear and heed prophetic voices of judgment against injustice and the gospel call to share in God's feast.

While there are both theological and historical reasons for the emergence of any Christian ecclesiology, including historical diversity among Lutherans about how much emphasis to place on word and sacrament respectively (perceptible in liturgical shifts like communing weekly rather than rarely), my ecclesiological reflections arise from my participation in mostly Midwestern Lutheran congregations from the last few decades of the twentieth century until today. I will first show how my ecclesiological intuitions came to consciousness through a series of encounters—especially with left-leaning activists—in which my responses were implicitly informed by Lutheran worship of word *and* sacrament, beginning in a small Upper Michigan town that was predominantly Lutheran and Catholic, with many Finnish-Americans, Native Americans, and "Finndians." Second, interpreting political polarization in the U.S. as an expression of too much spoken word and too little sacramental seeing, manifesting in what Luther called the sins of presumption and despair, I turn to Paul in Galatians for insight into a way of advocating one side in a debate while assuming one's opponents belong to the same ecclesial body of Christ. Third, drawing upon two of Luther's perspectives on truth-telling practice—the theme in his *Heidelberg Disputation* of "calling a thing what it is" from a cruciform viewpoint, and his commentary on the eighth commandment in the *Small* and *Large Catechisms*—I will suggest four kinds of truth-telling about our nation and our neighbors that, intertwined, might reflect the kind of word and sacrament-shaped seeing of one another that resists drives toward both tyranny (which President Trump's opponents fear he seeks) and polarization in our political discourse.

DISCERNING ECCLESIOLOGICAL INTUITIONS (AMID THE SOCIAL ACTIVISTS)

After exposure to Marcion's arguments against including any Jewish scriptures in a Christian Bible because he thought they depicted an evil Jewish deity who trapped us in a material world, other second century Christians became more aware of their working criteria for determining which books belonged in the scriptural canon. The same can be said when we come to an awareness of our working ecclesiology by observing the ways our participation in a particular church has been forming our sensibilities about identity, belonging, and the processes of political contestation and social change—within and beyond the church itself[4]—especially as we incorporate additional public identities (such as liberal, conservative, feminist, and activist). Here are some of the moments and contexts in which I became aware of how a Lutheran ecclesiology of word and sacrament encourages a worldview that frames denunciations of social injustice and activist calls for reform within a noticing of our already belonging to one another within the redeemed and redeeming body of Christ.

In high school, during a regional Lutheran youth workshop I met a remarkable teenager who was more politically aware than any other seventeen-year-old I knew. I will call her Lisa. Daughter of Lutheran missionaries in south Asia, she told me as we were walking along Lake Superior about the conflict between Tamil Hindus and Sinhalese Buddhists in Sri Lanka. When she returned abroad we exchanged letters, she writing about how she thought Christians she knew in Asia had a stronger concern for social justice for their neighbors than Buddhists she knew, who seemed more interested in using their religious rituals to secure well-being for their immediate material or family advantage. She introduced me to a progressive social justice form of

Lutheranism that I would absorb over subsequent years, though I initially resisted it because I felt as if she were rooting the gospel in a kind of works righteousness by conditioning Christian identity on becoming a social activist, rather than starting with the mystical sense of union with Christ and one another to which the gospel of John testified. I recall her replying that I had a point about John, but that the effects of that union should still manifest in our willingness to participate in social change movements for the common good. The gospel is about proclaiming what is (in our union with Christ) *and* what is supposed to be, as the reign of God is made manifest.

At Carleton College, I was thrown beyond my relatively introverted spirituality into a public arena by work with the college chaplain and by a course for activists with political science professor Paul Wellstone. These experiences at once challenged and confirmed an ecclesiological sensibility that begins with a vision of redemption, sensed as already present in and across the brokenness and division in our lives. The chaplain, Jewelnel Davis, was ordained in the African American Progressive National Baptist tradition, and she modeled living out of her particular tradition while supporting all the religious activities at Carleton. At her behest, I facilitated weekly interreligious dialogue conversations over dinner, co-led a Martin Luther King Jr. celebration, and tended the fire for dancing naked pagans as the chaplain's representative. I also soaked up Jewelnel's sermons, which combined the prophetic and the mystical, Martin Luther King Jr. and Howard Thurman, in ways that affirmed both points of view in the conversation between Lisa and me. Jewelnel's Baptist focus was on word rather than sacrament, but she helped me to better see and draw lines of connection as a North American Christian between the preached word and divine providence at work judging and transforming our country's history of racism and other forms of social injustice. I grew into a public identity as a progressive Christian, building on a childhood sense that the women's and civil rights movements were Spirit-driven.

A course on Grassroots Organizing and Social Change Movements with Paul Wellstone challenged me more pointedly, if implicitly, to emphasize the prophetic dimension of the word of God through participation in public protests. Later a U.S. Senator from Minnesota, Paul was then a political science professor and the most energetically patriotic citizen I had met (with the possible exception of a repentant former member of the Nazi youth movement I once met on a plane, who felt Franklin Roosevelt had saved the soul of his former country). A secular Jew who wore a Star of David necklace, a former wrestler, Paul believed in the American democratic project and in social change movements with the spirit of an evangelist. "Why don't the poor rise up in the streets?" he asked with messianic fervor. Indeed, Paul inspired many students to a lifetime of activism and political involvement, even as his own vision was more irenic than that of students sorting out their newfound political allegiances. I remember an evening gathering at which wealthy students from Republican families were asking one another if they needed now to distance themselves from their Republican friends. Paul listened attentively, but did not encourage this sort of break. With the steadfastness of a Jew or Christian determined to see each person as made in the image of God, Paul perceived every U.S. citizen as someone who had something positive to contribute to society.

I had never felt more existentially challenged to convert—in this case, into a social justice activist—yet also given my first opportunity to write from a theological perspective about community organizing for social change. Paul had us journal about our readings and class events (with guests who ranged from labor organizers to a homeless man, and a trip to the Twin Cities to protest at a company that did business with the military). I journaled about why I thought social justice activism should be grounded first (and as it unfolded) in a vision of the reign of God as already in our midst, that this made a profound, if paradoxical, difference. Paul said that what I wrote was too deep for him. He said it matter-of-factly, not dismissively, in a spirit of humility and affirmation of another that he was famous for one-on-one with others—alongside his publicly passionate calls for collective action. Encountering Paul deepened my identification with the history of U.S. civil rights, anti-war, and anti-poverty movements, even if it was becoming clear to me that identifying *exclusively* with those movements was neither sustainable nor expressive of a large-enough vision of identity and belonging.

Meeting both faith-based and secular activists over the years has fostered and clarified an ecclesiological sensibility that is as much about a sacramental vision of our shared life in God as about a prophetic word that names how reality ought to be. During a year in the Lutheran Volunteer Corps from 1989 to 1990 working with the Chicago Religious Leadership Network on Central America (now on Latin America), I met the Lutheran Bishop of El Salvador, Medardo Gomez, who told us that our speaking out about human rights violations gave space for Salvadorans to organize and act—something more needed, he said, than charity. A Presbyterian returning from mission work in Guatemala, Grace Gyori, spoke of how faith-based activists seemed to have a larger vision of the reign of God that was not dependent on the success or failure of particular efforts or elections. They seemed less thrown by political setbacks. I noticed the same when Marxists I knew in Nashville were despondent after Daniel Ortega lost the 1990 presidential election in Nicaragua, into whose Sandinista Communist revolution they had poured their hope. As a volunteer activist who co-led the protest against the Gulf War while I was an MDiv student at Vanderbilt Divinity School in Nashville, and later helped lead the local movement against the Iraq War in Macomb, Illinois, I noticed that protesters active in churches or mosques often sought bridge-building as well as peaceful public witness against the war; some withdrew from participating when they felt that too-strident voices dominated meetings or public events. And while attending in the 1990's a few meetings of the Chicago chapter of the Committees of Correspondence, a democratizing break-away from the more hierarchical Communist Party USA, I observed not only that lifelong communists (who called themselves "red diaper babies") attended meetings in church basements as if they were a secular church (replete with potlucks), but also that the most outspoken leader held a strong doctrine of original sin alongside a doctrine of salvation by works. When he expressed deep pessimism about the goodness of a capitalist American society, and began a speech urging us to attend a variety of labor protests across the state, making participation in many protests a litmus test of how left we *really* were, I suddenly flashed to an image of my hometown in winter, with everyone bundled up, finding a way to say hello to one another, despite the high rates of alcoholism, poverty, and depression in Baraga County. A political ideology like that of CoC didn't seem to be able to account for how everyday kindness could be sustained amid the very economic circumstances a communist vision seeks to reform. While I could have stayed to find or develop a more adequate form of socialist ideology, I realized then that I was not sectarian—that I preferred the way the mainstream political parties seemed to make space for a spectrum of commitment rather than conditioning belonging on intense and frequent participation in confrontational rituals (if only because mainstream parties' primary measure of commitment is the ritual of voting), even as various ideological perspectives vie for control of them. While some may be drawn to more sectarian politics precisely out of feeling the wounds of an unjust social order—an empathy made possible by a sacramental sense of identification with others—the temptation in radical politics to condemn those who don't participate in transforming the social orders too easily signals a dualistic worldview of the saved and the damned.

This narrative may seem far from an exposition of a Lutheran ecclesiology, yet I believe it is my liturgical and catechetical formation in a small-town Upper Michigan Lutheran church (a formation reinforced in other Lutheran as well as ecumenical and interfaith settings over the years) that shaped my instincts for participating in both the political process and social justice movements with a hunger to bridge polarized political and cultural divides, even as I've come to identify quite thoroughly with a progressive Christian narrative that perceives as Spirit-guided the liberation movements that seek to undo sexism, racism, heterosexism, the lingering effects of colonialism, economic injustice, and ecological devastation—among other forms of oppression that we are learning to name and engage with ever greater perspicuity. Of course, there is nothing inevitable about how a Lutheran ecclesiology will interface with particular political identities and social commitments, even if some tendencies might be noted. As Kathryn Tanner observes, drawing upon postmodern cultural theory, we engage in negotiated appropriations of circulating cultural and theological elements as we make *ad hoc* decisions about our participation in the public sphere, including in Christian debates about what constitutes the common good.[5] That doesn't mean we never deem some attitudes and actions unfaithful; indeed, we cannot avoid normative judgments about our understanding of word and sacrament, even as a tangle of opposing arguments peculiarly holds us together across a cultural divide. Certainly diametrically opposed perspectives on whether or not Donald Trump's election as president is *providential* render Trump-phobic and Trump-philic Christians nigh unintelligible to one another.

SINS OF PRESUMPTION AND A PAULINE CALL FOR SACRAMENTAL ATTENTION TO OUR BAPTISM IN CHRIST

Indeed, we may despair of our neighbor's political salvation more than we despair of their eternal salvation. The flip side of this despair, though, is a presumption of our own rightness. While Democrats often perceive themselves as more open to diversity, a conviction of liberal righteousness can lead to what Luther—and Catholic theologians before him—call the sin of presumption,[6] expressed here not as personal uprightness but as presuming to hold the right worldview *in contrast* to the worldview of (often white Christian) social conservatives, who seem to be on the wrong side of history and opposed to whole groups of people: women (at least as people with agency over our bodies and equal rights in the public sphere), people of color, sexual minorities, immigrants, and Muslims. Of course, the sin of presumption readily afflicts conservative Republicans as well, who are as convinced that they hold the right and righteous worldview, who are more likely than Democrats to oppose March for Our Lives rallies on behalf of gun control with rallies called March for Our Guns (whose ownership they declare both a constitutional and a God-given right[7]), and who believe liberals fail to value respect for the law (by supporting illegal immigrants), stable heterosexual families, and the lives of unborn babies.

While mirrored sins of presumption animate both (or all) parties in a polarized environment, I want to focus here on the temptation to the sin of presumption among Democrats and progressive Christians, because it is we who are most acutely tracking the tendency toward authoritarianism and tyranny under Trump, as many conservatives did under Obama.

In her presidential campaign, Hillary Clinton became an avatar for the liberal sin of presumption. Hillary Clinton analyzed her defeat in 2016 by saying, "If you look at the map of the United States, there is all this red in the middle where Trump won. I won on the coasts ... I won in the places that are optimistic, diverse, dynamic, moving forward, and his whole campaign, 'make America great again,' was looking backwards."[8] During her presidential campaign, Clinton also called half of Trump supporters "a basket of deplorables" who are "racist, sexist, homophobic, xenophobic, Islamophobic" and in some cases, "irredeemable"; but, she added, "thankfully they are not America."[9] Although she apologized and qualified her statement the following day, Clinton "calls a thing what it is" insofar as she names the attitudes of many liberals toward not only Trump supporters, but Republican-leaning states, especially rural regions of the Midwest (with its "flyover" states). The people in these red middle places are "not America"—even as Republicans and conservative Christians see precisely rural heartland regions as archetypal "real America."

Indeed, from Paul's day to our own, salvation—national and ecclesial—is a matter of identity and belonging. Clinton's depiction of "half" of Trump supporters as "irredeemable" evokes the language of salvation no less than Paul does when he argues that justification is by faith in Christ, not by works of the law. However, Paul's passion for ecclesial unity shapes the way he calls out Jews who want to condition belonging, and salvation in Christ, on Gentiles also becoming circumcised, kosher-keeping Jews.

On one hand, Paul holds nothing back in going after his opponents, since the very nature of the gospel and the church are at stake: if Gentiles cannot be part of the church unless they observe Jewish ritual law, then Gentiles are not becoming part of the church through baptism into the crucified and risen Christ, but by becoming an observant Jew. In his perhaps most tweetable insult against his circumcision-insisting opponents, Paul wishes they would go the whole way and "castrate themselves" (Gal 5:12 [NRSV]). Paul doesn't hesitate to stake out a clear position in a polarizing debate about the nature of the body politic—in this case, the church: "As we have said before, so now I repeat, if anyone proclaims to you a gospel contrary to what you have received, let that one be accursed!" (Gal 1:9).

On the other hand, Paul redefines the boundaries of the covenantal people of Israel itself by broadening them to include those who were once called "not my people" (Rom 9:25, citing Hos 1:10), the Gentiles: "There is no longer Jew or Greek, there is no longer slave or free, there is no longer male and female; for all of you are one in Christ Jesus" (Gal 3:28). Put another way—one that frames Jewish identity through an haggadic (narrative) rather than a halakhic (legal) interpretation of Torah[10]—Paul argues that Gentiles become part of the covenant of Israel not by becoming ritually observant Jews, but by keeping the heart of the Torah by loving their neighbors as themselves (Gal 5:13–14), and by doing what Abraham himself did, *before* the Mosaic Law ever appeared: experiencing righteousness through faith (Gal 3:6–29). Paul is engaged in a long-standing Jewish debate about the "real" nature of Israel, disputing with those who want to make Israel great again by shrinking its boundaries rather than expanding them in and through an identification with the particular Jew that Paul calls Christ Jesus. To include Gentiles, Paul uses Christ-centered midrash to create a different haggadah, to tell another kind of story of covenantal belonging.

While Paul's haggadah can imply an argument against the continued existence of all but a Messianic form of Judaism, Paul's drive toward covenantal inclusion moves from the opposite direction in Romans 9–11. In wrestling with the question why not all of "[his] own people," Israelites (Rom 9:3–4), affirm Jesus as the Christ, Paul ultimately argues that God predestines most Jews not to accept Jesus as Messiah by hardening their hearts so that Gentiles can join the covenant.[11] However, God "has not rejected his people whom he foreknew" (Gal 11:2); "all Israel will be saved" (Gal 11:26) in some divinely-mysterious way that Paul finds "inscrutable" (Gal 11:34): "As regards the gospel they are enemies of God for your sake; but as regards election they are beloved, for the sake of their ancestors; for the gifts and the calling of God are irrevocable" (Gal 11:28–29).

The modern and postmodern period has witnessed philosophical, ethical, and exegetical debates about how to reckon with a universalist orientation in Paul alongside a call for recognition of particular identities that resist assimilation into a Christian or any universalizing identity.[12] For our purposes here, it may suffice to note, along with many Jewish and Christian post-Holocaust Pauline interpreters, that Paul's insistence that first century Gentiles did not need to become observant Jews to belong to Christ coincided with his insight that divine providence lay behind the persistence of Jews in choosing not to belong to Christ at all. There is a kind of double-belonging here—two ways of belonging to the covenant community that has its roots in promises to Israel and branches that extend to Gentiles. Here Paul's eschatological vision encompasses the tension of the moment—feeling it fully, yet stretching beyond it to take his bearings from a glimpse of reconciliation across a painful division among Jews themselves and, as the church eventually comes to be called Christian, between Jews and Christians.

Likewise, in a move that shaped Luther's own articulation of ecclesial unity across deeply polarizing differences, Paul resists dividing the unity of the church insofar as he refuses to form a Gentile church that separates out from the mother church in Jerusalem. Although he will dispute with Peter on the matter of circumcision (Gal 2:11–14), he travels to Jerusalem to be assured that he and the other apostles were in basic agreement in their preaching of the gospel (Gal 2:1–10), and to agree to collect funds from churches he founded to support the church in Jerusalem (2 Cor 8–9). The Gentile and

Jewish churches are one church. Similarly, addressing sixteenth century church divisions in his 1535 commentary on the phrase "To the churches of Galatia" in Galatians 1:2, Luther builds on Jerome's patristic commentary on Paul to portray both the Catholic church and the more radically reforming churches as still all truly church.

> Jerome raises an important question here: Why does Paul call "churches" those that were not churches? For Paul, he says, is writing to the Galatians, who had been led astray and turned away from Christ and from grace to Moses and the Law. I reply: When Paul calls them the "churches of Galatia," he is employing synecdoche.... Writing in a similar vein to the Corinthians, he congratulates them that the grace of God was given them in Christ.... And yet many of them had been perverted by false apostles and did not believe in resurrection of the dead, etc. So today we still call the Church of Rome holy and all its sees holy, even though they have been undermined and their ministers are ungodly. For "God rules in the midst of His foes" (Ps 110:2) ... and even if it is surrounded by wolves and robbers, that is, spiritual tyrants, it is still the church. Although the city of Rome is worse than Sodom and Gomorrah, nevertheless there remain in it Baptism, the Sacraments, the voice and text of the Gospel, the Sacred Scriptures, the ministries, the name of Christ, and the name of God.[13]
>
> Therefore even though the Galatians had been led astray, Baptism, the Word, and the name of Christ still continued among them.... For Baptism, the Gospel, etc., do not become unholy because I am defiled and unholy and have a false understanding of them.... Therefore the church is holy even where the fanatics [radical reformers] are dominant, so long as they do not deny the Word and the sacraments; if they deny these, they are no longer the church. Wherever the substance of the Word and the sacraments abides, therefore, there the holy church is present, even though the Antichrist may reign there, for he takes his seat not ... in a congregation of unbelievers but in the highest and holiest place possible, namely, in the Temple of God (2 Thess. 2:4).... The church is universal throughout the world, wherever the Gospel of God and the sacraments are present.[14]

Luther adds that the "fanatics" are not part of the church insofar as they "deny these things" (word and sacraments)—nor are "Jews and Turks [Muslims]."[15] Luther's naming of who does *not* belong to the church reminds us that ecclesial unity cannot be conflated with a national identity per se, even if it can provide a lens through which to view other kinds of corporate identity and belonging, as well as one religious frame of reference for imagining the world's unity and redemption. While addressing the vital work of interfaith imagining is beyond the scope of this chapter, I am among those who find that conversation more compelling when we each bring forth the most-fleshed-out particularities of our respective visions of the world seen in its ultimate frames of reference. So, working with the theological conviction that the eschatological yet sacramentally present unity of the church matters for

Christian engagement with the affairs of all nations and peoples, I turn now to explore what a sacramental vision implies for our speaking a prophetic yet reconciling word together.

THE PROCLAIMED WORD: TRUTH-TELLING ABOUT NATIONS AND NEIGHBORS

Those of us shaped by liberation-minded theologies have internalized an understanding that the word of God is never less than a prophetic word—a word that denounces social injustice as systemic sin, calls us to collective repentance and conversion, and announces an in-breaking liberation from the bondage of oppressive social systems and for a freedom to form new personal and collective identities not marred by sexism, racism, colonialism, and other forms of hierarchical social patterning that locate each of us on spectrums of value, visibility, and personhood (and position long-range ecological attention beneath short-term comfort). But we may be less adept at communicating with Christians more familiar with conceptualizing sin in individual terms. To learn to hear a prophetic word of liberation involves a conversion of consciousness—and once we have made it, we can be as vulnerable to the sin of presumption against those of unconverted consciousness as the Corinthian believers who realized that idols didn't exist, so it didn't matter if one ate meat that had been sacrificed to them—whatever the feelings of believers of "weaker" faith (1 Cor 8). Like Clinton in her more presumptuous moments, we can turn prophetic truths into weapons we use not just against structural injustice, but also against persons we perceive as willfully ignorant of what we regard as radiantly clear prophetic truths—persons who look backwards into nostalgia for a patriarchal white supremacy instead of forward into God's dynamic new creation emerging in our midst (at least in U.S. cities and on U.S. coasts).

How then do we practice truth-telling, calling things what they are, at the level of both nations and neighbors, ideologies and persons? One kind of liturgy of the activist left demands a public confession of sin from those complicit in acts of racism, sexism, or heterosexism. It conditions belonging to the right side of history upon the recitation of a creed espousing equality and equity. In a time when the U.S. president stokes nostalgia for an imagined past golden (white) age and shows himself drawn to authoritarian uses of power, can fascist-fearing Lutherans practice boldly anti-tyrannical, justice-seeking truth-telling, yet avoid denouncing our neighbors—or whole regions of the country—as damned and irredeemable unless they undergo a politicized public penance and conversion?

If we take our cues from a theology of both word and sacrament, an adequate answer to this question does not avoid a call for conversion, but extends the call for repentance and new vision throughout the ecclesial body of Christ by listening not only to God's word against structural injustice, but also to divine judgment against the existential sins of presumption and despair to which we are tempted when we face systemic injustices or a dehumanizing response from our political opponents. While Luther perceived presumption as the sin of those who believe they are in the right by being personally righteous, presumption with regard to a self-righteous worldview signals that we can be among the "woke" to an ideological truth, but not yet "woke" to the ways we still fail to love our neighbors (not just our nation) as ourselves. Caught in a state of presumption, we who are progressive Christians may feel despair about our ideologically un-woke neighbors ever seeing the light—and so may despair about the future of our nation and planet. *The right view matters*; we stand firmly upon the prophetic word of God, which functions for us as the law in Luther's law-gospel dialectic—a law that presumably judges our neighbors more than ourselves, a law we hold to be self-evident to all who take the time to educate themselves. "So the law is holy, and the commandment is holy and just and good" (Rom 7:12). We know we too are complicit in the structures of injustice, but in our presumption that we are woke to the right direction that social justice takes in the reign of God, we might notice less easily ways we can be complicit in dividing our country into the saved and the damned—the damned being those politically wrong-thinking neighbors we might know mostly in the abstract. "For I delight in the law of God in my inmost self, but I see in my members another law at war with the law of my mind, making me captive to the body of sin that dwells in my members.... Who will rescue me from this body of death? Thanks be to God through Jesus Christ our Lord!" (Rom 7:24–25). And for Paul, as for us, the redeeming body of Christ includes the church itself; to say "there is no salvation outside the church" is to say that the *basileia tou theou* or dominion of God does not consist in an individual relationship with Jesus, but in belonging as individuals to the ecclesial body of Christ (cf. 1 Cor 12:27) whose head is the crucified and risen Jesus, the "image of the invisible God" (Col 1:15) in whom "all things hold together" (Col 1:17) and are reconciled (cf. Col 1:15–29). This image from Colossians was expressed in a spherical stained glass window in my hometown church depicting Jesus with outstretched arms resting on two globes, two earths—the old and new creations, the worlds of sinner and sinned against, the worldviews of polarized parties of every sort—with Christ between them.

To *hear* the converting, reconciling divine word as Christians who sense a new creation even in a still-unredeemed world, a Lutheran theology of word *and* sacrament invites us also to *see* one another with a sacramental imagination grounded in our baptisms and in communion. Our ecclesial identity, our belonging in Christ, draws us together as weeds and wheat, as old and new Adams and Eves, as a broken sin-soaked people who are already one even as we are being made anew in Christ by the guidance of the Spirit. As an ELCA study guide on "Faith, Sexism, [and] Justice" puts it:

> First and foremost for our conversations, it is important to recognize that our unity in Christ is a gift of God. It is not the result of agreeing about everything we discuss, even deeply held ethical convictions. The gift of unity is not the same thing as uniformity, and it is not our doing; it is given to us in our common baptism into Christ. This gift of unity calls us forward in the Spirit to seek relationships of "mutual conversation and consolation.... In conversations in which we try to discern what is good and right (Romans 12:1–2), we depend first upon the church's unity in Christ because we all see through a mirror dimly, and all of us must rely on the Holy Spirit's guidance, which is given within the community.[16]

No less in our time than in Paul's or Luther's, we may find it easier to identify our side of a contested issue than to recollect the unity in Christ that enables us to risk speaking to that issue in the first place. But truth-telling among Christians begins with announcing—beholding—the truth of our unity in Christ.

Luther framed truth-telling in two ways that can be theologically fruitful for contemporary Christian practices of truth-telling with regard to both the collective level of the nation and the interpersonal level of the face of our neighbors. The first way appears in thesis 21 of Luther's 1518 *Heidelberg Disputation*, where Luther depicts truth-telling as a practice of "calling a thing what it actually is" as viewed from "God hidden in suffering" rather than from the "puffed up" place of our own "good works": "A theology of glory calls evil good and good evil. A theology of the cross calls the thing what it actually is."[17] Because it speaks from the perspective of the underside, a position of apparent defeat than success, "calling a thing what it is" has become a favored motif among Lutherans speaking a prophetic and pastoral word about forms of oppression ranging from racism, to violence against women, to human rights violations in Central America enabled by US military aid.[18]

A second approach to truth-telling can be found in Luther's commentary in the *Small Catechism* on the eighth commandment, "You shall not bear false witness against your neighbor." Here truth-telling means approaching our neighbors with a charitable interpretation as much as possible:

> We should fear and love God, and so we should not tell lies about our neighbor, nor betray, slander, or defame him, but should apologize for him, speak well of

him, and interpret charitably all that he does.[19]

While Luther (like Paul) speaks plenty of cross words about his theological opponents like the pope, he does so because "the sin is public," "manifest to everybody" so "there can be no question of slander or injustice or false witness."[20] He further adds in his *Large Catechism* on the same commandment, "[N]obody has the right to judge and reprove his neighbor publicly, even when he has seen a sin committed, unless he has been authorized to judge and reprove,"[21] although following Matthew 18:15, one ought to "admonish" a neighbor who has sinned against one "privately so that he may amend."[22] This form of truth-telling has a bearing on when, and how, to "call a thing what it actually is."

In an effort to speak against structural injustice and potential tyranny in a nation, yet also to speak about our neighbors in a way that interrupts presumption about ourselves and despair about our fellow citizens, we might identify four forms of speaking truthfully that take the shape of "calling a thing what it is" while regarding our neighbors charitably. Together they draw on Luther's approaches to truth-telling and a Lutheran theology of word and sacrament.

A first kind of truth-telling involves attesting to empirical facts and resisting efforts to suppress them. This includes calling out the rhetoric of an authoritarian-leaning leader, whose "theology of glory" about himself manifests in a kind of "magical thinking" that confuses people about the nature of particular truths. Factual truth-telling is the kind that political progressives are the most keen to practice amid a "post-truth" culture with its "alternative facts." In *On Tyranny: Twenty Lessons from the Twentieth Century,* historian Timothy Snyder names lesson 10, "Believe in truth":

> To abandon facts is to abandon freedom. If nothing is true, then no one can criticize power, because there is no basis on which to do so. If nothing is true, then all is spectacle.[23]
> You submit to tyranny when you renounce the difference between what you want to hear and what is actually the case.[24]

Snyder cites Victor Klemperer's observations under Hitler that when a society moves toward totalitarianism, "truth dies in four modes": in "open hostility to verifiable reality, which takes the form of presenting inventions and lies as if they were facts"; in a "shamanistic incantation" that repeats a meme until it is plausible (like "Crooked Hillary" or "Build that wall"); through a "magical thinking, or the open embrace of contradiction" (like lowering taxes while promising to increase social and defense spending); and finally, through making truth "oracular rather than factual" and focused on a leader's own claim to speak for all and solve all.[25] Aware of how the dangers of a totalitarian worldview are present in the U.S. and globally, a renewed passion for empirical truth is finding a footing among progressives who had been drawn to viewing truth as contextualized or constructed, contingent on social location or performed identities. Now instead of resisting empire (or postcolonial legacies) only through a postmodern emphasis on plural forms of rationality and worldview, many progressives are calling for a common-sense kind of empirical truth-telling that resists "alternative facts."[26]

A second practice of truth-telling is the ideological sort that reveals underlying structures or patterns in our collective lives; construed theologically, it includes truth-telling about structural sin and its redress to a nation (or other collective identity) from the perspective of those marginalized or oppressed within it. Citing Luther's theme of "calling a thing what it is," Deanna Thompson names systemic racism in the U.S. in this fashion.[27] The most interesting (if also most contested) forms of ideological truth-telling are those that risk sketching a picture of our shared lives that is at once metaphysical and historically and culturally inflected. For example, J. Kameron Carter not only calls out white supremacy and joins Angela Davis in urging white people to "stop being white" (meaning no longer consenting to the privileges of a white identity, being a traitor to the idea of a white race); he also identifies life-generative patterns of perception he notices running across the centuries—through voices as wide-ranging as those of Marguerite Porete, Meister Eckhart, W. E. B. DuBois, and the poetry of M. NourbeSe Philip in *Zong!*—perceptions of a nonsubstantialist deity and a mysticism of the social, visible today in what he calls a black social life or "black churchicality" (in which blackness is not reducible to skin color, but represents that ebullient communal life which cannot be killed, even by the likes of a white supremacist shooter like Dylann Roof).[28] While an ideological form of truth-telling draws on postmodern ideas about multiple forms of rationality that depend upon social location, when it is "calling a thing what it is" from within the underside of a theology of the cross, it is involved in a prophetic naming of structural sin and a providential reading of our collective lives—the kind that many allude to when saying, "The arc of the moral universe is long, but it bends toward justice."[29] However, when we speak ideologically from a position of privilege, or from a position of resentment about losing our once-privileged status, we might read providence as running in the opposite direction—as arguably white evangelical Christians do when they see Trump's election as divinely ordained.[30] Are Christians who disagree correct in perceiving Trump and his allies as practicing a theology of glory rather than a theology of the cross? Theologically-inflected ideological truth-telling is risky. Still, the risk of ideological truth-telling is necessary, if insufficient: necessary because it is the means by which we identify patterns of sin and redemption, of that which destroys and that in the human spirit which cannot be destroyed, in a collective like a nation; insufficient insofar as through it we can be tempted to hypostasize oppressive patterns themselves (capitalism or Marxism; white supremacy become a supra-personal force with a will) in a way that prevents us from seeing the particular faces of our neighbors. It is then that we can fall into the sin of presumption by identifying fiercely with a justice-seeking trajectory of divine providence we know to be true, but in a way that does not acknowledge other sorts of truths—and may tempt us to slander our neighbors through the very kinds of name-calling memes associated with totalitarian thinking.

A third kind of truth-telling practice is precisely about the search for ways to speak properly of our neighbors when they oppose the ideological kind of prophetic truth-telling that we are staking our vision of justice upon. Even if we are speaking God's prophetic word about our nation correctly, we may be just as much in danger of turning our neighbors into stereotypes or monsters when we are convinced they are wrong as if we were doing the same in the name of a fascist ideology that prefers feelings to facts. And so Luther intentionally frames his commentary about the eighth commandment with a theocentric awareness—"We should fear and love God, and so we should not tell lies about our neighbor, nor betray, slander, or defame him"—because otherwise we might make ourselves gods of our neighbors, rather than their servants in love, and conversation partners in discerning where the Spirit is leading us together. In the context of an issue that divides a country, this may be easiest to practice when we can readily see something worthy of respect in our neighbor's resistance to sharing our own public policy concerns. For example: insofar as the March for Our Lives movement has voices within it that seek to ban all guns, there is an at best ignorant denial of the ordinary place that rifles have in the lives of those of us who grow up in rural areas and who hunt, protect livestock, or simply take time away from school (like my sixth grade class did) to learn outdoor skills, including gun safety and shooting a BB gun. When ignoring these, it is as if one neighbor is saying to another: your way of life is irrelevant to me, or backwards and passing away. Here there is a need for a more richly storied, even ethnographic understanding of one another as neighbors. Otherwise, that which is righteous and good becomes the occasion for causing another to stumble; or to use a parable of Jesus rather than a saying of Paul, the blind leads the blind, and both fall into the pit (cf. Rom 14:13–23; Luke 6:39).

Ethnographic or narrative truth-telling about our neighbors means beginning not with the ideological level of truth-telling about our nation—viewed through structural sin and its correlate of social justice—but with the ways our neighbors make meaning of their everyday lives. It is at the second, ideological level of truth-telling that Allen Jorgenson calls for a repentant resistance to an "ecclesiology of entitlement" by those who immigrated to North America, displacing indigenous peoples from their lands. Christians—including the ELCA in 2016[31]—have only begun to repudiate the Doctrine of Discovery, a 1493 papal bull that depicted all American lands not settled by Christians as lacking ownership. Jorgenson cites North American indigenous political theorists who reject Canadian and U.S. identities and passports. But alongside being accountable to these prophetic forms of truth-telling about the structural sin of colonialism, we do right also to include a richer ethnographic sense of contested Native perspectives on identity and belonging in relationship to the U.S. or Canadian nation states—to remember that our Native American neighbors are not reducible to a radically indigenous political ideology, but hold diverse views on every contested national or Native subject (as anyone who follows the radio talk show *Native America Calling* will quickly notice). As one who grew up white in a town surrounded by an Ojibwe (Anishinaabe) reservation, I cannot think of accountability to Native neighbors—friends and former classmates—without an awareness that a vocal minority support Trump's views on immigration. A "Finndian" truck driver in my hometown (who is both a descendant of a former president of Finland and a member of the Keweenaw Bay Indian Community) won't hesitate to voice anti-immigrant, pro-Trump, pro-gun-owning comments in response to a Facebook post I made about how deportations are upsetting small town friendships and businesses—even as he then praises me for being one of the few liberals he knows who won't block him for doing that. While I could accuse him of false consciousness for identifying with the United States instead of exclusively with Native sovereignty, it is even harder to do that when I think of Native veterans from my hometown who, even recently, have lost their lives in U.S. wars. Another Native friend, a Catholic who votes Republican, told me during our debate team years that she opposes abortion because of the history of forced sterilization of Native American women (and also told me that the land my family lived on had been sold by someone Ojibwe under the Dawes Act, and the tribe hoped to buy it back one day). To speak truthfully about my neighbors, I need to be aware of their complex identifications and the stories that make sense of them, to more accurately see the textures of their, and our, lives as variously shaped by colonialism—as one factor among many in the always intersectional identities of our neighbors and ourselves.

    A fourth sort of truth-telling relates at once to our neighbors and to an ultimate vision of our belonging to one another in the ecclesial body of Christ, and so circles back to where I began: with the intuitions opened up by participating in a Lutheran liturgy of word and sacrament. While the church is not the nation, Lutheran congregations and theology are the prism through which I have learned to see all creation as beloved in the crucified and risen

Christ—a gift of sight we receive and bear. Telling the truth of the gospel involves telling stories of grace, of ongoing conversion, of how those who were "not my people" are now being called "my people" (cf. Hos 2:23; Rom 9:25). In the small-town Midwest and South of the U.S., these include stories of white Lutheran churches calling as women pastors from South Korea, India, and the West Bank; and of a priest from Uganda in my current western Illinois town telling me that in Africa, the Midwest is spoken of as the place in the U.S. that is actually the most open to priests from their continent. Many other everyday stories of neighbors deepening their ties across differences tell the truth of belonging by grace, even before we know one another fully; and these everyday stories join the testimonies of those with graced vision who find a way to love their enemies as neighbors, even while disagreeing with them.

CONCLUDING REMARKS

I have tried to tease out the implications of a Lutheran theology of word and sacrament for practices of a truth-telling law and gospel proclamation that is accompanied by *noticing* what already draws us into a beloved community in and through the ecclesial body of Christ. We can learn to rightly proclaim the prophetic divine word—in a way that resists both tyranny and polarization—when we begin by seeing sacramentally: remembering the sacrament of baptism that names our deeper belonging to one another in Christ, and viewing our common life together in light of redemption from the fracturing of sin—an eschatological vision whose proleptic fulfillment we taste in the sacrament of communion. Seeing our lives, past and present, in relationship to eschatological redemption is what I have called a fourth kind of truth-telling—one that interacts in a background way with other sorts of truth-telling (empirical fact-telling, ideological naming of structural in/justice, and ethnographically-rich depictions of our neighbors). In this way, by balancing word and sacrament, by proclaiming law and gospel (the prophetic and the evangelical) while seeing sacramentally the gathering of all God's wounded and wounding people, Lutheran liturgy fosters a non-sectarian sensibility that can spark a Spirit-driven instinct to participate in social justice movements and the political process with a hunger to bridge polarized and social divides.

NOTES

1. The Lutheran Church in America (LCA), 1962–1987, was formed by the merging of German, Finnish, and various Scandinavian immigrant-rooted Lutheran churches. The Evangelical Lutheran Church in America (ELCA) was formed in 1988 by the merging of the Lutheran Church in America with the American Lutheran Church (ALC, also a denomination formed out of mergers among immigrant Lutheran churches) and the Association of Evangelical Lutheran Churches. The congregations with which I have been involved the longest are United Lutheran Church in L'Anse, (Upper) Michigan; Augustana Lutheran Church of Hyde Park in Chicago; and Trinity Lutheran Church of Macomb, Illinois.

2. Martin Luther, "Freedom of a Christian," *Martin Luther: Selections from His Writings*, ed. John Dillenberger (New York: Anchor Books, 1962), 60–61.

3. Dietrich Bonhoeffer, "Costly Grace," in *The Cost of Discipleship*, rev. edn., trans. R. H. Fuller and Irmgard Booth (New York: Collier Books MacMillan, 1963), 46–60.

4. For an account of postmodern cultural theory in relationship to theological formation and debate, see Kathryn Tanner, *Politics of God: Christian Theologies and Social Justice* (Minneapolis, MN: Fortress Press, 1992).

5. Tanner, *Politics of God*.

6. "[H]e is a true Christian who neither is presumptuous in his works nor despairs in his sins." Martin Luther, *Luther's Works*, vol. 16: *Lectures on Isaiah Chapters 1-39*, ed. Jaroslav Pelikan, trans. Herbert J. A. Bouman (St. Louis, MO: Concordia Publishing House, 1969), 15. Luther pairs presumption and despair as two sides of idolatry in his commentary on the first commandment in the *Large Catechism*: "notice how presumptuous, secure, and proud people are because of [idolatrous] possessions, and how despondent when they no longer exist or are withdrawn"—the latter "doubts and is despondent, as though he knew of no God." In *Christian Classics Ethereal Library*; online at https://www.ccel.org/ccel/luther/largecatechism.i_2.html (accessed Feb. 11, 2020). See also the Catholic *Baltimore Catechism*, Lesson on the First Commandment, Q's 1182–87; online at http://www.baltimore-catechism.com/lesson30.htm (accessed Feb. 11, 2020).

7. "On a Day of Gun Protest, Some Montanans Will March for Their Guns," *National Public Radio* (March 23, 2018); online at https://www.npr.org/2018/03/23/596253830/on-a-day-of-gun-protest-some-montanans-will-march-for-their-guns (accessed Feb. 11, 2020).

8. Cokie and Steven V. Roberts, "Respect Your Voters," syndicated editorial (March 21, 2018); online at https://www.uexpress.com/cokie-and-steven-roberts/2018/3/21/respect-your-voters.

9. Angie Drobnic Holan, "In Context: Hillary Clinton and the 'basket of deplorables,'" *Politifact* (Sept. 11, 2016); online at http://www.politifact.com/truth-o-meter/article/2016/sep/11/context-hillary-clinton-basket-deplorables/ (accessed Feb. 11, 2020).

10. Charles B. Cousar, *Galatians, Interpretation: A Bible Commentary for Teaching and Preaching* (Louisville, KY: Westminster John Knox, 2012), 75–77, 82. Cousar

cites here James A. Sanders's essay "Torah and Paul," in *God's Christ and His People*, ed. Jacob Jervell and Wayne A. Meeks (Oslo: Universitetsforlaget, 1977), 132–40.

11. Rom 11:25, and Rom 11:7–25 more broadly.

12. Compare, for instance, Alain Badiou's *Saint Paul: The Foundation of Universalism*, trans. Ray Brassier (Redwood City, CA: Stanford University Press, 2003); and Daniel Boyarin's *A Radical Jew: Paul and the Politics of Identity* (Oakland, CA: University of California Press, 1997).

13. Martin Luther, *Luther's Works*, vol. 26: *Lectures on Galatians (1535)*, ed. Walter A. Hansen, trans. Jaroslav Pelikan (St. Louis, MO: Concordia Publishing House, 1963), 24. In his 1519 commentary on Gal 1:2, written before his excommunication in 1521 by Pope Leo X, Luther stressed avoiding schism amid disagreement (here too following Jerome and other patristics); Luther, *Luther's Works*, vol. 27: *Lectures on Galatians (1519)*, ed. Walter A. Hansen, trans. Jaroslav Pelikan (St. Louis, MO: Concordia Publishing House, 1964), 168–69.

14. Luther, *Lectures on Galatians (1535)*, 25–26.

15. Luther, *Lectures on Galatians (1535)*, 26.

16. "Faith, Sexism, Justice: Conversations toward a Social Statement," A Study from the ELCA Task Force on Women and Justice: One in Christ (Evangelical Lutheran Church in American, 2016), 26–27; online at https://download.elca.org/ELCA%20Resource%20Repository/FSJ_LnCall-ProposedStmntIRs-March-7.pdf (accessed Feb. 20, 2020). The quote within the quote is from Martin Luther, "Smalcald Articles Part III, Article iv," in *The Book of Concord*, ed. Robert Kolb and Timothy J. Wengert (Minneapolis, MN: Fortress Press, 2000), 319.

17. Martin Luther, *The Heidelberg Disputation*, online at http://bookofconcord.org/heidelberg.php (accessed Feb. 12, 2020). In his fuller "proof" of the thesis, Luther states, "He who does not know Christ does not know God hidden in suffering. Therefore he prefers works to suffering, glory to the cross, strength to weakness, wisdom to folly, and, in general, good to evil. These are the people whom the apostle calls 'enemies of the cross' (Phil. 3:18), for they hate the cross and suffering and love works and the glory of works. Thus they call the cross evil and the evil of a deed good. God can be found only in suffering and the cross.... Therefore the friends of the cross say that the cross is good and works are evil, for through the cross works are dethroned and the 'old Adam,' who is especially edified by works, is crucified. It is impossible for a person not to be puffed up by his 'good works' unless he has first been deflated and destroyed by suffering and evil until he knows that he is worthless and that his works are not his but God's."

18. See, for example, Deanna Thompson, "Calling a Thing What It Is: A Lutheran Approach to Whiteness," *Dialog: A Journal of Theology* 53, no. 1 (2014): 49–57; Mary M. Solberg *Compelling Knowledge: A Feminist Proposal for an Epistemology of the Cross* (Albany, NY: SUNY Press, 1997).

19. Luther, "Small Catechism," in *The Book of Concord*, ed. Theodore G. Tappert (Philadelphia, PA: Fortress Press, 1959), 343.

20. Luther, "Large Catechism," in *Book of Concord* (1959), 403.

21. Luther, "Large Catechism," 400–401.

22. Luther, "Large Catechism," 402.

23. Timothy Snyder, *On Tyranny: Twenty Lessons from the Twentieth Century* (New York: Tim Duggan Books, 2017), 65. Critical reviews of *On Tyranny* caution against historical analogies, especially as prophetic warnings; see e.g. Jacob Mikanowski, "The Bleak Prophecy of Timothy Snyder," *The Chronicle Review* (April 12, 2019); online at https://www.chronicle.com/interactives/20190412snyder?cid=at&utm_source=at&utm_medium=en&cid=at (accessed Feb. 12, 2020).

24. Snyder, *On Tyranny*, 66.

25. Snyder, *On Tyranny*, 66–71.

26. Thomas Tweed made a confession of this sort in his plenary talk at the Midwest American Academy of Religion, "Religion in Higher Education," Muncie, IN, March 4, 2017.

27. Thompson, "Calling a Thing What It Is," 52–54.

28. M. NourbeSe Philip, *Zong!* (Middletown, CT: Wesleyan University Press, 2008). For a taste of J. Kameron Carter's depiction of black churchicality, see his essay "What Was Dylann Roof Shooting At?," in "In the Shadow of Charleston: Politics, Religion, and White Supremacy," *Syndicate* (July 30, 2015); online at https://syndicate.network/symposia/theology/in-the-shadow-of-charleston/ (accessed Feb. 12, 2020). See also his forthcoming volume *Black Rapture: A Poetics of the Sacred*.

29. This phrase seems to originate with nineteenth century Unitarian minister Theodore Parker with regard to the anti-slavery movement; see "The Arc of the Moral Universe Is Long But It Bends Toward Justice," *Quote Investigator* (Nov. 15, 2012); online at http://quoteinvestigator.com/2012/11/15/arc-of-universe/ (accessed Feb. 12, 2020).

30. In his sermon at Trump's inauguration, Robert Jeffress said, "I believed that you would be the next President of the United States. And if that happened, it would be because God had placed you there." In "Read the Sermon Donald Trump Heard Before Becoming President," *Time* (Jan. 20, 2017); online at https://time.com/4641208/donald-trump-robert-jeffress-st-john-episcopal-inauguration/ (accessed Feb. 12, 2020). See also Amy Sullivan's review of Stephen Strang's book *God and Donald Trump* (Barnsley, England: Frontline Books, 2017) in "Millions of Americans Believe God Made Trump President," *Politico* Magazine (Jan. 27, 2018); online at https://www.politico.com/magazine/story/2018/01/27/millions-of-americans-believe-god-made-trump-president-216537 (accessed Feb. 12, 2020).

31. See Jorgenson's article "Embodying Truth in Ecclesial Practices," in ch. 3 of this volume; the ELCA 2016 statement is online at http://download.elca.org/ELCA%20Resource%20Repository/RepudiationDoctrineOfDiscoverySPR2016.pdf (accessed Feb. 12, 2020); see also "Statement from ELCA Presiding Bishop Eaton on Standing Rock," online at https://www.montanasynod.org/elca-statements.html (accessed Feb. 12, 2020).

Chapter 8

Creation Piety and Spiritual Formation

Gordon J. Straw

My task here is, first, to explore spiritual formation from my own experience of formation in an American Indian Christian context and in the theological traditions of a Lutheran witness. Second, to provide a framework for our encounters with God, both as mystery and as revealed, in the world, in our lives, and in the interaction between spiritual formation and leadership formation for the sake of the ministry to which each of us is called through baptism, for the sake of the world and for the building up of the Body of Christ. And third, approach spiritual formation both as an academic subject and as a spiritual practice, in the context of theological higher education.[1]

I begin with my story of spiritual formation. When I was eight years old, my great uncle—a Minnesota state senator for twenty-seven years—took me aside at a family gathering. He told me that my skin color was light enough that I could pass for a White person, and that I should never let anyone know that I am an American Indian. At the time, it was just one more confusing conversation with one of my elders. It did not make sense then. I thought it might make sense later. It did make sense later and it hurt. I think I understand now why he said what he did. He meant well. He was hoping to spare me from the pain of his own life, a pain that came with darker skin and a life lived—as successful as it was—in a society that saw Native people as less— less human, less worthy, of less concern to God. That was the day I began my spiritual journey, although I did not realize it at the time. It has been a journey of struggle. A journey that took me in and out: in and out of American Indian communities, because I was part White; in and out of dominant society, because I was part Native; in and out of the church, because Native people have no faith in Jesus, right? I searched for a spiritual center—a place to call home, to feel like I belonged. I caught glimpses of the mystery of God in all these places, yet it felt like I was looking in from outside.

When I was twenty-seven years old, a senior at Luther Northwestern Theological Seminary, I met the Rt. Rev. Steven Charleston, a Choctaw from Oklahoma and an Episcopal priest. He walked alongside me ... he was a spiritual mentor in a way that no one was before ... a guide in my journey ... a gift from the Holy Spirit who showed me that my journey had a *telos*—a purpose. It was not endless struggle. He showed me that it *is* possible to be an American Indian/cross-blood and a Christian at the same time. I did not have to choose. He guided me through an understanding that all my life has been a weaving of spiritual relations, manifested in mind, body, spirit, and community, so that I might take my place in this web of relationships and to care for these relationships, woven in with all that is within and around me. I am made, just as I am, by the Creator of all life, to inhabit this particular spiritual place in the web called life. This spiritual journey, connected with all that is around me, is what I have come to know as Creation Piety. I want to develop this idea in three parts: Native Insights into Creation Piety, biblical insights into Creation Piety, and theological insights into Creation Piety.

CREATION PIETY: NATIVE INSIGHTS

The Lakota/Nakota/Dakota people tell a story of the beginnings of the world we live in. It is the story of Inyan, The Rock. I am paraphrasing this story from a composite of oral tellings, written in the book, *Lakota Star Knowledge: Studies in Lakota Stellar Theology*, by Ronald Goodman.[2] A very long time ago, before anything was created, there was Inyan, the Rock. Inyan was spirit, without shape or form, like a cloud. Inyan's spirit had great power, the power of life, and it was everywhere. Inyan is Wakan Tanka, the Great Mystery. This is what the Christians call God. Han also existed, but Han is not a being. Han is simply darkness. Inyan longed to use this power, but since there was nothing else that existed, there was nowhere to use it. So, Inyan opened himself up and created a disc, called Maka (Earth). On this disc, Inyan poured out his blood, the spirit of Inyan. This blue spirit covered Maka the earth. Inyan continued to create. Each time Inyan created, Inyan gave more of his blood, and each time Inyan did so, he shrank, becoming rigid and powerless. So ... all of Creation contains the blood of Inyan, water, the power of life. It is Inyan's gift to us all. This same blood ... this same creative energy ... this same Spirit ... courses through all of Creation. All things in Creation are related by the blood of Inyan. This is the story of Inyan.

The Lakota people call this "blood-relation" *mitakuye oyasin*, literally, "all my relations." Its primary connotation is that all things in creation, by virtue of their source in the Creator, are related. However, it is not a monism ... a more natural version of *Star Trek's* "Borg Collective." The character of these relations are not merely related to proximity. The Lakota understand the universe to be moral, i.e., it is a power that each creature has by virtue simply of participating in reality (life-giving or life-destroying). It occurs each moment, as a condition of existence. No creature, by trait or condition, is either life-giving or life-destroying, however. These two realities of the moral universe do not exist independently of each other. Both came into existence simultaneously, by virtue of the act of Creation. Living as a creature in Creation, I participate either in life-giving relations or in denying (destroying) such relations. From this vantage point, spiritual formation, then, with its attendant spiritual practices, is the journey you and I take by *living* in the places we inhabit.

Maintaining right-relations is spiritual practice. For Native people, a spiritual universe and living a spiritual life are natural. Materialism, which reduces the universe to a mere material reality, devoid of spirit, denies these spiritual relations. The implication for spiritual formation, in a reality reduced to materiality, is that living a spiritual life or practicing spirituality is an "other-worldly" thing. It is unnatural. For much of the modern West's history since the Enlightenment, the materialist view of the universe has been predominant. When Philip Sheldrake, a long-respected authority in the study of Christian spirituality, delivered the prestigious Hulsean Lectures at the University of Cambridge, England, he addressed the predominance of a materialist view in these lectures, titled "Place, Memory and Identity." It has since been published as *Spaces for the Sacred: Place, Memory and Identity*.[3] Sheldrake argues that scholars are moving away from this view that space, which is empty, infinite, absolute, and *a priori*, is the fundamental reality of the universe and that place is a secondary, human social construction. He argues that this view is inadequate for several reasons: 1) There is no objective reality to space outside of how humans interpret it. It is an interpretation to favor the universal and general over the particular and local, the abstract and objective over what we garner from experience. 2) The notion of space as three-dimensional, geometrical, evenly extended and divisible is seriously being challenged by Einsteinian physics, particle theory, and the psychology of perception. Space is not an objective thing, a Kantian *Ding-an-sich*. It is experienced by all based on one's subjective experience. 3) The view that nature is a morally neutral reality, on which we can impose whatever value we choose, is not only a philosophical problem, but a political, ethical, and finally a spiritual problem.[4] All of Creation is not merely a backdrop to human activity, it is alive and making right-relations in the same places humans inhabit. Sheldrake concludes that "a sense of *place* actually precedes and creates a sense of space. Space is an abstract, analytical concept whereas place is always tangible, physical, specific and relational."⁵

All things are formed spiritually through relations of the power we call life. Yet, because of the nature of space (the distance between related things) and time (the duration of relations), spiritual relations are bound to space and time along a continuum of direct to indirect relations; these spiritual relations become material. The notion of "place" gives honor or recognition to those relations which are most direct and intimate with our own lives and existence. From these "places," one experiences life as having a center, from which direct spiritual relations become less and less direct, though always in relation. These centers are located not by some universal law of culture, but through relative associations. As these associations are bound by time and space, these relative centers share permeable boundaries, radiating out, connecting with other spiritual relations.

These places where cultures and people (and all of their constituent relations) encounter each other are great and glorious places—gifts from the Creator—like a confluence of rivers. The rivers may run fast or slow, but still they intermingle. The landscape, then, is shaped by the interaction of these fluid relations. Without a center, life in its specificity has no identity. Diversity wouldn't make much sense. It wouldn't make sense to talk about Lakota culture or spirituality in comparison to Norwegian American Haugean culture and spirituality ... or Franciscan ... Ignatian ... or Benedictine spirituality with their cultural centers in Europe. As I have described my own spiritual journey, it is a journey of relations as a bi-racial person, growing up in a rural Norwegian community in Minnesota, a short drive from three Dakota Indian reservations, interacting with farmers and college professors alike. This is the richness of spiritual formation. Stories that each of you tell, which are the ground of the formal, academic study of spirituality that you engage in today.

CREATION PIETY: BIBLICAL INSIGHTS

I coined the term Creation Piety as I was preparing for an Ash Wednesday sermon, actually. I chose Matthew 6 as my sermon text. I did not get very far into the Greek text before I stumbled on a phrase in Matthew 6:1: "Beware of *practicing your piety* before others in order to be seen by them; for then you have no reward from your Father in heaven." The phrase, ποιεῖν δικαιοσύνην, grabbed me. Δικαιοσύνη is one of my favorite Greek words, in fact. Connected to ποιειν, the Theological Dictionary of the New Testament (TDNT) describes δικαιόσθειν as "a title for exercises and expressions of piety. It illustrates the typical sense of the word as 'action before and for

God.'"[6] That is fine and dandy as it is, as a definition of a process of spiritual formation. But if you also look at the use of δικαιοσύνη in secular Greek, specifically in Plato, Aristotle, Josephus, and Philo ... and in the Septuagint (LXX), its meaning becomes even richer. Generally, its translation into English is rendered either "righteousness" or "justice." As an expression of Creation Piety, I choose to translate it, "making right-relations." Δικαιοσύνη, according to secular Greek usage, is a "second stage" in the development of δίκη (legal right). It refers to "a *civil virtue* of observance of law and fulfillment of duty."[7] As a δύναμις, it refers to "spiritual harmony and balance," particularly in Plato.[8] In Aristotle, a close connection with the legal view is kept. "For alongside the view of δικαιοσύνη as civil virtue there always lies the use of δικαιοσύνη as a basic legislative principle, e.g., justice."[9] In Josephus and Philo, it is "right conduct in the sense of virtue."[10]

Its use in the Septuagint (LXX), as a translation of הקדצ, goes even deeper for the notion of Creation Piety. It implies "relationship." "One is righteous when one meets certain claims which another has on one in virtue of relationship…. God's covenantal rule in relationship with God's people."[11] In the *Theological Wordbook of the Old Testament* (TWOT), קדצ refers to conformity to an ethical or moral standard. But, some scholars, such as Achtemeier, "hold that righteousness is the quality of relationships between individuals."[12] Thus, translating ποιεῖν δικαιοσύνην as "making right-relations," I believe, is true to its history of usage. It also fits nicely with Dr. Martin Luther's understanding of "communion," i.e., *communio* is a two-fold relationship: a vertical relationship to God and a horizontal relationship with the rest of Creation, each of which carry "right conduct" as part of the relationship. As a spiritual practice, making right-relations—practicing one's piety—can be interpreted, from a Lakota perspective, as *mitakuye oyasin*. By virtue of our place in Creation, we participate in it by the spiritual practice of maintaining right relations. Rather than viewing "piety" as a rigid set of moralistic and prudish rules, Matthew speaks of conduct of a more encompassing virtue, relationship with God and with God's Creation.

CREATION PIETY: THEOLOGICAL INSIGHTS

Now, I want to turn to some theological insights into Creation Piety.

A theology of place, from a Native perspective, begins with a Native understanding of "the sacred." There is a fundamental aversion for placing any limits, conditions, or parameters around the sacred, in Native theology. "Sacred," as Natives understand it, is complete mystery. Wakan Tanka, as the Lakota say. The word "Wakan" is usually translated "mystery" in English, but its connotation goes well beyond "something that cannot be solved." Another

English translation is "spirit." This is closer to the Lakota meaning. Wakan are those things which are so old, no one remembers a time when they did not exist. Wakan are those things and people who are so new (infants, e.g.) that we do not know yet what or who they will be. Wakan are those things that defy explanation or expectation. Wakan is mystery. From this, come all things ... source and ground. A personified God is a limited God. It is a weakening of mystery, thus of the sacred. God does not enter or break into world history, but simply is ... the ground and source of all. To answer the charge that this is pantheism, God-understanding is more similar to panentheism: Creation, in its totality, does not equal God. God is distinct from what is created, by virtue of being the Creator.

From this, continuity between the spiritual universe and all its spiritual relations and concrete reality lies in "place." Being aware of one's place and what is happening at the present moment is the stuff of theology for Native people. This means that neither the past, nor the future, completely determines our understanding or behavior in the present. The past (including tradition) is only helpful if it helps make sense of the present moment. Dr. Eugene Begay, a holy man of the Lac Courtes Oreilles Nation in Wisconsin, urges young people to return to their traditional beliefs and ways. However, one cannot simply repristinate what once was. Instead, young people (and we) should pray to Creator to receive new instruction in how to live in the present moment, for the sake of maintaining right relations in the places we inhabit. This emphasis on the present, however, is not an "anything goes," "live in the present moment" philosophy. The place one occupies in one's family, clan, tribe, order, congregation, and nation comes with responsibilities inherent to that place. These are the "relations" that become spiritual practice and bring us further along in our spiritual formation. There is continuity in these places from which one's identity comes. These places are the resting place for the bones of our ancestors, going back millennia. Our sacred sites mark out the spiritual geography of these places.

Covenant is the theological key for a theology of place. The first covenant that the Creator makes with Creation is in the act of creation itself. As a Native Christian, I see this in the story of the first covenant which God makes with all of Creation, after the Great Flood. But, so too, the covenants established in the specific places of specific peoples, who live in those places. For Native people, place is always covenanted place, given to them by the Creator, not as an exclusive possession, but to maintain concrete relations in that place, for the benefit of all that exists in that place, not only for humans. Sheldrake comments that even though "place is a human construct, it is equally vital not to lose sight of the fact that the natural features are part of the interrelationships that go to make up place."[13] Covenanted place is a way of living on a specific land. It contains traditions of ceremony and ritual used to maintain right-relations within that land, for the benefit of all who live there. A particular place is covenanted with a particular people because of the intimate knowledge they possess about the land: what rituals are required, an intimate knowledge of the relationships between all the beings within the land, and a collective memory of events which have taken place on the land. This intimate knowledge implies a responsibility to live in a "good way" on the land and perform the necessary rituals to keep spiritual relations of the land in harmony and balance.

The unique role humans play in Creation is to keep these relations alive through story ... maintaining the narrative of the concrete relations of a particular place. Humans are not superior to the rest of Creation because they communicate in symbols. Humans, instead, have a responsibility to the flourishing of *all* who inhabit a specific place. Sheldrake speaks to the importance of narrative, not only in its telling and remembering, but in its honoring of all the voices within a place. "Narrative is a critical key to our identity."[14] We live by story because it helps us to make sense of otherwise seemingly unrelated events. Sheldrake urges us not to get rid of narrative because it has been used as a tool to suppress so many stories, but rather to pry the "elitist history" open, creating an entry point for stories that have been excluded from public narrative. He says, "Rather than abolish narrative we need to ask, 'Whose narrative has been told?' 'Who belongs within the story of this place?'"[15]

This, it seems to me, is the ground upon which #decolonizeLutheranism stands. The #decolonizeLutheranism movement desires not the end of Lutheranism as a narrative, but an opening up of the Lutheran narrative to include all of the voices that inhabit the "place" called Lutheranism. The Rt. Rev. Steven Charleston writes in his essay, "The Old Testament of Native America": "It means seeing Jesus not as a white plastic messiah taken off the dashboard of a car and dipped in brown to make things look more Indian, but a living Christ that arises from the Native covenant" as much as the European narrative that dominates on this continent.[16] Sister Eva Solomon, a Chippewa spiritual leader from Canada, affirmed this too (I paraphrase here): "I used to think that the Indian people had the Old Testament and Jesus Christ is the New Testament, which fulfills the Old Testament. But, as I've thought about it, I now think that the Indian people have their original testament and Jesus Christ lived, died, and rose again, so that Indian people would and could return to their testament, that is tied to their land, their place on Mother Earth."[17]

CREATION PIETY AND SPIRITUAL PRACTICE: AN EXAMPLE

"Day by day ... they broke bread from house to house and ate their food with glad and generous hearts, praising God and having the good will of all the people" (Acts 2:46–47). Perhaps you have thought of eating as a spiritual practice (even better, eating *together* as a spiritual practice). I do all the time. The brief description of life for Christians in the early days of the church, in Acts 2, is about eating together and the spiritual rewards that ensue: glad and generous hearts, praising God, and good will. Much of this has been lost because of the ways our society and lifestyles have discouraged or ignored eating together. We have convinced ourselves that, in our overly busy lives, we do not have time to eat together as family or as friends, except on rare occasions. We rush past each other in the kitchen. We stand in line at the microwave or in the refectory. Even if we do sit together, the TV is on or cellphones are in hand. Children, at school, are given twenty minutes to eat (if that), but it is also the only time they have to interact with their friends during the school day, so they take a few minutes to scarf down their food and run to the gym. As adults, we think we are being more productive by conducting business over lunch or dinner, poring over spreadsheets and memos, papers and agendas. Yet, with all this distraction in our lives around the table, there is little chance of noticing the gift before us. It is not always this bad, of course, but it certainly is more a routine than it is an exception. We are losing the sense of eating together as a gift from God, a sacred meal. With great anticipation, we wait for an experience of mystery to envelop us at the Lord's Table, and miss the same spiritual refreshment occurring at the dinner table. The message we give ourselves is that eating is simply providing for our physical, bodily requirements. Enjoying it is optional. Enjoying it with *someone else* is optional. Celebrating it as a spiritual gift is ridiculous. What is missing is the biblical notion that eating is a *community* activity. The early Christians ate *together*. They shared food, each other's company, and gratitude for God's blessings in their lives *together*.

I have been fascinated by the Netflix documentary series, *Cooked*. Michael Pollan, through an examination of the industrialization of food production, identifies what we have lost in the connection between the food we prepare, whether one does it alone or in a group, and our spiritual relationship with the rest of Creation, hence with our gracious Creator, who gives us an abundant life. As a way of spiritual practice, I encourage you to consider committing to eating a home-made meal with others once a week. Perhaps even make the meal together! If it fits, commit to two or three times a week. Be mindful of the gifts as you receive them and the gratitude you experience in this practice of connecting with the Creator and all your relations around you, in the simple act of eating together.

SPIRITUAL FORMATION: A ROLE FOR THE SEMINARY

Justo González, in his recent book, *The History of Theological Education*, asserted that seminaries are a relatively recent phenomenon within the history of theological education.[18] It has been only since the Council of Trent that an institution, called a seminary, existed. This does not imply, González argues, that there was no theological education. The church has always had some form of theological education. What is unique in the past five hundred years is that theological education moved more and more to an identity as places where people become credentialed for professional ministry. For the first fifteen centuries of the church, the identity of theological education was more in line with Jesus' admonition in the Great Commandment, to love the Lord, your God, with all your mind (cf. Luke 10:27; Deut 6:4). The purpose of theology and theological education was not to grant degrees, but to express devotion and obedience to God in one's life. The life of the Christian is inherently a life of studying the Bible, exploring the connections between God's love and action and the world we live in through theological study, hearing and telling the stories of the history of the church, not unlike the stories we heard sitting on our grandpa's knee as a child. For the first fifteen centuries of the church, the church's leaders have always been well educated, even in the worst of times in the church. Pastors and bishops at least were educated enough to read, a function of their role. This education most often took place in the university setting. The seminary developed out of the Roman Catholic Church's need to respond to and reform itself in a world that now included Protestants. The seminary served two roles in this: First, to provide for the spiritual formation of its leaders, through spiritual practices and living in community. And second, to combat heresy. Seminary students needed to know how to answer the questions and challenges of those who no longer were "in the fold."

These two roles still exist for seminaries five hundred years later. The Carnegie Foundation for the Advancement of Teaching published a study, *Educating Clergy: Teaching Practices and Pastoral Imagination.*[19] In their study, the authors identify two approaches to forming students, intricately woven into each other, which address the formational needs of a pastoral imagination (as they describe it): pedagogies of formation and practices of formation. Alongside the instructional content of courses in seminaries, pedagogies and practices of formation are integral to the life and goals of a seminary. Pedagogies and practices of formation and content instruction do not operate separately from each other, but are interwoven within the curriculum, as well as in important aspects of seminary life outside the task of teaching the curriculum, most commonly a seminary-wide worship experience. Spiritual formation of leaders in the church, both rostered and laity, includes both spiritual formation as academic study and spiritual formation as spiritual practice. The academic study of spiritual formation not only presents us with a history of such practices, but more broadly, invites us to enter into an engagement with spiritual traditions from around the world and throughout history—as resources for our own spiritual well-being and as opportunities to enrich these traditions through mutual learning and respectful observance in all its rich variety. Spiritual practices are more than techniques to be mastered as one leads a congregation. Rather, they are opportunities to explore the presence of God within and without me.

SPIRITUAL FORMATION IN A PUBLIC CONTEXT

Spiritual formation in a public context is often not seen as spiritual formation. Spiritual formation, to many, is inward focused—spiritual development of my inner being, heart, mind, and soul. It is not seen as moving outward, into the world, experiencing the presence of God in the people and circumstances that exist around me and that shape me in significant ways. As an example, one of these public contexts for the Lutheran School of Theology at Chicago (LSTC) is confronting racism as a nation and as a seminary community. A fundamental flaw with most anti-racism models is, I think, not their ineffectiveness against racism, but their inability to reach people in concrete ways and to offer practical and practice-able solutions for the issues we confront.

Traditional anti-racism work treats both racism and anti-racism as commodities, products of intellectual pursuit and assent, rather than the real behaviors of real people. Both racists and anti-racists operate from this same view of reality. It is an ideal to be aspired to, whose opposite must be attacked. Thus, our efforts never seem to reach the level of behavior. Employing power analyses and post-colonial theory in confronting racism is essential, but it is not enough. Unless it is put into practice, it has no reality in people's lives. The answer is not to peddle more of *our* product, to combat *their* product. The solution is to create a whole new reality by simply doing something else, practicing other values, walking away from what is destructive.

Confronting racism involves a few principles: 1) Racism and anti-racism are practices! They are not legislated, cajoled, or packaged. They exist because people practice them. The only way to combat racism is to offer people something else to practice other than racist behaviors, to give them another option—minus the condemnation. 2) By inviting people to experience other ways of being with each other, we present them with a choice to do something different. Rather than trying to convince others that they are wrong, we teach people how to walk away from concrete acts of prejudice and bigotry and build their lives around a positive, *new* life—not a life *without* racism. 3) This new life is an act of embracing diversity, which increases unity. Rather than seeing diversity and unity as inversely proportionate (as one increases, the other decreases), Charles Hartshorne argued that unity and diversity are directly proportional to each other: diversity strengthens unity, it does not weaken it. Increased diversity increases the points of contact and relations between us, just as by sanding wood before you paint it, you create more points to which the paint can adhere. 4) The choices that we make are based on real needs and actual situations, rather than upon theories. There is no "right way" to combat racism. It is a spiritual struggle within a particular place. Choices can be: looking at actual data, using asset maps to discover actual solutions at hand, and using Open Space Technology or Talking Circles, rather than immersion experiences which are little more than trips to the zoo, to discover the real needs and solutions *together* as a community.

Let me conclude by making a few comments about how I see spiritual formation from a Lutheran Christian perspective. First, I am not advocating that these comments reflect how Lutherans are right or do things better. Rather, they reflect a few of the unique contributions Lutherans have made to life in the whole Body of Christ. Second, the Lutheran idea of vocation (at least the use of the term) has been limited to "following a call to public or professional ministry." Indeed, this is an important and necessary function of the seminary. However, I argue that a call to public ministry is more properly placed with the idea that there are people who are called to maintain a regular order in the church, to oversee the office of ministry, which belongs to the whole community, not individuals. Rather, vocation, from a Lutheran perspective, is more like the idea I have been sharing today, Creation Piety. My vocation is the place that I inhabit, with all its constituent relations, encountering others in my journey, maintaining right-relations with others through the responsibilities I have as a father, husband, brother, son, pastor, friend, and teacher. I believe that the role of a seminary is not simply to grant degrees for professional ministry. Rather, the seminary plays a vital role in helping every member of the church to discern the call to ministry they received in their baptism. And when each member discovers where that call lies, they receive the resources necessary to fulfill that call. My hope is that every member of the Evangelical Lutheran Church in American (ELCA) would go to seminary, just not only to become a rostered leader.

Tied to my own personal journey, I believe that Lutherans have a rich resource for spiritual formation in "theologies of the cross." The spiritual life is not a life of ease or entitlement. Jesus promises that if we follow him, trouble, even death, is sure to follow. Spiritual formation is developing ways to trust in the web of relations around us, even in the midst of deep doubt and not feeling connected. We look, in these moments, to see our Lord, broken and bleeding, defeated in every worldly sense. But in this is life, abundant life, offered freely to all of Creation.

Finally, spiritual formation is our resource to bring this message of hope in the midst of despair, confidence in the midst of fear. We are "little Christs" in the places we inhabit. Spiritual formation is not only a process or mastering a technique, it is a life-long trust in the promise of God in Christ for *this place* where I live; it is a life-long development of the resources and practices that I can use to maintain right-relations—δικαιοσύνη—in this place and all the other places the Lord God, Creator of all, sends me.

NOTES

1. [Ed. note] This chapter is an edited form of a lecture given at the Lutheran School of Theology in Chicago on Feb. 27, 2017, when Dr. Straw was candidate for the Cornelsen Chair of Spiritual Formation.

2. Ronald Goodman, *Lakota Star Knowledge: Studies in Lakota Stellar Theology*, ed. Alan Seeger, 3rd edn. (Mission, SD: SGU Publishing, 2017).

3. Philip Sheldrake, *Spaces for the Sacred: Place, Memory and Identity* (Baltimore, MD: The Johns Hopkins University Press, 2001).

4. Sheldrake, *Spaces for the Sacred*, 6.

5. Sheldrake, *Spaces for the Sacred*, 7.

6. Gerhard Kittel and Gerhard Friedrich (eds.), G. W. Bromiley (trans.), *Theological Dictionary of the New Testament*, 10 vols. (Grand Rapids, MI: Eerdmans, 1977), vol. 7:199. Hereafter abbreviated as TNDT.

7. TNDT 7:192.

8. TNDT 7:193.

9. TNDT 7:193.

10. TNDT 7:193.

11. TNDT 7:195.

12. Paul Achtemeier, "צדק," in *Theological Wordbook of the Old Testament*, ed. R. Laird Harris, Gleason L. Archer Jr., and Bruce K. Waltke (Chicago, IL: Moody Publishers, 2003), 1879.

13. Sheldrake, *Spaces for the Sacred: Place*, 15.

14. Sheldrake, *Spaces for the Sacred: Place*, 19.

15. Sheldrake, *Spaces for the Sacred: Place*, 19.

16. Steven Charleston, "The Old Testament of Native America," in *Native and Christian: Indigenous Voices on Religious Identity in the United States and Canada*, ed. James Treat (New York/London: Routledge, 1996), 69.

17. From a personal conversation at Catholic Theological Union (CTU).

18. Justo L. González, *The History of Theological Education* (Nashville, TN: Abingdon Press, 2015).

19. Charles R. Foster, Lisa E. Dahill, Lawrence A. Golemon, and Barbara Wang Tolentino, *Educating Clergy: Teaching Practices and Pastoral Imagination* (Stanford, CA: The Carnegie Foundation for the Advancement of Teaching, 2006).

Chapter 9

Remembering the Immigrant Experience

The Body of Christ as a Borderless Space to Embrace Our Shared Humanity in the Face of Rising Xenophobia

Man Hei Yip

In *Expanding Space*, Elaine Padilla writes:

> Space expands via movement. Like a cosmic ocean with its myriad ripples, it enfolds and explicates a manifest order. The universe, the largest living organism, knows the pain of such expansions, and sheds tears at every rupture that each of these migrations cause. It expands at the beckoning of the stars and planets, whose orbits leave a light trace of their presence in its darkness. The human footprints in this expansive universe likewise extend the limits of earthly borders, boundaries that one might hope become more fluidly porous. Yet, one wonders if the root systems needfully characteristic of the earth can perhaps be made repottable beyond the hostile tendencies of geopolitics.[1]

The debate over immigration in the United States became more controversial since Donald Trump took office. Federal agents are given tremendous power to arrest, detain, and deport individuals of suspicious nature. Cases of immigrants being arrested by Immigration and Customs Enforcement (ICE) soared, since then. In one of *The Atlantic*'s reports on the life of detained immigrants, solitary confinement has been extensively used against the detainee population. The news source reveals, "Contraband sugar packets, calling a border guard a 'redneck,' menstruating on a prison uniform, kissing another detainee, identifying as gay, [and] requesting an ankle brace" could be some of the reasons that allow ICE officials to send detained immigrants to solidarity confinement.[2]

I am sickened. As an immigrant myself, I am faced with similar challenges and difficulties. I can tell how hurtful it was when asked in an unfriendly manner about my reasons to live here, or being ignored simply by virtue of my skin color. But far more than that, as someone who was born and raised in Hong Kong, a city where thousands of migrant workers and new immigrants are drawn to work and live, I know how ugly the immigrant debate can get. I have been protected from systems and institutions that function to privilege those like me, the majority in society, yet the very systems and institutions fend off outsiders or unwanted minorities. I can well imagine the danger of reinforcing the "us versus them" mentality. Fear and distrust of others will only intensify, rather than lessen. The cycle of xenophobia must stop before it spirals out of control.

Our discussion should go beyond fulfilling legal expectations. It must unveil the problem of authority that devalues one's immigrant experience. How we, as church, speak against dehumanizing immigration policies and respond to the hostility sowed to divide people are important topics to ponder. This article seeks to contribute to the conversation by subverting the narrative of immigrants to see how it informs ecclesiological practice toward immigrants and vulnerable communities, and how it expands the ecclesiological space to embrace shared humanity. To deepen the meaning of being church, the body of Christ is highlighted as a metaphor to both describe and shape the community of faith and its prophetic call. It affirms the church's role and responsibility in the public by creating a space without borders to resist hegemonic forces that deprive respective communities of their dignity in the process. This renewed vision of being church attends to the aspect of relationality, which will inevitably change the way we imagine ourselves, others, and the world.

LOVING AND CARING FOR THE IMMIGRANTS IS NOT A PROGRAM (OPTIONAL)

There are people who do not care about unfair treatment toward immigrant communities or who continue to obsess about their (il)legal status. Let us be clear: Supporting immigrant justice is an urgent task of Christian witness in a violent world. As dehumanizing immigration measures intensify, more religious leaders are speaking against presumptive otherness and publicly denouncing abuses of powerless individuals. This is encouraging, but we should also take note of the reality that each congregation's involvement in fighting for immigrant rights varies. While congregations generally agree that taking care of the poor is the primary moral obligation, some are hesitant and wonder if the church should take a stand on immigrant reform. Some may want to avoid getting themselves into trouble when clashing with authority. They are doing the minimum they can to help undocumented immigrants. Loving and caring for the immigrants will likely be treated as some kind of outreach program, which can be opted out of when necessary.

While, also, resources are widely accessible to groups to discuss God's love for strangers and ways of caring for them, some may sound too familiar and some too radical. Anything that is labeled supplementary will be easily ignored. Christians have a tendency to first check the Bible and fixate on particular texts. The discussion sometimes divulges into a conversation arisen from certain randomly selected verses. I refrain from giving an exegesis on those texts, but a discussion on immigration and immigrants based on one or two verses is really an issue that needs our attention.

Two most frequently cited texts in the Old Testament include: "When an alien resides with you in your land, you shall not oppress the alien. The alien who resides with you shall be to you as the citizen among you; you shall love the alien as yourself, for you were aliens in the land of Egypt: I am the Lord your God" (Lev 19:33–34 [NRSV]). And "For the Lord your God is God of gods and Lord of lords, the great God, mighty and awesome, who is not partial and takes no bribe, who executes justice for the orphan and the widow, and who loves the strangers, providing them food and clothing. You shall also love the stranger, for you were strangers in the land of Egypt" (Deut 10:17–19 [NRSV]). The use of these two passages aims to show God's indiscriminate love toward strangers and aliens, and ask God's people to do likewise.

In the New Testament, Jesus' interactions with the socially stigmatized are best references to criticize those who are indifferent to human suffering. For instance in Matthew 25:35–46 (NRSV), it is written "For I was hungry and you gave me food, I was thirsty and you gave me something to drink, I was a stranger and you welcomed me, I was naked and you gave me clothing, I was sick and you took care of me, I was in prison and you visited me.... Truly I tell you, just as you did it to one of the least of these who are members of my family, you did it to me."

Church leaders' disposition of appealing to the authority of scripture intend to give instructions and remind congregants or parishioners of their moral obligations toward others. Thus, by incorporating the moral obligations into the church agenda, church leaders hope to engage better in evangelism and outreach.

Welcoming strangers in our midst indeed captures an important part of what our call is like. But how effective is randomly citing scripture to promote moral appeals? What if welcoming and helping strangers is reduced to a kind of patronizing sympathy? When loving and caring for the immigrants remains merely an add-on program, it does not help Christians understand the church's role in society. Doing good work only makes us feel good about ourselves, which fails to challenge our social behaviors and ways of relating to others.

Christianity and immigration are inseparable in the United States. Christians in the U.S. can trace their immigrant roots and remember how their immigrant ancestors embarked on adventures and started a new life in a new land against all odds. But how does that past immigrant experience meet the challenges of new immigrants and how does that encounter inform a new way of being church?

The issue is multi-layered, however. Factors, such as gender, race, class, and religious backgrounds all intersect with one another. Not all races or peoples or cultures are made equal across the United States. Immigrant women are most vulnerable to poverty and exploitation. Hellena Moon points out that white women in the U.S. are taking advantage of "the cheap labor of immigrant women to clean their homes, take care of their children, cook, do the gardening, etc., so that they can have fulfilling, meaningful careers and enjoy leisure time" and the discriminatory practice including but not limited to the insufficient legal protection of immigrant women "reveals the nature of power that sustains, as well as further exacerbates, inequalities among women."[3] Simply by being charitable, such as providing food and clothing to the immigrants does not address issues of inequity, but obscures widespread socioeconomic and institutional injustice.

Even within the body of Christ, immigrant congregations are not on par with their counterparts of European descents. For congregations that show great eagerness to preserve the legacy of their ancestors primarily from Europe, they tend to measure religious experience by their own standards. They would love to see new immigrant churches become like them. Immigrants' otherness is thus allowed but it is regulated through worship and religious events. Some even expect new immigrants to assimilate into American society fully and quickly, and the American (religious) way is understood purely in the framework of ethnic European identities. The promotion of cultural diversity remains a slogan, when there are no meaningful and intentional interactions between different groups of people. Working with ethnic groups or immigrant communities without being willing to sacrifice one's power proves superficial. These efforts perpetuate the implicit bias and prejudice within the ecclesial body.

Loving and caring for immigrants is anything more than an outreach program. It requires us to pause and ponder who the people are and how we share our common humanity. Unveiling forced identity for immigrants is needed, and it will inevitably lead us to re-discover our identity in Christ.

PROBLEMATIZING THE IMMIGRANT LABEL

There are many reasons why immigrants choose to leave their home countries. Some move to other countries because of economic hardship, political strife, religious persecution, and natural disasters. Others simply want to pursue their dreams of living abroad. The immigrant identity is unfortunately loaded with negative connotations and generalizations. Immigrants are described as poor, dirty, uncivilized, and uneducated. Immigrant becomes synonymous with welfare recipients. Furthermore, differences in skin color, language, and culture provoke powerful feelings of otherness. Politicians and leaders know how to manipulate public opinion by using hateful rhetoric and blaming immigrants for everything. Calling people "bad hombres," "criminals," "thugs," "drug addicts," etc., is a making of excuses to get rid of all undesirable ones.

Institutionalized scapegoating against vulnerable communities has reached an unprecedented level. The President of the United States ended the Deferred Action for Childhood Arrivals (DACA) program in September 2017. The program used to give legal protections for young unauthorized immigrants, but the termination of that is jeopardizing the lives of many currently living in the U.S. and others hoping to survive and escape from harsh realities.

Immigration restrictionists who have largely benefited from chain migration are relentlessly advocating an end to the family-reunification system. Family-based migration, which allows close relatives of U.S. citizens and lawful permanent residents to legally migrate to the country, has inevitably been targeted. New rules are also aimed at legal immigrants who rely on welfare programs, including food stamps and housing. Who is next?

According to the Pew Research Center, foreign-born population in the U.S. reached 44.4 million in 2017, representing 13.6 percent of the total population.[4] This figure was however less than that in the 1890's (14.8 percent). Most of these immigrants from the past (77 percent) received legal permanent residence status, and close to half of them were naturalized. Undocumented immigrants accounted for 23 percent of the immigrant population in the U.S. The findings further show: "By 2017, that number had declined by 1.7 million, or 14 percent. There were 10.5 million undocumented immigrants in the U.S. in 2017, accounting for 3.2 percent of the nation's population."[5]

The decline in both the numbers of immigrant population and undocumented immigrants suggests a close correlation to anti-immigrant policies; meanwhile, it implies a larger problem of how the U.S. understands the nation and the people. The United States was created by settlers, or to be exact, immigrants who shared similar dreams and aspirations regardless of language and culture. They fled to the new world to escape war, violence, famine, and misery. They saw opportunities in this land they fervently called home. The U.S. is a nation of immigrants, so would people think.

The promise of America, however, did not bring equality; as a matter of fact, not everyone had equal access to economic betterment in the past. People were divided along the lines of race, ethnic/cultural background, education, gender, religious affiliations, and the like. We must be alert to the fact that becoming American is not simply about assimilation, but also the endorsement of a few who have the power to define, name, and label the other. Immigrants are allowed to reside in the U.S., but they have been studied, assessed, and put into different categories. It becomes clear that some groups of immigrants enjoy privileged status in society, whereas others do not. Some are thought to be inferior, thus less favorable, and some are considered more dangerous than other groups. The ideology of exclusion is actively at work in the making of the American identity. Paradoxically, xenophobia, the fear and hatred of foreigners takes place within the nation of immigrants.

Now anti-immigrant rhetoric stokes up hostility to outsiders, American attitudes toward immigrants are increasingly polarized. Things become worse when irresponsible speeches lead ordinary people to believe they have the right to decide what is true or untrue about other ethnic/cultural groups. The breaking of America's promise as "a nation of immigrants" runs the risk of fabricating its past by erasing other groups' history and preserving only the memory of a few.

IMMIGRANTS REVISITED: RESILIENCE, COURAGE, AND DETERMINATION

A lot has been said about how the previous administration habitually used insulting words to describe immigrants. The vigorously obtrusive rhetoric has proved successful especially when the labor market is undergoing fundamental changes. Supporters of the previous POTUS tend to believe immigrants take jobs away from Americans, and popular sayings go: "They are taking our jobs." "They are hurting our workers." "They are invading our country." Negative feelings and emotions, including unfriendliness, antagonism, and resentment prevail in the wider society and are seriously affecting public attitudes and behaviors toward immigrants.

It is necessary to debunk stereotypes about immigrants. To subvert the narrative of immigrants aims to change the public's understanding of immigrants and immigration. We need to be open to discuss how society capitalizes on their labor. I cited studies about the hiring of immigrant women as caregivers, which evidently increases economic productivity in the U.S.; however, a high percentage of these women or domestic workers are not fully compensated.

They neither receive retirement benefits nor health insurance from their employers who have better chances to pursue higher paying careers. Without enjoying their deserved benefits, these immigrant women continue to give care to their employers. Life goes on.

While immigrants are blamed for low wage growth in the U.S., entrepreneurs indicate that immigrants are needed and willing to do the work unwanted by white Americans. Certain industries, particularly agriculture, are heavily reliant on undocumented workers. This is an open secret. David McIlwain, owner of a small landscape business in New Jersey, says, "Americans don't want my kind of jobs.... I ran 'help wanted' ads in my area, and not a single American applied. You can guess why they wouldn't: Who naturally gravitates toward hard labor for eight months and then four months of no work?"[6] Experts note that immigrants are good for the economy. Immigrants that made their way to the U.S. are determined to make this their new home; they raise families, and they raise honest children. They pay taxes every year, and support local businesses. They are as hard-working as other citizens.

Not only are immigrants making contributions to the economy. They also bring their wisdom and rich spiritualities to make positive changes in society. The United States is becoming increasingly pluralistic. Immigrants who come from different parts of the world have come with their faith and belief systems. With immigrants' diverse geographic origins, the religious demographics in American society has gradually been shifting. The religiosity of our new neighbors is a window to the world. The different kinds of worldviews will eventually widen our horizons and quest of greater truth.

In addition, the changing religious landscape has seen another shift in Christian denominational affiliation. Gemma Tulud Cruz, a theologian deeply involved in the issue of migration, asserts that "immigrants have played a significant role in shaping American religious life not only by contributing to the de-Europeanization of American Christianity but also in witnessing to a kind of public Christianity or by becoming a 'social congregation.'"[7]

These immigrant churches are oftentimes misunderstood as congregating among themselves and speaking their own languages. These immigrant churches do not show a desire to assimilate into society, but make themselves an ethnic enclave. However, Cruz argues these immigrant churches are outward-looking and take seriously the call to be witnesses to the gospel. Cruz continues to point out that these immigrant churches "catered to the most urgent needs of the most vulnerable communities, provided religious instruction and training for the next generation of Americans, and supplied vital social services that contributed to public well-being."[8] They constantly bring in new stories of compassion and commitment. Many of these immigrant churches have experienced growth numerically and spiritually. Their gifts and talents, religiosity and enthusiasm to build relationships are valuable lessons for churches that are experiencing decline in worship attendance and wrestling to be relevant in today's world.

The immigrant issue persists throughout American history, and the presence of immigrants, including those incoming ones, should motivate people to rethink what it means to be American. Their presence should help remind Americans that their ancestors were once newcomers to the United States. Those who have forgotten this important piece of history are setting boundaries and legal obstacles to hinder immigrants from coming and thriving in society. Confronting the immigrant stereotypes also prompts us to consider the question of who we are. "Who are the immigrants" and "who are we" are never independent of each other. They are not two questions, but one. People of the U.S. should honestly reflect on the past. How we remember history is crucial to how we understand our identity and how we relate to others and the world.

JESUS THE IMMIGRANT: (RE)CONNECTING US THROUGH HIS BORDER-CROSSING PASSION AND COMMITMENT

Remember one's immigrant roots. We are all connected. Memory and connection work both ways. The connection goes beyond the one that is artificially made or intended for self-serving purposes, but emerged naturally from the act of remembering. Stories, feelings, and experiences flow through our bodies and that memory transcends time and geographic limits. The memory can inspire our lives in ways that we do not even realize.

In the ritual of remembrance, we are immersed in the history of our immigrant ancestors that enables us to see, feel, and hear the struggles and challenges of starting a new life in a new land. In remembering the tears of our immigrant ancestors, we are connected not only to the cries of those who are suffering from the broken immigration system, but also the agony of Jesus, who endured pain and mockery in his days as an immigrant body traversing borders and finding ways to break down boundaries.

Jesus' experience as a stranger in a foreign land began with Mary and Joseph's journey to Egypt. The narrative birth in the Gospel of Matthew indicated that Jesus was a threat to King Herod's regime, and Herod's paranoia subsequently led to the killing of innocents, especially babies and children. Jesus was born during a time of violence. Driven by fear, Mary and Joseph fled with their child to Egypt, a safer place to live and raise the child.

Jesus knew what it means to be a stranger, for he was one of them. His solidarity with the poor and oppressed, and in this case the strangers and marginalized immigrants is made concrete.

As Cruz says, "Jesus himself, as the stranger *par excellence*, paves the way for forging a church of the stranger."[9] Cruz focused more on the Lukan account, and described the coldness and unfriendliness Jesus received while being a stranger in the land. Though being "the perfect (fellow) stranger," as Cruz highlights, Jesus remembered all the marginalized and oppressed and insisted in practicing hospitality toward them.[10] Cruz concludes, "Thus, it could be said that Jesus not only forged the path for struggle for the 'estranged' of this world; he also laid the foundations for a church of the stranger."[11]

Earlier than Cruz's observation, Peter Phan regarded Jesus as "the Immigrant and Border-Crosser Par Excellence" in his theologizing and contextualizing of the Vietnamese-American experience.[12] Phan argued that Vietnamese-Americans, either immigrants or refugees, live between two worlds. They are not considered fully Vietnamese or fully American, but in reality, they are both. They embrace two worldviews and they navigate between the two worlds and help others understand the difference. Given such a vantage point, Phan can relate to Jesus' immigrant experience and find links between it and Jesus' incarnation, death, and resurrection. Phan insists, "The mystery of the Word of God made flesh in Jesus can certainly be viewed as an act of border-crossing."[13] The incarnation of Jesus is therefore, as Phan continues, "the culmination of that primordial border-crossing by which the Triune God steps out of himself (sic)" and walks and struggles with others in the person of Jesus.[14] Right at the borders, it is where diverse worlds meet and the meeting of these different worlds is not always appreciated. There is sometimes conflict. People are marginalized by those who are resourceful to form the center of power. And right at the borders, Jesus shuts down the conflict by creating a space to embrace. Phan asserts, "In Jesus, the margin where he lived became the center of a new society without borders and barriers, reconciling all people," and therefore, "Strangers and guests as they are, immigrants are invited to become marginal people, to dwell at the margins of societies with marginal(ized) people, like Jesus, so as to be able to create with them new all-inclusive centers of reconciliation and harmony."[15] In that sense, strangers, immigrants, and all those who are marginalized have nothing to be ashamed of. They are redeemed people who rejoice in the promise of Jesus.

For Phan, inviting strangers and immigrants to the church body is fundamental to the life of the church. If the church regards the welcoming of the stranger as a goal, then it will omit other core beliefs of the Christian faith. Put differently, one simply cannot be satisfied with Jesus' promise without looking seriously at his suffering and particularly his death. Thus Phan claims, "Jesus' violent death on the cross was a direct result of his border-crossing and ministry at the margins, which posed a serious threat to the interests of those occupying the economic, political, and religious center."[16] Again, Jesus' death is not the end of the story. Phan points out, "Jesus did not remain within the boundaries of ... death," which also means Jesus was not overcome by "failure, defeat, destruction."[17] In stark contrast, the resurrection of Jesus has perfectly demonstrated his power to overcome death. In Phan's observation, Jesus who "crossed the borders of death" becomes the hope that gives life and leads people to the path of freedom and a "life in abundance."[18]

Deirdre Cornell took the discussion of Jesus' immigrant experience to the next level by linking up human mobility with the history of Christianity. Cornell argued that human mobility is deeply rooted in the Christian tradition. Cornell puts forward, "Jesus belonged to a people indelibly marked by stories of Exodus and exile. His life and ministry are framed by these narratives.... For two millenniums, as Christians have interiorized the great biblical stories of human mobility, migration has figured prominently in our faith."[19]

If human mobility is not anything new and it occasionally happens in later generations, the only difference will be the "types of migratory experiences."[20] Cornell made clear that forced migration is completely different from voluntary migration.[21] The presence of immigrants presents a challenge to our faith and requires us to find our true selves. Cornell postulates, "For all Christians—not just Catholics—human mobility lends its language to the articulation of our identity. Once we perceive our lives of faith as a journey, we look toward human acts of migration with a new openness to what those experiences might tell us."[22]

Apparently, we have inherited a faith stemming from the context of immigration. Jesus' life as a stranger, in conjunction with other biblical narratives of border-crossing, should expose us to a new kind of identity, that is: to witness to the one who suffered alongside people on the move. We are all connected by, in, and with Jesus' immigrant experience. Our story is inseparable with the story of Jesus the immigrant.

Jesus' immigrant story is neither a single episode, independent of his other life events, nor optional for learning about his life and mission; however, Jesus' immigrant experience offers a unique perspective that links up with his incarnation, death, and resurrection. Each time when we gather at the table in remembrance of Jesus, we are reminded of the self-giving love of Jesus. We are not asked to count our own blessings, but to contemplate the entirety of Jesus' life including his immigrant identity. In our self-emptying, we are able to participate in Jesus' death; because of that, the cross together with resurrection hope can refresh anew our way of remembering history and also inform our behaviors when relating to people on the margin.

THE BODY OF CHRIST AS A BORDERLESS SPACE: EMBRACING OUR SHARED HUMANITY IN THE FACE OF RISING XENOPHOBIA

As Jesus' immigrant experience becomes the focal point of re-connecting people far and near, it sheds new lights on being church, specifically how the church's self-understanding connects with God's justice and mercy to the world.

The Greek term for "church" is *ekklesia*. It is generally translated as a gathering or assembly and widely understood as a group of faithful assembling before the Lord. In that sense, the church is about people and not the building. One common metaphor used to refer to the assembly of God's people or simply the church is the *body* of Christ (Eph 1:22–23; Col 1:18).

I found the metaphor of the body of Christ particularly helpful in the context of immigration. The image of the body of Christ can both describe and illustrate how the church responds to the suffering bodies from within and without. These are real people who are under tremendous stress and hardship, and yet they are determined, resilient, and courageous. When it comes to real people on the move, we are not talking about the kind of church that aims at maintaining church membership or gathering the faithful and perpetuating structures and practices based on a particular cultural heritage or tradition. Church is not a place intended for entertaining the privileged, but giving hope to those who are suffocated by layers of borders and boundaries, and longing for freedom and redemption. The very presence of immigrants before our eyes is calling for an emergent ecclesiology that engages God's salvation with Jesus' immigrant experience at a deeper level and speaks to both us and them as one dignified body without borders.

I now focus mainly on Colossians 1:18–20 (NRSV) that reads: "He is the head of the body, the church; he is the beginning, the firstborn from the dead, so that he might come to have first place in everything. For in him all the fullness of God was pleased to dwell, and through him God was pleased to reconcile to himself all things, whether on earth or in heaven, by making peace through the blood of his cross." The text spells out the ABCs of Christianity, but I want to first emphasize the point that we are members of the body, in which Jesus is our head. Affirming that Jesus is the head of the body as Colossians 1:18 is neither asking Christians to be totally submissive to the authority of the church nor promoting the hierarchical structure of the church. Even Jesus does not place himself above anyone. Being the beginning of all things and the firstborn from the dead, Jesus did not assume first place in everything. He made himself God's dwelling place to actualize reconciliation to the world through his suffering on the cross.

The affirmation is an important reminder because when we become members of the body of Christ, we are dismantling our sense of self in terms of self-serving interests and self-righteousness. In other words, we give up our desire to regulate the body of Christ. We do not have absolute power over who is in and who is out, how the body moves, and when it should place admission on hold. One immediate result is to re-discover the inclusive nature of the body of Christ. Including others—including but not limited to those who cross the borders and speak a language different from us—in the body of Christ does not exhaust the vision of the church. Contrarily, it complements it.

When the body of Christ moves, it expands. As Elaine Padilla rightly puts it, "Space expands via movement."[23] More people are welcome to be part of the body along the way. We can say that the body of Christ is porous, fluid, and to be exact, borderless. The movement of the whole body headed by Jesus is meant for all creatures of God, which is not hindered, deterred, and alienated by any boundaries of human construct.

The idea that the body of Christ is borderless totally subverts toxic narratives on immigrants and immigration. This much-needed ecclesial expression is good news to dehumanized individuals and embedded in the renewed identity of church is a call to re-imagine religious space in the midst of rising xenophobia.

Before I go into the details, let me come back to Elaine Padilla's concept of space. Padilla clearly stated that human mobility is never a thing, but concerned with a group of people on the move. Padilla says, "Space expands via movement."[24] It looks like as if this is a simple rule, but Padilla is not simply describing a phenomenon and drawing a conclusion: It is what it is. Padilla writes about what follows human mobility is something that should concern us all. Immigrants are moving from one place to another, but the spaces to which they traverse do not necessarily promise joy. Conversely, those spaces can be haunted by terror and fear. Space may expand whichever way people are moving, but expanding space fails to communicate with the realities of people. People suffer as the space expands. Padilla laments that the space continues to be "scarred by the wounds of hostility"[25] and fabricated again by "the hostile tendencies of geopolitics."[26]

How can we turn hostility into hospitality? How can we create a space that provides a deep communal experience for all? The task of redefining space becomes more urgent than it needed to be in the past. Building on Frida Kahlo's painting *The Embrace of the Universe*, Padilla illustrates how transformation can happen in a place where people are committed to "welcoming spaciousness." Central to the idea, space becomes sacred because it is defined by the divine and the space is actually the realm of the divine. Humanity, regardless of race, ethnicity, gender, and so on has a share in this dwelling place; everyone is invited and simultaneously encouraged to share the dwelling with others. Padilla postulates, "Embracing a way of dwelling cavernously means that space is vital, that it imbues the everyday with transcendence in a lively way.... It involves the economy but by taking another form, an embodied rather than an impersonal, distant, and objectifying mode of exchange."[27] Transcendence can be experienced in every ordinary moment, because of the indwelling of others in the space. Each one reveals the glory of the divine. Since people are interconnected with one another, that interconnectivity enables goodness and kindness to flow through the web of relationships.

Padilla's idea of expanding space provides new insight into reconceptualizing the body of Christ as a borderless space to effectively respond to the fear, resentment, and hatred toward immigrants and refugees. Being inspired by Jesus' immigrant experience, the body of Christ as a borderless space seeks a larger role of church in the public that aims to break the cycle of xenophobia, re-order relationships, and facilitate mutual transformation.

The body of Christ will need to take the initiative to re-humanize the immigration experience. On the first level of this endeavor, the body of Christ creates space for cultivating meaningful connection.

Being borderless, the body of Christ is not intimidated by any boundaries of human construct, but works with others to defy a long history of narrative used to target immigrants. Resistance consists of speaking against family separation and other humiliating policies that deprive immigrants of their dignity. It also consists of extending networks to support those who have lived in the US long enough to seek a pathway to citizenship.

In addition to advocating for immigrant rights and reform, there are congregations committed to providing sanctuary to those who feel insecure, threatened, and isolated under the existing systems and institutions. The body of Christ, headed by Jesus Christ, is redeemed and protected from the dark powers of destruction through his cross. People who are invited and welcomed into this borderless space should accordingly be entitled the same protection. In fact, more than 700 parishes and congregations in the U.S. have provided sanctuary and offered refuge to immigrants and communities at risk of deportation since Trump was elected in 2016, according to the National Sanctuary Movement. The Evangelical Lutheran Church in America (ELCA), for instance, voted to become a "sanctuary church body" at its Churchwide Assembly in Milwaukee on August 7, 2019. Becoming a sanctuary denomination, as the ELCA website indicates, "means that the ELCA is publicly declaring that walking alongside immigrants and refugees is a matter of faith."

The act of turning the church into a dwelling place for immigrants and refugees who are tired and weary and are looking for shelter and protection is certainly sensible and appropriate. But the body of Christ should not be limited to and easily satisfied by welcoming the otherized immigrants into the church building. The body of Christ is encouraged to step out of its comfort zone to be with the people, that is to eat, laugh, and sit with those who are trampled and socially disconnected.

Making the space borderless in the body of Christ thus attempts to cultivate a common ground where people meet to see and listen to one another. Through re-establishing bonds and communicating with one another in this ever-expanding body of Christ, we embrace our shared humanities. As explained earlier, all bodies are connected in Jesus' immigrant story. The connection that emerges from Jesus' incarnation, death, and resurrection reminds us that we are all receivers of God's grace in Jesus, and no one is above anyone else in the dwelling place. To say that we embrace our shared humanities also means that we share our vulnerabilities. We were once strangers to one another, but we are now invited to become part of Christ's body. The connection with one another and, actually, our interconnection motivates us to pursue the call God has placed on us through Jesus the immigrant. Remembering Jesus' immigrant experience awakens our awareness, compassion, and sensibilities toward others so that we can hear the cry of those bodies, rejected, unwanted, and dead while fleeing and seeking refuge across borders. This communal experience is powerful in ways that it resists subjugation, hegemony, and exclusion, and furthermore, addresses a deeper need through remembering peoples' stories of resilience and honoring the humanity in them.

On the second level of re-humanizing the immigrant experience, the body of Christ must learn to appreciate cultural and linguistic differences and bring together diverse gifts and talents to build a healthy society for all. Padilla observes, "Through encounters with the others, whether human or nonhuman, space may be redefined and place may become hospitable."[28] True encounter requires us to give up our biases against and prejudices of others. When these invisible walls stand between us and them, we are unable to see rightly and justly the beauty of the others. Constructing a space that increases interactions between one another will enable us to get to know better these individuals. It is also vital to recognize the strength and wisdom of the others. These individuals have thoughts, feelings, and they know how to get things done right.

Can these others really gain our admiration and affection? Or do they remain a homogenous group waiting to be saved, redeemed, and empowered? It is hard to imagine practicing hospitality without respecting and recognizing peoples' strength and wisdom.

Mutual learning and growth is possible only when we give up our desires to regulate how, when, and where the space expands. Failing to attend to this aspect will drag us down to the trap of repeating the same old patronizing sympathy that praises: we are doing good things for the others and we do not have any problems. In reality, we ignore the root causes of systemic violence against our immigrant neighbors.

Recognizing the agency of immigrants authenticates what it means by a borderless space. It can seriously disrupt the status quo that privileges only a certain group of people. With a diversity of cultures and gifts, the body of Christ will furthermore create a borderless culture that does not aspire to linear growth but radical change in systems and institutions; meanwhile, a culture without borders keeps us accountable so we are always aware of how we remember history and how we imagine ourselves, others, and the world.

CONCLUSION

Discriminative immigration policy under the Trump administration that seeks to reduce the number of "foreigners" living in the United States devastates the life of many communities. Dreamers, refugees, undocumented immigrants, and other lawful permanent residents are living in constant fear of deportation.

How church resists hegemony through the task of re-humanizing immigration and the immigrant experience in a culture that condones xenophobia becomes both urgent and relevant. I have demonstrated that the topic of being church cannot be analyzed in isolation, but must be contextualized by the topic of immigration. I have also explained how Jesus' experience as a stranger breaks down borders and (re)connects all people. Jesus' immigrant story that links up with his incarnation, death, and resurrection reminds us that we all are receivers of God's grace, and in his suffering on the cross, Jesus remembered all, including those who have been discriminated against and unfairly targeted. We all are interconnected in the sacred dwelling place. That memory and the interconnection emerged from the rituals of remembrance not only re-direct the way we remember history and imagine ourselves, but also motivates us to pursue the call God has placed on us through Jesus the immigrant.

Being borderless, the body of Christ is the space that transcends geographical limitations and legal expectations. Within this borderless space, people meet, talk, embrace common humanities and share vulnerabilities together. Everyone has the potential to thrive in this space. Whether the body of Christ expands or contracts, it depends on how we redefine the religious space and how ready we are to disrupt the status quo.

Immigrants are human beings. Only when we see others as human beings, are we able to liberate ourselves for higher ideals. For now, the task of re-humanizing the immigrant experience benefits not just others but also ourselves. It helps make us more human.

NOTES

1. Elaine Padilla, "Expanding Space: A Possibility of a Cavernous Mode of Dwelling," in *Contemporary Issues of Migration and Theology*, ed. Elaine Padilla and Peter C. Phan, Christianities of the World (New York: Palgrave Macmillan, 2013), 53.

2. Ian Urbina, "The Capricious Use of Solitary Confinement Against Detained Immigrants"; online at https://www.theatlantic.com/politics/archive/2019/09/ice-uses-solitary-confinement-among-detained-immigrants/597433/ (accessed June 1, 2020).

3. Hellena Moon, "Immigrant Mothers of Color, Pastoral Theology, and the Law," *Pastoral Psychology* 61, no. 3 (2012): 349.

4. Jynnah Radford, "Key Findings about US Immigrants"; online at https://www.pewresearch.org/fact-tank/2019/06/17/key-findings-about-u-s-immigrants/ (accessed June 1, 2020).

5. Radford, "Key Findings."

6. David McIlwain, "Americans Don't Want the Job I Offer. Immigrants Do"; online at https://www.newsweek.com/americans-dont-want-jobs-visa-seasonal-1403512 (accessed June 1, 2020).

7. Gemma Tulud Cruz, *Toward a Theology of Migration: Social Justice and Religious Experience* (New York: Palgrave Macmillan, 2014), 90.

8. Cruz, *Theology of Migration*, 90.

9. Cruz, *Theology of Migration*, 93.

10. Cruz, *Theology of Migration*, 93.

11. Cruz, *Theology of Migration*, 93–94.

12. Peter C. Phan, *Vietnamese-American Catholics*, Ethnic-American Pastoral Spirituality (Mahwah, NJ: Paulist Press, 2005), 108.

13. Phan, *Vietnamese-American Catholics*, 108.

14. Phan, *Vietnamese-American Catholics*, 108.

15. Phan, *Vietnamese-American Catholics*, 111.

16. Phan, *Vietnamese-American Catholics*, 111.

17. Phan, *Vietnamese-American Catholics*, 111.

18. Phan, *Vietnamese-American Catholics*, 111.

19. Deirdre Cornell, *Jesus was a Migrant* (Maryknoll, NY: Orbis Books, 2014), 5.

20. Cornell, *Jesus was a Migrant*, 7.

21. Cornell, *Jesus was a Migrant*, 7.

22. Cornell, *Jesus was a Migrant*, 6.

23. Padilla, "Expanding Space," 53.

24. Padilla, "Expanding Space," 53

25. Padilla, "Expanding Space," 65.

26. Padilla, "Expanding Space," 53.

27. Padilla, "Expanding Space," 66–67.

28. Padilla, "Expanding Space," 65.

Chapter 10

Practicing Jesus Christ in Public, Embodying Resistance

Craig L. Nessan

"May you live in interesting times!" The words of the Chinese curse haunt. We live in an era of deep divisions over core convictions, what to believe and how to act. Church and society are polarized to the edge of political disintegration. How do Christians navigate such times, when there are twenty new causes for outrage every day?

LOCATING OURSELVES IN AMERICAN HISTORY

We are not the first generation to live in moral peril, although there remain developments without precedent. The epic films of Ken Burns—documenting American history in the Civil War, World War I through the Great Depression (*The Roosevelts*), World War II, and Vietnam—serve to locate us in the struggle for justice over time.[1] We are not the first followers of Jesus Christ to search for what it means to remain faithful amid controversy and conflict.

These films chronicle the issues faced by the American nation that called for decisions from Christians about the cost of discipleship: slavery, economic disparity, wars, and the civil rights movement. Each of these periods tested the character of Christian people during presidencies that included those of Abraham Lincoln, Franklin D. Roosevelt, Harry S. Truman, John F. Kennedy Jr., Lyndon B. Johnson, and Richard Nixon. We witness over time the exercise of executive power in relation to the legislative and judicial branches of government, the trials of the electoral process, the use of military force, the expansion of corporate interests, and calculated efforts to control public opinion.

The manipulation of radio and television messaging anticipate in kind, if not degree, the impulse to use social media to mislead and deceive for the sake of maintaining political power. It has always been difficult for common people to know what is going on. Today the manufacture of consent through fear is intense.[2] Terrorism, nuclear threats, climate change, racism, and immigration policies keep us off balance and reactive. Times of crisis generate causes for deep fear that can either be channeled to scapegoat designated enemies or sublimated into constructive energy toward movements for nonviolent resistance and social justice.

How did the church and its leaders respond to the challenges of previous generations? Which moral stances by Christian people have been validated when we look at the arc of history? Opposition to slavery, rights for minority people, advocacy for the poor, equality for women, social programs to protect the vulnerable, welcome to immigrants, checking the impulse to make war, and nonviolent movements for civil rights: these are some of the courageous stances taken by Christians in previous generations now vindicated. We are summoned to such as these.

CENTRALITY OF THE GOSPEL OF JESUS CHRIST

To redirect our fear, anger, and outrage into constructive energy requires strenuous spiritual work. Sublimation names the process by which strong emotions are transformed and channeled into constructive behavior and action. Our tumultuous times have seen the virtual disintegration of shared discourse about the common good, an era characterized by intransigent partisanship.[3] After the postmodern arises post-truth, hyper-individualized construction of truth claims, and the closing of ranks among the like-minded.[4] The breakdown of genuine democratic process stymies the possibility of compromise toward an approximation of the common good.[5]

Remaining centered in such times requires clarity about what the gospel is and is not. To make appeals to the authority of "God" is something different from drawing strength from the gospel of Jesus Christ. The gospel is that message which performs the reality of Jesus Christ. This message is not partisan but for all. And in order to be for all, it pays special attention to the weak, those most in harm's way. Paul contrasted being "in Christ" to being "in the flesh." As Jesus Christ is performed in word and sacrament, the reality of Jesus Christ is performed on us and in us. We not only eat the body and blood of Jesus Christ "but it is the bread and the wine which eat us. We are to become what they are: the body and the blood of Christ."[6]

To know Jesus Christ is to know his benefits. To receive the benefits of Jesus Christ is to share those benefits with others: forgiveness, mercy, grace, love, generosity, hope. These always are manifest under the proviso of the *simul* character of Christian existence, but nonetheless real. The death and resurrection of Jesus Christ become enacted upon us in daily repetitions. We become the body of Jesus Christ for the life of the world. The gospel is the only source of energy for the struggle and the *sine qua non* of Christian unity. The gospel allows us to live with open questions yet remain one body in the midst of difference.

Remaining centered in the gospel above all things is a great leadership challenge.[7] When we become distracted by twenty new causes for outrage occurring every day, we lose our focus on the cost of discipleship. Richard Rohr writes:

> The Gospel offers a way to make our action sustainable and lasting over the long haul. People on the Right tend to be perpetually angry, fearful, and overly defensive, and people on the Left tend to be perpetually cynical, morally righteous, and outraged. The Gospel calls forth a refined instrument beyond these two falsehoods that can really make a difference because it is a new level of consciousness altogether. Such activists are themselves "a new creation" (Galatians 6:15) and the lightning rods of God's transformative energy into the world.[8]

It is one thing to proclaim the gospel as true for others; it is an entirely different thing to trust the gospel as the center for your own life. How do we avail ourselves of the means of grace? Worship, dwelling in the word, prayer, meditation, spiritual practices, collegial relationships, spiritual direction, and Sabbath time, including mini-sabbaths. These provide the way to the sublimation of the negative into the spiritual energy necessary for the vocation of practicing Jesus Christ in public.

THE CHRISTOLOGICAL IMPERATIVE

Christology has provided the foundation for resistance by the church throughout Christian history. During the first three centuries, the early church—pre-Constantine—immersed itself in the Way of Jesus Christ. The teachings, life, death, and resurrection of Jesus Christ constituted the matrix for a way of life. Within the diversity of religious alternatives in the late Roman Empire, Christianity prevailed in the fourth century to become the religion authorized by emperors, Theodosius and Constantine.[9]

Three features of earliest Christian practice contributed to this emergence. First, at worship and by catechesis Christians were intentionally brought into conformity to the shape of Christian existence. The followers of Jesus Christ immersed neophytes into the mysteries of faith through a deliberate formation process. Second, Christians were formed to speak the promises of Jesus Christ to others. The practice of evangelizing spread the Good News through words spoken by members of the Christian community. Third, the early church acted as the body of Christ to minister to the needs of neighbors in their society. Christians shared bread with the hungry, practiced forgiveness by living nonviolently, and risked their own lives taking care of the sick, including those suffering from the plague. Through these practices the early Christian community attracted new followers to the Way.

After the establishment of Constantinian Christianity, the enmeshment of church with empire diluted the formation of Christian persons in those practices that contributed to its earlier vitality.[10] Throughout church history, however, reform movements arose by the power of the Spirit to restore clarity to the church's identity and mission. These movements included monasticism with its practice of a life ordered by prayer and acts of charity, the Protestant reformation retrieval of the gospel of Jesus Christ as central to the church with its power to set people free to live out the baptismal vocation of serving neighbors, classical Pietism with its dual focus on devotional practices and service to the weak, the Social Gospel movement summoning believers beyond the privatization of Christian faith to assume public responsibility for the marginalized, the Confessing Church calling Christians to resist the captivity of National Socialism through costly discipleship, the Civil Rights movement through nonviolent direct action led by African American leaders from historic black churches, and multiple expressions of liberation theology that bring the resources of Christian faith to engage and transform suffering caused by human oppression.[11]

Robust Christology lies at the heart and soul of each of these movements of resistance and hope. Jesus Christ is the foundation upon which Christian transformative practice is grounded. The red thread running through those movements that demonstrated the capacity to differentiate between church and empire is the person and way of Jesus Christ. "Give therefore to the emperor the things that are the emperor's, and to God the things that are God's" (Matt 22:21). In the teaching and practices of Jesus Christ, purity of heart led to his crucifixion by the Roman Empire.[12] "Whenever Jesus Christ calls us, his call leads us to death."[13]

CASE BONHOEFFER

The witness of Dietrich Bonhoeffer within the context of the Confessing Church in Nazi Germany provides a compelling case for the centrality of Christology in exercising resistance to political tyranny. Together with Karl Barth, primary author of the Barmen Declaration, Bonhoeffer grounded his resistance to fascism on the Lordship of Jesus Christ. This conviction was articulated in Article One of Barmen:

> 8.11 Jesus Christ, as he is attested for us in Holy Scripture, is the one Word of God which we have to hear and which we have to trust and obey in life and in death.
> 8.12 We reject the false doctrine, as though the church could and would have to acknowledge as a source of its proclamation, apart from and besides this one Word of God, still other events and powers, figures and truths, as God's revelation.[14]

Those theologians making concessions to the German Christian movement did so by making allowances for other forms of revelation—based on race, nation, language, history, and soil—that functioned to validate National Socialism.[15] This found an extreme form in the Institute for the Study and Eradication of Jewish Influence on German Religious Life, founded in 1939, which provided education and publications supporting Aryan Christianity.[16]

Bonhoeffer provides a defining case of a theologian whose concentrated focus on Jesus Christ gave him the grounds for political resistance from his earliest academic work to the time of his execution for participating in the conspiracy to assassinate Hitler. This began with his definition of church as "Christ existing as church-community" in his doctoral dissertation, *Sanctorum Communio*.[17] His commitment was sharpened during his year of study in New York both by his conversion to Christian nonviolence in his relationship to his fellow student, Jean Lasserre, and by his immersion in the worship, teaching, and social activism of Abyssinian Baptist Church in Harlem.[18]

Through his Christology lectures at the University of Berlin in 1933, Bonhoeffer made clear to his students that we are called to pay attention to "Who" Jesus Christ is as a living person *pro me* and not only to the "How" of doctrinal formulations. Jesus Christ is the center of human existence, history, and nature.[19] As director of the underground seminary at Zingst and Finkenwalde, Bonhoeffer formed students in the way of Jesus Christ through individual and communal practices that would sustain them for pastoral leadership in congregations of the Confessing Church. Jesus Christ binds the community together by mediating every relationship.[20] In his book, *Discipleship*, Bonhoeffer provided a commentary on the Sermon on the Mount to teach the costly grace of following Jesus Christ.[21] The shape of this commitment came to expression in the *Ethics* as the call to be "conformed" to the crucified and risen Christ.[22] By the time of his imprisonment, Bonhoeffer focused the character of Christian existence in a "world come of age" even more precisely: "we can be Christians today in only two ways, through prayer and in doing justice among human beings."[23]

The witness of Bonhoeffer provides a case study for Christian political resistance, whose parallels to the requisites of our crisis are striking. As in previous generations, centering on Christology places ground under our feet for distinguishing between false gods and the God revealed in the person and way of Jesus Christ.

WHICH GOD?

To say that one believes in God begs the question: Which God? The Bonhoeffer case demonstrates the struggle between competing Christianities under fascism: the first made Christianity subservient to the self-interested policies of the nation, while the other confessed a Christocentric theology that authorized resistance to nationalistic appropriation of Christian theology.[24] We are engaged in a comparable contest over the entanglements of Christianity in American civil religion and the character of the God revealed in Jesus Christ.

The Christian religious right construes God according to American nationalism with its inextricable entanglements with global capitalism; God, capitalism, and patriotism merge together into a single whole.[25] William Connolly describes this nexus as the "evangelical-capitalist resonance machine."[26] According to civil religion, America is God's New Israel, a unique nation chosen to be God's agent in history with a manifest destiny for accomplishing divine purposes.[27] No other nation has this holy calling from God. This undergirds the claim to "American exceptionalism," which authorizes deviance from international law and human rights.[28] Furthermore, as Catherine Keller writes:

> To outgrow our anthropic exceptionalism may, oddly, mean outing the string of white-heterosexist-nationalist-classed-religious exceptionalism that so unexceptionally rule.[29]

This entangled web of American exceptionalisms requires analysis, prophetic denunciation, and deconstruction. For example, Christian nationalism includes an individual work ethic as the way to success, prosperity in this world for the righteous, a traditional family structure with the man as the head, support for the right to keep and bear arms, and obeying the law as the way of godliness.

The Bible is interpreted as authorization for an American capitalist theocracy within a dualistic worldview. God is on the side of the Christian religious right and against those who oppose them, including Muslims, atheists, and progressive Christians. This dualistic worldview contributes to the vitriol generated by Christians on the religious right, insofar as their opponents are not only wrong but against God. In recent history the Christian religious right has defended the cause of white nationalism, abiding public racist rhetoric, and support for discriminatory immigration policies. One can discern true Christians from false according to well-defined litmus test issues: abortion, homosexuality, creationism, and climate change denial. The refusal to engage scientific findings, particularly related to the devastating consequences of climate change, contributes to the actualization of perilous end time scenarios depicted in the literature of millennialism. The theology of the Christian religious right is embedded within an apocalyptic worldview, in which unconditional support for the State of Israel accords with the Bible's predictions for the end times.[30] The mission of the church is to convert people to its theological paradigm as they make individual decisions for Jesus Christ.

The substitutionary death of Jesus Christ on the cross is the chief feature in the Christology of the Christian religious right. God sent his Son to die for the sins of the world and all those who accept Jesus Christ as their personal Savior will obtain everlasting life. Salvation is other-worldly with heaven as the reward for right belief. Because we are living in the end times, the focus shifts toward escaping this evil age and preserving Christian purity until the rapture when true Christians will receive life after death. There is little attention to the teachings of Jesus Christ as the basis for social action by Christians to improve this world, insofar as this world is passing away. By contrast, there is much focus on preserving Christian values within American society during this time of waiting for God's deliverance of the righteous.

SEVEN PUBLIC PRACTICES OF JESUS CHRIST

What is at issue among Christians is the very identity of God and the character of Jesus Christ. If the Christology of the religious right concentrates primarily on substitutionary atonement, the Christology of the confessing church interprets the crucifixion of Jesus "from below." It is not possible to understand the cross and resurrection of Jesus Christ without seeing these within the entire trajectory of his life and teachings. The centrality of the reign of God to Jesus' proclamation, the epitome of Jesus' teaching in the Sermon on the Mount, and the provocative table hospitality as practiced by Jesus need to be interpreted coherently with his royal entry into Jerusalem on Palm Sunday, his public demonstration of "cleansing" the temple, and his crucifixion as a pretender king by Roman authorities. Interpretations of the cross "from above" after Easter begin with the recognition that the resurrection was God's vindication of Jesus Christ as the one who taught and performed the reign of God in contrast to the rule of Rome.[31] Only after affirming the historical context for Jesus' resurrection can we proceed to understand it according to the many other biblical and theological metaphors that contribute to the full significance of the death-resurrection event.

In contrast to the narrowing of Christology by the Christian religious right, a Christology of resistance is funded by a range of practices embodied in and authorized by the teachings and life of Jesus Christ. These practices constitute a Way that was characteristic of Jesus Christ, followed by the disciples of Jesus Christ in the early church, and sources of renewal by the reform movements that have emerged over the course of Christian history. This description of seven practices should be understood as representative and not exhaustive as resources for a resistance Christology.

1. *Radical Hospitality.* In extending welcome to others, Jesus broke boundaries based on gender, age, class, purity, ethnicity, and status. Jesus welcomed women, children, the poor, public sinners, foreigners, and the unclean into his company. The table of Jesus was characterized by "open commensality."[32] Jesus eating with outcasts and public sinners was a cause for offense to those religious people who maintained boundaries based on purity and righteousness (Lk 5:29–32). This radical hospitality was extended also to Gentiles on occasion by Jesus with the full implications for inclusion realized in the early church, especially through missionary activity of Paul (Acts 15:1–21). Jesus instituted a meal of God's reign by which he was to be remembered by his disciples (Lk 22:14–20). The Eucharist is a meal of radical hospitality at which all are welcome.
2. *Excessive Generosity.* Jesus demonstrated generosity and care, especially to the undeserving. Living in gratitude for God's beneficence, Jesus pointed to the birds of the air, lilies of the field, and clothing of the grass as instances of God's caring provision (Matt 6:25–34). Because God is generous to all, special attention must be given to those who are otherwise disregarded: "Give to everyone who begs from you; and if anyone takes away your goods, do not ask for them again" (Lk 6:30). Jesus taught that those who only worked one hour should be paid the same daily wage as those working the entire day (Matt 20:1–16). In a parable that topples all social norms, Jesus promised that as we are generous to the hungry, thirsty, stranger, naked, sick, and imprisoned, so we are acting in generosity to him, because Jesus meets us in the least of these neighbors (Matt 25:31–46).
3. *Feeding the Hungry.* Central to the teachings and ministry of Jesus was providing food for the hungry. The Gospels are replete with miracles where hungry people are fed. Jesus ministers to the whole person, body and soul. Jesus also invited his followers to participate in the ministry of feeding hungry people: "They need not go away; you give them something

to eat" (Matt 14:16). The early church took up this command from Jesus in its common life (Acts 2:43–47) and implemented the office of deacon for "the daily distribution of food" (Acts 6:1–6). The Lord's Supper represents the abundant economy of God's reign in contrast to all conventional economies. Here is the anticipation of an eschatological meal where not only are all welcome but a meal where there is sufficiency for all. This makes the Eucharist an alternative economy to the economies of competition and scarcity in conventional society.

4. *Challenging the Status Quo.* Jesus challenged many conventional religious and social practices of his time. When Jesus replied: "Give therefore to the emperor the things that are the emperor's, and to God the things that are God's" (Matt 22:21), this was not about separation of church and state but encompassing devotion to God above all things. Jesus challenged the authority of Herod: "Go and tell that fox for me" (Lk 13:31); and Pilate: "You would have no power over me unless it had been given you from above" (John 19:11). Jesus also challenged on many occasions the authority of the scribes and Pharisees: "[F]or he taught them as one having authority, and not as their scribes" (Matt 7:29). The agitation of Jesus against the political and religious leaders led to his being singled out for attention and eventual arrest. The basis for the challenge by Jesus to the status quo was contained already in the Great Commandment: "'You shall love the Lord your God with all your heart, and with all your soul, and with all your mind.' This is the greatest and first commandment. And a second is like it: 'You shall love your neighbor as yourself'" (Matt 22:37–39). Wherever the understanding of God was too limited or the interpretation of neighbor too narrow, Jesus challenged those claims (Lk 10:25–37, Parable of the Good Samaritan).

5. *Healing the Sick.* Jesus was renowned as a healer. He healed persons who were lame, blind, deaf, and mute, and many others of their diseases and sickness. Jesus also cast out demons and evil spirits from those afflicted by these maladies. The crowds knew about the healing power of Jesus and sought him out: "When he went ashore, he saw a great crowd; and he had compassion for them and cured their sick" (Matt 14:14). Jesus was acclaimed even for raising the dead back to life. The disciples of Jesus were sent out on journeys that included the commission to pray for and heal the sick: "[C]ure the sick who are there, and say to them, 'The kingdom of God has come near to you'" (Lk 10:9). The early apostles, Paul and Barnabus among others, shared the healing of Jesus with others (for example, Acts 14:8–10). Healing belongs to the core ministry carried out by the church in Jesus' name.

6. *Demonstrating for the Kingdom.* The kingdom of God was the central metaphor by which the message of Jesus was characterized (Mk 1:15).[33]

Core to the prayer that Jesus taught his disciples was an invocation of the reign: "Our Father in heaven, hallowed be your name. Your kingdom come. Your will be done, on earth as it is in heaven" (Matt 6:9–10). The Hebrew Bible provides the antecedent for describing God as King and God's rule over the earth as kingdom, especially evident in the Psalms (for example, Psalm 97). The implications of the reign inaugurated by Jesus should not be spiritualized, rather the kingdom had material consequences: "But if it is by the Spirit of God that I cast out demons, then the kingdom of God has come to you" (Matt 12:28). Jesus was received into Jerusalem with the welcome of a king: "Hosanna to the Son of David! Blessed is the one who comes in the name of the Lord!" (Matt 21:1–11). Both the cleansing of the Temple ("My house shall be called a house of prayer; but you are making it a den of robbers" [Matt 21:12–17]) and the royal entry into Jerusalem were public demonstrations challenging political and religious authorities in the name of the kingdom. Together with other provocations—for example, the question about paying taxes (Matt 22:15–22) and the lesson of the fig tree (Matt 22:32–35)—these led consequentially to Jesus' arrest, trial, and execution on the cross by the Romans.

7. *Countercultural Peacemaking.* Jesus taught and practiced nonviolence. The coming of the reign resonates with expectation for God's reconciliation and peace: "Blessed are the peacemakers, for they will be called the children of God" (Matt 5:9). Jesus radicalized the meaning of peacemaking: "You have heard that it was said, 'An eye for an eye and a tooth for a tooth.' But I say to you, do not resist an evildoer. But if anyone strikes you on the right cheek, turn the other also" (Matt 5:38–39). Even more, Jesus taught his disciples: "You have heard that it was said, 'You shall love your neighbor and hate your enemy.' But I say to you, Love your enemies and pray for those who persecute you, so that you may be children of your Father in heaven" (Matt 5:43–45). As his passion approached, Jesus prayed as he wept over Jerusalem: "If you, even you, had only recognized on this day the things that make for peace!" (Lk 19:42). The witness of Jesus to peacemaking culminates with his words from the cross: "Father, forgive them; for they do not know what they are doing" (Lk 23:34). A nonviolent interpretation of the cross sees Jesus' death as the end of all spirals of violence by the unmasking of the scapegoat mechanism.[34] The Way of Jesus is nonviolence, peacemaking, and reconciling.[35]

These seven practices characterize what it means to practice Jesus Christ in public, embodying political resistance. While these practices need to be implemented creatively, courageously, and imaginatively in particular contexts, they constitute a Way that is in continuity with the discipleship taught and embodied by Jesus. The matrix formed by these practices contradicts the reductionist Christology prominent in the Christian religious right. Moreover, the Way marked by the performance of these practices was embodied by the church in the first centuries and revived by Reform movements throughout church history.

NEIGHBOR POLITICS, NOT RELIGIOUS IDENTITY POLITICS

These seven public practices of Jesus constitute a neighbor politics that contradicts what can be described as the religious identity politics of the Christian religious right. The religious identity politics of the Christian religious right is driven by a theocratic impulse that aims at the implementation of biblical teaching, interpreted according to its peculiar theological hermeneutic and paradigm, as public policy. This aims at a virtual one-to-one correspondence between definitive biblical commandments and political advocacy that these be implemented as legislation to govern all of society. This strategy can be seen, for example, in the efforts to enact restrictive abortion laws, restrict the teaching of evolutionary science in public schools, or define marriage exclusively as between a man and a woman. The political agenda of the Christian religious right has gained momentum through the election of leaders, selection of public appointees, and appointment of judges who share, or are beholden to, this theological paradigm.

The religious identity politics of the Christian religious right is motivated by the desire to bring society into conformity with its construal of biblical truth enforced through the rule of law. Neighbor politics, by contrast, aims not at the theocratic imposition of biblical teaching as law of the land and public policy. Rather, neighbor politics aims to translate the practices of Jesus into a political agenda that persuades others through publicly accessible reasoning and by building coalitions with people who share these convictions, regardless of their religious convictions.[36] The focus of neighbor politics shifts away from implementing the "truth" of its theological convictions toward public reasoning that prioritizes policies that best address the concrete needs of neighbors. Furthermore, in order to attain a rule of law that is fair and equitable to all persons, a neighbor politics pays special attention to the welfare of those on the margins, who may be treated with less regard than those with greater wealth, status, or privilege.

The translation of neighbor politics into social policy, in accord with the public practices of Jesus, can be illustrated through the Social Statements and Social Messages of the Evangelical Lutheran Church in America. The purpose of social policy is to mediate between church teaching and political engagement according to the following commitments:

- be a community where open, passionate, and respectful deliberation on challenging and controversial issues of contemporary society is expected and encouraged;
- engage those of diverse perspectives, classes, genders, ages, races, and cultures in the deliberation process so that each of our limited horizons might be expanded and the witness of the body of Christ in the world enhanced;
- draw upon the resources of faith and reason—on Scripture, church history, knowledge, and personal experience—to learn and to discern how to respond to contemporary challenges in light of God's word;
- address through deliberative processes the issues faced by the people of God, in order to equip them in their discipleship and citizenship in the world;
- arrive at positions to guide its corporate witness through participatory processes of moral deliberation;
- contribute toward the upbuilding of the common good and the revitalizing of public life through open and inclusive processes of deliberation.[37]

In relation to the seven public practices of Jesus, it would be of value to explore how these come to expression in the social teaching of the church: for example, radical hospitality in the message on immigration; excessive generosity in the statement on caring for creation; feeding the hungry in the statement on economic life (*Sufficient, Sustainable Livelihood for All*); challenging the status quo in the statement on race, ethnicity, and culture; healing the sick in the statement on health care; demonstrating for the kingdom in the statement on church in society; and countercultural peacemaking in the statement on peace.[38] Such social statements and messages demonstrate the necessary work of translating the public practices of Jesus into a neighbor politics to inform political engagement. They function as "middle axioms" between the witness of the New Testament to Jesus Christ and engaged praxis by members of the body of Christ speaking and acting in context today.[39]

While the work of political advocacy at the national and state levels needs to remain vigorous—including active participation in the electoral process with all citizens provided equal access—today we are called to build movements for the common good from the grassroots up. Substantial political change in our time is unlikely to be implemented from the "top down" without renewed energy and activism generated from local communities.

Wendell Berry long has advocated that the well-being of the whole depends first on paying attention to our local places. Among the "17 Sensible Steps" for a sustainable community Berry proposes for local implementation, we cite four:

1. Always ask of any proposed change or innovation: What will this do to our community? How will this affect our common wealth?
2. Always include nature—the land, the water, the air, the native creatures—within the membership of the community.
3. Always ask how local needs might be supplied from local sources, including the mutual help of neighbors.
4. Always supply local needs first. (And only then think of exporting their products, first to nearby cities, and then to others.)[40]

While the argument may appear counterintuitive, attending to the care of the local community contributes most to the well-being of the whole.

When surveying the infrastructure of many local communities, the most intact and vital organizations equipped to contribute to the common good are religious congregations. Leaders of religious communities should not underestimate their ability to contribute to the process of moral deliberation leading to participation in movements for change.

> Ordinary people are able to listen to diverse opinions, consider the nuances of issues, and make substantive recommendations.... Imagine the cumulative effect of many citizen's assemblies across the country helping to shape public conversations and recognize the deliberative skills of citizens.[41]

Pastors have authority to call for and convene public conversations about matters affecting the common good, starting with issues that impinge on the local population and place. Moreover, religious congregations are positioned by purpose and values to equip their members for their vocations in daily life, including the vocation of citizenship.[42]

Practicing Jesus Christ in public, embodying resistance, involves the call to discipleship under the sign of the cross.[43] An ethics of the cross looks less to success and more to faithfulness in the Way of Jesus Christ. "It is the hope, the chance, the faith that the future is always better, not because it is, but because that is what we hope and that is what hope means."[44] An ethics of the cross means participating in the suffering of the world and choosing to take that suffering upon oneself. How do we persist in the face of the many causes for outrage, discouragement, and conflict? In words that echo Martin Luther King Jr., Keller asks:

> In the fierce urgency of our all too human now, what local planetary solidarity might emerge? Never quite all in all, and yet nonetheless—all in. Why not become the new earth, the new public, we imagine?[45]

In a time of festering cynicism and despair, we are called to the challenging spiritual work of transforming these into daring hope, resistance, and practicing Jesus Christ in public: "See, I am sending you out like sheep into the midst of wolves; so be wise as serpents and innocent as doves" (Matt 10:16).

NOTES

1. See the listing of documentaries by Ken Burns; online at http://kenburns.com/the-films/ (accessed Aug. 15, 2019).

2. Edward S. Herman and Noam Chomsky, *Manufacturing Consent: The Political Economy of Mass Media* (New York: Pantheon, 2002).

3. Keith M. Parsons and Paris N. Donahoo, *Polarized: The Collapse of Truth, Civility, and Community in Divided Times and How We Can Find Common Ground* (New York: Prometheus, 2019).

4. Lee McIntyre, *Post-Truth* (Cambridge, MA: MIT Press, 2018).

5. Cf. Timothy Snyder, *The Road to Unfreedom: Russia, Europe, America* (New York: Penguin Random House, 2018).

6. Rubem A. Alves, *The Poet, The Warrior, The Prophet* (London: SCM, 2002).

7. Norma Cook Everist and Craig L. Nessan, *Transforming Leadership: New Vision for a Church in Mission* (Minneapolis, MN: Augsburg Fortress, 2008), 46–47.

8. Richard Rohr, "Nonviolence," *Daily Meditations* Week 34 (Aug. 19, 2019) on "Creating Peaceful Change"; online at https://cac.org/creating-peaceful-change-2019-08-18/ (accessed Sept. 30, 2019).

9. Rodney Stark, *The Rise of Christianity: How the Obscure, Marginal Jesus Movement Became the Dominant Religious Force in the Western World in a Few Centuries* (Princeton, NJ: Princeton University Press, 1997).

10. Douglas John Hall, *The End of Christendom and the Future of Christianity* (Eugene, OR: Wipf & Stock, 2002).

11. Cf. Lilian Calles Barger, *The World Come of Age: An Intellectual History of Liberation Theology* (New York: Oxford University Press, 2018).

12. John Dominic Crossan, *Who Killed Jesus?: Exposing the Roots of Anti-Semitism in the Gospel Story of the Death of Jesus* (San Francisco, CA: HarperCollins, 1995).

13. Dietrich Bonhoeffer, *Discipleship*, ed. Gefferey B. Kelly and John D. Godsey, trans. Barbara Green and Reinhard Krauss, Dietrich Bonhoeffer Works 4 (Minneapolis, MN: Augsburg Fortress, 2001), 87.

14. "The Theological Declaration of Barmen," *Confessions of the Presbyterian Church U.S.A.*; online at http://www.westpresa2.org/docs/adulted/Barmen.pdf (accessed Sept. 30, 2019).

15. Robert P. Ericksen, *Theologians Under Hitler* (New Haven, CT: Yale University Press, 1985).

16. See Susannah Heschel, *The Aryan Jesus: Christian Theologians and the Bible in Nazi Germany* (Princeton, NJ: Princeton University, 2008).

17. Dietrich Bonhoeffer, *Sanctorum Communio: A Theological Study of the Sociology of the Church*, ed. Clifford J. Green, trans. Reinhard Krauss and Nancy Lukens, Dietrich Bonhoeffer Works 1 (Minneapolis, MN: Augsburg Fortress, 1998), 141.

18. See Reggie L. Williams, *Bonhoeffer's Black Jesus: Harlem Renaissance Theology and an Ethic of Resistance* (Waco, TX: Baylor University Press, 2014).

19. Cf. Dietrich Bonhoeffer, "Lectures on Christology," in *Berlin: 1932-1933*, ed. Larry L. Rasmussen, trans. Isabel Best and David Higgins, Dietrich Bonhoeffer Works 12 (Minneapolis, MN: Augsburg Fortress, 2009), 308–15 and 324–27.

20. Dietrich Bonhoeffer, *Life Together/Prayerbook of the Bible*, ed. Geffrey B. Kelly, trans. Daniel W. Bloesch and James H. Burtness, Dietrich Bonhoeffer Works 5 (Minneapolis, MN: Augsburg Fortress, 1996), 30–35.

21. Bonhoeffer, *Discipleship*, 43–56 (ch. 1).

22. Dietrich Bonhoeffer, *Ethics*, ed. Clifford J. Green, trans. Reinhard Krauss, Charles C. West, and Douglas W. Stott, Dietrich Bonhoeffer Works 6 (Minneapolis, MN: Augsburg Fortress, 2005), 93–102.

23. Dietrich Bonhoeffer, *Letters and Papers from Prison*, ed. John W. DeGruchy, trans. Isabel Best, Lisa E. Dahill, Reinhard Krauss, and Nancy Lukens, Dietrich Bonhoeffer Works 8 (Minneapolis, MN: Augsburg Fortress, 2009), 389.

24. Victoria Barnett, *For the Soul of the People: Protestant Protest Against Hitler* (New York: Oxford University Press, 1992).

25. For example, Stephen E. Strang, *God and Donald Trump* (Lake Mary, FL: Frontline, 2017).

26. William E. Connolly, *Capitalism and Christianity, American Style* (Durham, NC: Duke University Press, 2008), 39–67 (ch. 2).

27. Philip Gorski, *American Covenant: A History of Civil Religion from the Puritans to the Present* (Princeton, NJ: Princeton University Press, 2017).

28. Roberto Sirvent and Danny Haiphong, *American Exceptionalism and American Innocence: A People's History of Fake News—From the Revolutionary War to the War on Terror* (New York: Skyhorse, 2019).

29. Catherine Keller, *Political Theology of the Earth: Our Planetary Emergency and the Struggle for a New Public* (New York: Columbia University Press, 2018), 161.

30. Cf. Mitri Raheb, *Faith in the Face of Empire: The Bible through Palestinian Eyes* (Maryknoll, NY: Orbis, 2014).

31. Richard A. Horsley and Neil Asher Silberman, *The Message and the Kingdom: How Jesus and Paul Ignited a Revolution and Transformed the Ancient World* (Minneapolis, MN: Fortress, 2002).

32. John Dominic Crossan, *Jesus: A Revolutionary Biography* (New York: HarperCollins, 1994), 74–79.

33. See Bruce Chilton, *Pure Kingdom: Jesus' Vision of God* (Grand Rapids, MI: Eerdmans, 1996).

34. On René Girard's interpretation of the cross as the disclosure and overcoming of the scapegoat mechanism, see Gil Bailie, *Violence Unveiled: Humanity at the Crossroads* (New York: Crossroad, 1995).

35. Walter Wink, *Jesus and Nonviolence: A Third Way* (Minneapolis, MN: Fortress, 2003).

36. For further discussion of neighbor politics, see Craig L. Nessan, "Luther's Two Strategies and Political Advocacy: Law, Righteousness, Reason, Will, and Works in Their Civil Use," in *Lutheran Theology and Secular Law: The Work of the Modern State*, ed. Marie A. Failinger and Ronald W. Duty (New York: Routledge, 2018), 63–74.

37. "Church in Society" Social Statement (Chicago: Evangelical Lutheran Church in America, 1991); online at http://download.elca.org/ELCA%20Resource%20Repository/Church_SocietySS.pdf?_ga=2.30095289.721768161.1565980088-1973750146.1565640965 (accessed Aug. 16, 2019).

38. Evangelical Lutheran Church, Social Statements and Social Messages; online at https://elca.org/Faith/Faith-and-Society/Social-Statements (accessed Aug. 16, 2019).

39. Paul Ramsey, *Basic Christian Ethics* (Louisville, KY: Westminster John Knox Press, 1993), 349–51. On the origin of the term, see William J. Danaher, "Healing Broken Bodies: The Missional Ecclesiology Behind J. H. Oldham's Middle Axioms," *Anglican Theological Review* 92 (Spring 2010): 297–321.

40. Wendell Berry, "Community in 17 Sensible Steps," online at https://www.utne.com/community/communityin17sensiblesteps (accessed Sept. 5, 2019).

41. Editorial, "Deliberate Citizens," *The Christian Century* 136 (Aug. 14, 2019): 7, which comments on the value of Citizens' Assemblies as practiced in Ireland.

42. On living out the baptismal vocation in daily life, see the purpose and resources of the Life of Faith Initiative, see online at http://lifeoffaith.info/ (accessed Aug. 16, 2019).

43. Cf. John D. Caputo, *Cross and Cosmos: A Theology of Difficult Glory* (Bloomington, IN: Indiana University Press, 2019).

44. John D. Caputo, *The Insistence of God: A Theology of Perhaps* (Bloomington, IN: Indiana University Press, 2013), 247.

45. Keller, *Political Theology of the Earth*, 180.

Chapter 11

Seelsorge for Those Who Resist

Timothy L. Seals

In his iconic speech to the assembled throng of a quarter of a million people encamped around the Lincoln Memorial in the summer of 1963, Dr. Martin Luther King Jr. said, "I have a dream that one day down in Alabama, with its vicious racists, with its lips dripping with the words of interposition and nullification, one day right there in Alabama little black boys and black girls will be able to join hands with little white boys and white girls as sisters and brothers." The little black boys and girls and little white boys and girls to whom King referred were my generation, the children of the Civil Rights Movement. We were too young to contextualize his words in American history; yet, we were old enough to have his words contribute to the formation of our identities. As a six-year-old I watched King's speech on television together with my family. It was at that point that King entered my pantheon of heroes. Some four years later when I learned to play the clarinet, the first song I taught myself was *We Shall Overcome, so indelibly imprinted on my psyche was the signature hymn of the Civil Rights Movement.*

Years later, my heart was crestfallen when I first learned of King's moral failings: my hero had clay feet. The first revelations of such failings were disseminated in the 1989 publication of Rev. Ralph Abernathy's *And the Walls Came Tumbling Down*.[1] Abernathy, King's long-time confident and lieutenant, spoke openly of King's sexual proclivities and moral indiscretions. At the time of the publication of Abernathy's book, I was a young pastor four years into my ministry of an African American, Lutheran congregation in South Central Los Angeles. To make sense of Abernathy's revelations to my congregation and myself, I recall saying over a course of a few sermons that King's dream transcended him. He was an ambassador of a divine dream of social justice. Though King proved all too human, that did not, however, nullify a dream that was in reality a corporate dream of all African Americans who experienced slavery, Jim Crow, and diverse kinds of discrimination in education, employment, and housing throughout the United States. King was not the sole proprietor of that dream; he was one of many apostles of its dissemination under the directive of a divine imperative.

Now, as I gaze upon a picture of King in my office, a picture of King waving to the sea of humanity gathered before the Lincoln Memorial in 1963, I invariably ask myself, "How did Martin Luther King Jr. care for his soul?" How did he alleviate the stress of his demanding schedule that had him living out of a suitcase for most of his life after leading the Montgomery Bus Boycott in 1955? Did he ever find quiet spaces and moments to do proper *Seelsorge*? Anyone who is an emissary of the Light gets attacked in profound ways. The questions that I pose to King are informed by my reading of Howard Thurman. Thurman was King's teacher, friend, and mentor at Boston University. I imagine how a hypothetical conversation between the two over the issue of *Seelsorge* might have gone. No doubt Thurman had to be impressed by the gains King had made by 1965 in being considered one of the most admired personages in America. Nevertheless, Thurman would want to know about King's disciplines in the spirit. Was King placing himself in a position where he could experience God and thereby be healed of the attendant stresses and strains of being a conveyor of the dream? Essentially, Thurman would want to know about King's infrastructure of prayer. King was the consummate modern man, a man prompted by the big designs of reason, the hegemonic, universal scripts foisted on the many by the few. The active life was where King derived meaning. The active life always leaves one wanting, however. Thurman, on the other hand was the consummate postmodern man, a man of the heart who paid attention to the swirling emotions of the heart as all mystics are wont to do, for the frontline of the renewal of humanity occurs in the heart where one confronts one's fears, compulsions, and attachments to this life. For instance, Emir Abd el-Kader, the nineteenth-century Sufi mystic and Algerian fighter against French colonialism in North Africa, understood his retreat from the battlefield as an opportunity to engage in the greater holy war with himself. He was following the directive of the Prophet Muhammed who taught that fighting an external enemy who threatens the land of Islam (*Dar al-islam*) is a lesser war compared to the greater holy war in one's inner life.[2] Howard Thurman would agree with the great Sufi mystic and the Prophet Muhammad. For King's mentor and teacher, the experience of God derived from his disciplines in the spirit. His infrastructure of prayer and contemplation were his valued currency. These were the practices that kept one's humanity intact as one faced the principalities and powers of darkness. Resisting these powers, speaking truth to the universalizing script of the powerful, gnaws and scrapes at one's soul, whereby the joy and satisfaction of one's calling are rendered nonexistent. Over time speaking truth to power can render one numb and listless. King had to feel this way, as all reformers of humanity do. Martin Luther, after whom the young Michael King was renamed by his father, certainly felt the negative, psychic consequences of speaking liberating truth to power.

Those who resist, accordingly, must care for their souls. They must engage in an empowering *Seelsorge* that enables them to say with St. Paul, "Whether I live, whether I die, I am the Lord's." Paul, together with many early Christians, resisted the imperial script of the *Imperium Romanum*. As emissaries of the Light they suffered martyrdom. However, their acts of courage were not without precedent. The wise teachers (*maskilim*) who produced the book of Daniel in the second century BCE resisted the hegemonic script of Antiochus IV. They proffered the figure of Daniel as an example of how to face the religious terror of the Seleucid ruler that sought to destroy the Jewish people. Daniel has an infrastructure of spiritual practices that enable him to face the cruelty of the time, to speak out against Antiochus IV's absolutizing of himself and his Hellenistic culture above God. He also uses an infrastructure of spiritual practices to keep his psyche open to the new thing God would do through him and his people suffering the duress of religious terror.

Daniel's spiritual infrastructure, moreover, is driven by the typical, mystical modalities of the purgative, the illuminative, and the unitive. These modalities have become so ingrained in our approach to God that the traditional liturgy in the West is organized around them. The worship service begins with the purgative element through the confession of sin. Through such confession, one cleanses one's psyche and readies it for the illuminative experience. The illuminative experience occurs through the liturgy of the word, which culminates with the oral proclamation of the Word of God. The unitive experience occurs in the liturgy of the Eucharist, where Christ joins himself with those who partake of the consecrated bread and wine. It is the unitive experience *par excellence*. In the Book of Daniel, there are texts that are purgative in nature, illuminative, and unitive. These texts constitute Daniel's infrastructure of spiritual practices that prepare him for an experience of God that can cleanse him of the negative impact of Antiochus IV's universal script that called for the suppression of their religion and the destruction of their very humanity. Daniel answers the question of how one cares for one's soul when speaking to power. Daniel proffers an empowering *Seelsorge* for those who resist by speaking to power. Activism in the form of truth–telling must be coupled with an empowering *Seelsorge* that affirms our humanity. Activism without caring for one's soul leaves one jaded and disappointed. Caring for the soul as end in-itself is mere self-absorption. In a world where God is essentially related to all that exists, God demands a reciprocal mutuality of relatedness that uses power for the empowerment of others. Martin Luther hinted at this in his explanation of the seventh commandment. Christians are not only to concern themselves with the productivity of their own private property; they are to aid and assist their neighbors in the overall productivity of their private property as well.

POLITICS AND VIOLENCE

Before looking at Daniel's infrastructure of spiritual practices that constituted his *Seelsorge*, a survey of the history of the crisis-filled second century before Christ may be in order. The Hellenistic kings who succeeded Alexander the Great were military leaders.[3] They extracted other people's resources through conquest. Greek conquest was for economic gain primarily and not the dissemination of Greek culture. Hellenization was an epiphenomenon of conquest, as it caused the elites in subjugated societies to alter their culture to curry favor with their imperial overlords for economic, political, and social patronage.

However, the imperial strategy of extraction through military conquest is not a long-term solution for access to a people's resources. It is too costly: supporting a military expedition is economically prohibitive. The long-term subjugation of a people must be backed up by a hegemonic ideology. The Hellenistic ideology was promulgated through coins, statutes, architecture, and the cult of the ruler.[4] Horns were a prominent motif in Hellenistic iconography that served ideological purposes, as horns were associated with Seleucus I, renowned for his physical strength. Physical strength as an organizing value precipitated the violence that was an ever-present reality of life under the Hellenistic potentates. Judea was in the middle of perpetual chaos and violence, as the Ptolemies in Egypt and the Seleucids in Asia Minor and Mesopotamia vied for control of Judea, ever important as it laid on the trade route to Egypt. Alexander's death in 323 BCE initiated the era of violence, when his generals fought over control of his vast empire. Dividing his empire in several ways, a treaty by the victorious generals in 301 BCE awarded Syria-Palestine to Seleucus I. The four main *Diadochi* were Ptolemy I who ruled Egypt, Palestine, and Cilicia, Petra, and Cypress; Seleucus I who ruled Mesopotamia, the Levant, and east Asia Minor; Lysimachus who ruled over Thrace and west Asia Minor; and Cassander who ruled over Macedonia, the Greek (Macedonian) home of Philip and Alexander. Ptolemy I and Seleucus I both claimed Syria-Palestine as their possession. When the victorious generals gave Syria-Palestine to Seleucus I, the armies of Ptolemy I had already occupied the area and he refused to pull them back and cede Syria-Palestine to Seleucus I. Consequently, violence became the quotidian reality of life in the region, as a total of six Syrian Wars between the Ptolemies and the Seleucids occurred between 274 and 168 BCE. Ever aware of the political exigencies of his time, the author of Daniel mentions the violent milieu in the eleventh chapter of his book. He is clear and historically correct about the protagonists and the antagonists in the third century BCE, unlike his take on the Babylonian era earlier in his work. His historical miscues in the first half of his work reveal that he did not live during the Babylonian Exile.

Seleucid rule began in 200 BCE at the conclusion of the Fifth Syrian War. Antiochus III finally defeated the Egyptian (Ptolemaic) armies. He took over sovereignty of Palestine and Phoenicia. During the Fifth Syrian War Jewish leaders threw their support behind Antiochus III, as they wanted the Egyptian garrison and the citadel that housed them out of Jerusalem. Because of their support, Antiochus III reciprocated with substantial benefits. For instance, he granted them life-long tax exemption and resources to refurbish the Temple. Various leaders were singled out for perks in Antiochus III's letter sent to Ptolemy in the aftermath of the war: members of the council, priests, and Temple scribes, and singers. Two letters written by Antiochus III to Ptolemy, preserved in Josephus's *Antiquitates Judaicae*, form the cornerstone of the Seleucid's operating policy in Jerusalem: *The Letter to Ptolemy* and *The Programma*.[5] The aforementioned leaders singled out for privileges may have played a role in the production of *The Programma*, as it is replete with their interests in returning Jerusalem to the status of a holy city under the guidance of its ancient traditions. *The Programma* decrees only Jews who have purified themselves may enter the Temple. It emphasizes the ancient traditions of the Jewish people, as it reinforces priestly distinctions between pure and impure. The Jew is separated from the foreigner, as the Torah calls for Jews to be holy, distinct. Despite being under foreign occupation, Judea would assert its distinctive identity informed by its ancestral laws. The Temple and its precincts were once again to be a sacred space that testifies to the holiness of God and those who serve in the Temple. Kosher laws, moreover, were to be followed. *The Letter to Ptolemy* and *The Programma* established the precedence of an irenic relationship between the inhabitants of Jerusalem and their Syrian overlords until it was altered subsequently by Antiochus IV.

The stated objectives of *The Letter to Ptolemy* and *The Programma* are one thing; reality is quite another. Because they were a people whose land was occupied by a foreign power, Jews were at the mercy of their overlords. They lacked real political autonomy. What may be granted through the good graces of one emperor may later be taken away by another. That was always an imminent threat. Without political autonomy they were vulnerable to imperial exploitation. Their resources were not theirs and could be extracted on a whim. Seventy thousand troops were still bivouacked in Jerusalem at the close of the Fifth Syrian War. Together with these troops, there was an elephant corps of one hundred and fifty elephants that exhausted agricultural resources. The presence of so many troops, moreover, occasioned violence and the rape of girls and women. There was social and economic hardship;

yet, some fared better than others, as there was an unequal distribution of economic and political privileges.[6]

In this milieu just after the Fifth Syrian War, there was another key stressor. There was debate over what constituted authoritative tradition and the contours of that tradition. Portier-Young writes, "Ancestral laws as tradition is not a fixed tablet, but are in the process of being articulated and performed."[7] Tradition is never merely inherited; it is in the process of being produced. Hence, in this era there was an ongoing debate about the content of tradition and its place in informing identity. The engagement with tradition is "an imaginative and creative process."[8] A product of the creative, imaginative engagement with tradition is that God is reimagined as king.[9] The products of imagination are put down in writing, which was the important tool of empire. Writing was a powerful tool of empire not merely to catalog and inventory its possessions, but also the medium through which to disseminate its ideology. The subjugated Jews use writing to counter the ideology of Hellenistic emperors. For them, God is a sovereign king. Portier-Young notes, "In this period the use and invention of scriptural tradition will be a crucial resource for the construction of Jewish identity, practice and belief in relation to colonizing powers and providing authorization for resistance when those powers threaten the peace, well-being and survival of the Jewish people."[10] The production of this tradition that may be used in varied and sundry ways occurs in the context of debate. Such debate was a significant stressor for the Jewish people.

Ten years after Antiochus III's defeat of Ptolemy V in the Fifth Syrian War, Rome defeated Antiochus III in its battle with the Syrians over control of Greece. After the battle of Magnesia in 190 BCE, the terms of the established treaty were severe.[11] Seleucid activity in Europe and Asia Minor was limited. To depower the royal family, Rome demanded that twenty hostages be sent to Rome every three years. Antiochus IV was one such hostage sent to Rome. The Syrian empire was forced to pay a substantial indemnity, which strained its resources. Antiochus III and his successors, Seleucus IV (187–175 BCE) and Antiochus IV (175–164 BCE) were forced to identify new sources of revenue within their own empire. Antiochus III died in an attempt to extract funds from a temple of Baalzeus in Elam.[12] Seleucus IV extracted resources from the Jerusalem Temple. The Temple came under Seleucid control, which vitiated the previous agreement in *The Letter to Ptolemy* and *The Programma* that gave a semblance of protection of the Temple and its environs from foreign control. Seleucus IV sent his minister Heliodorus to the Jerusalem Temple sometime between 178 and 175 BCE.

Antiochus IV had been held hostage many years in Rome. After being released, on his way home to Syria he heard of the assassination of his brother Seleucus IV in 175 BCE.[13] He took advantage of the opportunity to take the throne. The high priest at the beginning of Antiochus IV's reign was Onias III. The high priesthood had been in the Oniad family for generations; yet, a rival family, the Tobiads of the Transjordan, desired the high priesthood as access to more power and wealth. Joseph Tobiad had eight sons, of whom three were priests, namely Simon, Menelaus, and Lysimachus. The Tobiad family made its wealth as tax farmers for the Greek crown.[14] The precipitating factor leading to the wholesale simony of the high priest office was not Hellenization. Both families were Hellenized to one degree or another. The elites of a city such as Jerusalem were quite comfortable with Greek ways. Before Alexander's conquest the Greeks had long been present in the Levant. The precipitating factor, then, was competition between three powerful families when the Sanballats (the family of the governor of Samaria) were thrown into the mix together with the Oniads and the Tobiads. Though these families intermarried among themselves, they were nevertheless bitter rivals.[15] Their rivalry dates to the third century BCE over tax farming rights.

A dispute arose between Simon (Tobiad) and the high priest Onias (Oniad).[16] Simon went to Seleucus IV to make his case. He accused Onias of conspiring with the Ptolemies. Subsequently, Onias went to Antioch to defend himself against Simon's charges. Before he got there, however, Antiochus IV had come to the throne. Onias's defense of himself proved unsuccessful with the new emperor. Jason, Onias's brother, took advantage of Onias's misfortune. He lobbied for himself the high priesthood, offering Antiochus IV a large sum of money and the promise of making Jerusalem into a Greek city equipped with a gymnasium and an *ephebeion* for Greek education.[17] Jason held the high priesthood for three years. Menelaus, a Tobiad, copied Jason in procuring the office of high priesthood illegitimately. Menelaus promised Antiochus IV an even higher sum of money. He was granted approval to remove Jason from the highest office and drive him from the city. Antiochus IV was impelled to accept Menelaus's offer, as he was perennially strapped for cash. From his perspective, it was merely a pecuniary decision. From Menelaus's perspective, it was a power play among rival families.[18]

Menelaus offered Antiochus IV an exorbitant amount of money, which he failed to pay. Antiochus IV summoned him to Antioch. While waiting for Antiochus IV, Menelaus allegedly instigated the murder of Onias III, the former high priest, who had divulged his unsavory machinations. While he was away from Jerusalem, Menelaus deputized his brother Lysimachus as high priest to attend to the affairs of the Temple and the city in his absence. It was rumored that he, Lysimachus, and their allies were plundering the Temple, selling off various golden vessels. A riot broke out. Lysimachus was killed. The council of leaders, the Gerousia, brought charges against Menelaus. He gained his acquittal from Antiochus IV through bribery. Menelaus's accusers were subsequently killed. While Menelaus was away from Jerusalem, Jason, the former high priest ousted by Menelaus, gathered about him an army of one thousand soldiers. A rumor had it that Antiochus IV was killed in Egypt in a battle against the Ptolemies. Based on the canard, Jason made his bid for the city. He entered the city with his army in 169 or 168 B.C.E. Civil war ensued. The Jerusalem populace's religious sensibilities had been offended because of the theft of the Temple vessels and the presence once again of Jason, the usurper. The religious issue that animated the people was the treatment of the office of high priesthood and the Temple and the wholesale theft of the sacred items of the Temple. Hellenization was not the animating cause per se.[19] Amid the chaos, Jason slaughtered his own people. Support for him waned. He fled the city. Various factions in the city kept Jerusalem in an uproar. This was the pretext that Antiochus IV needed to enter Jerusalem to abate the chaos. Antiochus IV entered the city to pacify it and gain a solid control over all of Judea.

In an age replete with violence, terror was a mechanism used by Hellenistic kings for control and domination. Terror was purposed to shatter any illusions that a subjugated people may entertain relative to their autonomy. It was meant to break their spirits, to make them into the walking dead. Antiochus IV's army killed forty thousand people. Forty thousand were sold into slavery. The objective of the terror was to remake the city in his own image and to so scare the people psychologically that they would think twice about fomenting future rebellion. Menelaus stood silent as Antiochus IV plundered the Temple. The theft served both a pecuniary purpose and an ideological one: to demonstrate to the subjugated people that their God was powerless to save them.

Antiochus IV issued an edict outlawing the practice of Judaism. This was unheard of in the ancient world. After the initial forty thousand were slaughtered, further public killings and torture ensued to bolster his ideological objectives. It was sanctioned torture by a political authority and the Jews were powerless. Antiochus IV compromised their sacred space at the Temple and their safe havens at home. He caused emotional chaos by disrupting the staid relationship between the cosmos, time, and human life.[20] The natural rhythms of the people in their social space were disrupted, keeping them on pins and needles. His sanctioned torture of the Jewish people was complete: outlawing Torah, circumcision, and the daily sacrifices at the Temple. The Temple was repurposed for the worship of Zeus, naming it in honor of the Olympian Zeus.

The edict, moreover, outlawed traditional practices; it also ordained new ones backed by the threat of death, like the compulsory monthly celebration of Antiochus IV's birthday. The celebration of festivals honoring Dionysius was also made compulsory. All privileges granted the Jewish people by Antiochus III as the space wherein to develop their identity and govern themselves according to ancestral laws were revoked. The Jews resisted. Key to the resistance movement was writing. This chaotic milieu also catalyzed the author of Daniel to write to encourage his circle of wise teachers to remain faithful to their God and their traditions that codified their people's engagement with their God over centuries. Writing is a powerful tool of expression. People look to leaders for strength in such trying moments. Resistance was as varied as the groups that resisted: some chose violent actions. The author of Daniel and his fellow *maskilim* chose faith and trust in God to deliver them, preferring the transcendent power of nonviolent engagement over the "little help" of violence. Establishing spiritual practices that open up spiritual possibilities of transformation is the course of action the author of Daniel and his fellow *maskilim* take. Those spiritual practices are contained in texts that are organized by the purgative, the illuminative and the unitive.

SPIRITUAL PRACTICES

The purgative texts that constitute the first phase of Daniel's *Seelsorge* are Daniel 1:18–21 (living kosher); Daniel 9:1–3; Daniel 10:1–5 (fasting); Daniel 2:17–23; and Daniel 9:4–19 (prayer). Living kosher, fasting, and prayer are the foundational elements of the purgative phase of spirituality, which empties one and readies one to receive what God may give in the illuminative phase of spiritual practice.

In Daniel 1:18–21, the author presents the protagonists and the antagonist, namely Daniel and his colleagues and the Babylonian king. New names have been imposed upon the Jewish youths to remind them of their new reality away from home. They are forced to live a hybrid existence, negotiating two cultures. While the chapter is about Daniel's hybrid existence in Babylon, it also narrates Daniel is not powerless in defining the contours and extent of that existence. Hybridity is a negotiated reality. His antagonist may cart his body away from home; ultimately, however, Daniel will not allow the king to have unilateral control over his body. This text reveals what informs Daniel's resistance. He wants to keep kosher. He will not defile his body through unkosher living. He chooses to eat those things that will not cause him to violate the kosher laws of his religion. The narrator is the primary voice throughout chapter one; the narrator introduces the various personages and gives emotional color especially to Daniel and his colleagues. The chief of the eunuchs speaks once and Daniel twice. The structure is snap and quick. It arrives quickly to the denouement, namely how to be faithful to ancient traditions and the consequence of such faithfulness is that God may reward such faithfulness either now or later in the resurrection in the case of those whose faithfulness leads them to be martyred. The faithfulness of Daniel and the faithfulness of God are mutually informing and empowering. Without this mutually interacting faithfulness at both ends of the divine/human spectrum why would one ever consider resisting? This chapter signals the theme of the book and displays in stark relief the theological organizing principle that unifies the whole work: the חֶסֶד (hesed) ("faithfulness") of both God and humans participating in a mutuality of faithfulness.

Daniel, moreover, is proffered as a holy man whose feats of faithfulness are meant to catalyze the audience to follow him in faithfulness. The legendary contours of the chapter are seen specifically in Daniel refusing to eat of the king's portion, the king's food. Like the legendary lives of the saints from the Christian, medieval era, the story of Daniel standing in defiance and resisting is meant to elicit a response of wonder in the audience. This is the purpose of legend. Historic figures are made bigger than life to inspire a response of faithfulness in the hearers of their feats.

The historical setting for Daniel 1:8–21 is the years 169 to 164 BCE, when Antiochus IV entered Jerusalem to terrorize it into submission after the rioting fomented by the abuse of the high priesthood and the robbing of the Temple of its treasured items. Those events precipitated a crisis of identity, a crisis of survival as a people, as what was essential to their identity was compromised. Their existence was at stake. Daniel choosing to be faithful and follow the kosher laws of his people would have spoken to many in the second century facing the same challenge to be faithful, even faithful unto death. Loyalty and faithfulness to food laws and other traditions had become a matter of life and death in mid-second century BCE.[21] Given that Daniel's audience finds itself in a life-and-death situation, they choose to demonstrate fidelity to God by observing their laws and traditions, the source of their identity as a people. Daniel 1:8–21 intends to resist. One sees what resistance in Daniel's context looks like. It is commitment to one's traditions; yet, it is also excellence in the public square controlled by empire. Daniel engages in the knowledge and benefits of imperial civilization; yet, he uses the tools of such knowledge to cast another vision of God as the imperial one. In Daniel, the conceptual language of empire is applied to God. God is the sovereign one, the imperial one, who is active in chaos not only to structure it but also to use it to break up some things in the established order to reconstitute that order. Daniel is faithful to this God alone. Antiochus IV is not God.

Daniel 9:1–3 and Daniel 10:1–5 are fasting texts. Daniel uses fasting for two different reasons. In Daniel 9:1–3, fasting serves as a cleansing from sin, coupled with an honest confession of both individual and corporate sin. After fasting, the angel Gabriel appears to him to give him enlightenment. In Daniel 10:1–5, Daniel also fasts in order to get enlightenment. In both cases, what occasions the fasts is Daniel's troubled spirit. It is eased only after the fast that yields a communication from God.

In Daniel 10:1–5, furthermore, something in Daniel's reading of the prophet Jeremiah disturbed him. He is impelled to pray with intensity. The intensity is borne out by how he prayed: he prayed with fasting, sackcloth and ashes, the traditional expressions in the Hebrew Bible for mourning, penitence, and importunity of prayer. Jacob tore his clothes and donned sackcloth upon hearing of the death of Joseph, his favorite son. When the child born to Bathsheba hovered on the precipice of life and death, David prayed, buttressing his prayer with fasting. And the prophet Joel called on his audience to repent with fasting and weeping. This example of fasting in Daniel is catalyzed by emotional distress. Perhaps there is emotional distress over the validity of the word of God to Jeremiah. He did not understand it. He needed a revelation. As the word of God had become his people's anchor in the absence of the Temple, it must be trustworthy. In the background of Daniel in Babylonian captivity is the second century author for whom the trustworthiness of scriptures is a major issue, especially amid crises involving the Temple, the center of their communal life. Since the destruction of Solomon's Temple, the Jewish people had begun to live without the Temple in exile. Ezekiel harkened to the substantial Temple in heaven, to which they had access outside Jerusalem. Though the Temple was important to them, the Jewish people were evolving their religion beyond it. The inhabitants at Qumran were in the process of doing that. The anthropological factor embedded in the structural analysis of the text is whether scriptures can be trusted. The stress over that issue drives Daniel to fast.

What disturbs Daniel in the aftermath of the completion of Jeremiah's prophecy is that there is not a word for the present. Have the voices of the prophets gone silent? God speaks in a new way. To hear God's voice anew one must prepare oneself through a spiritual infrastructure that includes fasting. Fasting is necessary for the emptying of oneself to be filled by God with revelation, illumination, and enlightenment. Daniel fasts; God reveals. The prophets practiced purgation; the prophets fasted. In 1 Kings 19, the prophet Elijah flees Jezebel after embarrassing her prophets of Baal in a contest of miracles. The prophets of Baal failed; God heard Elijah and answered his prayer on Mount Carmel. Jezebel vowed to murder Elijah; so, he fled. After fleeing, he got so depressed that he wanted to die. He asked God to take his life. God comforted him by feeding him. He got up. And, on the strength of that feeding, he fasted forty days as he took a spiritual journey to Mount Horeb. The spiritual practices of the prophets and the consequences of those practices in illumination, revelation, and empowerment were available to the author of Daniel and his circle of *maskilim*. God still speaks; God speaks to the mystic, at least to the person who readies herself or himself through fasting.

There is a place where the abusers of power cannot tread: it is the heart. A heart informed by the liberating power of God through an exposure to one's transcendent self leaps over the quotidian aspects of one's self. Transcendence does not mean flight from reality, but the freedom to engage reality with a fuller version of oneself. The most mundane things about oneself can occasion resistance, from singing to the clothes one wears and the food one eats or refuses to eat. Choosing not to eat, to fast, is a powerful weapon of resistance. It is a most fundamental exertion of one's volitional capability over one's own life. Through a fast Mahatma Gandhi resisted the British *Raj*, protesting the diminution of Indian political power through the separation of the Indian people into voting castes. While seated in the Birmingham jail, Dr. Martin Luther King Jr. fasted to get the world's attention; he especially fasted to demonstrate to his racist jailers they did not have ultimate power over what he did with his body. Fasting is resistance. Fasting says that one owns oneself. Fasting limits the reach and scope of imperial hubris, for through fasting the mystic and religionist alike engages his/her body in such a way to assert their power of self-determination. They also open themselves up to possibilities of hearing from God through visions, epiphanies, and illumination. Fasting appears to focus the practitioner to pay attention to voices other than the ones that scream limitless consumption.

Daniel 2:17–23 and Daniel 9:4–19 are two prominent prayer texts in the book of Daniel. Prayer is a purgative element because it puts people in separated, consecrated, physical space and gives them the disposition to receive illumination and guidance from God. Daniel faced Jerusalem, got on his knees, and prayed to God with praise and thanksgiving as he was wont to do every day, three times a day according to Daniel 6:10. In these texts we hear the content of Daniel's prayer. Also, these prayers readied Daniel to receive illumination about certain exigent circumstances. The author goes out of his way to tie Daniel's spiritual practice to a response from God. Prayer is not a quid pro quo, however. Like living kosher, prayer is a daily feature of the mystic's life.

Daniel 2:17–23 is a doxological prayer that occurs in the overall context of Nebuchadnezzar's dream which disturbed him and his whole court. A stringent test is proposed to the sages; they had to repeat the dream to the king and interpret it. It is an exacting standard that no sage can meet, unless that sage were illuminated by God. After hearing from Arioch, the king's captain, and the peril in which he and the sages faced, Daniel returns home. Daniel is confident. He moves with alacrity. He proposes that he and his companions pray. Consequently, illumination comes on the heels of prayer: not only is the actual dream revealed to Daniel, he also receives the interpretation. The author is inculcating the importance of prayer, the importance of remaining faithful to one's spiritual practices. Such spiritual practices are the power not only to resist; they are also the way to enlightenment. With such enlightenment, one can reconfigure one's identity and especially cleanse one's psyche from the repressive script of the oppressor.

The prayer establishes the sovereignty of God. God is sovereign to reward those who are faithful to their traditions. Daniel outpaces the Babylonian sages not through some inherent quality in himself; he does so because he is faithful to God. He opens himself up to God through his practice. Both Daniel and God show ḥesed.

The prayer in Daniel 9:4–19 is darker than the previous triumphant prayer. The spiritual preparation through fasting has occasioned an honest assessment of Daniel and his people. Spiritual experiences are not all saccharine sweet. There are dark nights of the soul when God seems distant, where the believer focuses on his/her private failings and the corporate failings of humanity. It is appropriate to balance the earlier prayer of thanksgiving with a darker prayer of repentance. At the end of this prayer there will be illumination like the earlier prayer. Illumination can occur when one approaches life with alacrity and joy; or, it can occur when there is melancholy over the past, for it is grounded in the sovereignty of God who gives such illumination at God's behest.

The prayer has affinity with Deuteronomistic theology and with other prayers, speech patterns, and other perspectives informed by the Deuteronomist.[22] It is a liturgical prayer from the era when Deuteronomistic ideas were current. It is the production of piety, as no responsibility is placed on God for the fate of the Jewish people losing their resources to empire. Deuteronomistic piety goes out of its way to protect God. Hence, all the blame is placed on God's covenanted people to remain faithful to the *Berit Olam*, the eternal covenant.

Though at the center of Daniel 9 is a prayer that is a traditionally Deuteronomistic, liturgical prayer that was current in the Second Temple era, it nevertheless is an intentional production of the author of Daniel. It is one of the traditional pieces, together with other cultural elements, that he uses to forge an identity in defiance of a political power that dehumanizes them. Subalterns seek to hold onto their traditions in the face of imperial encroachment onto their psyches. Though the Deuteronomistic prayer is monological, it ultimately gets counterbalanced subsequently by the apocalyptic genre. This traditional prayer and the apocalyptic genre will stand in a contrapuntal relationship with each other. The author of Daniel creates a polyphony of hybridity among his monological traditions, allowing other voices to speak. The Deuteronomist faults the people for the loss of their land, culture, and identity. Apocalyptic, however, will posit that the loss must be placed in a bigger, cosmic horizon, where God is sovereign over all possibilities for all people. God controls the sea of possibilities, be those possibilities good, bad, or ugly. A persecuted people want a big God, a sovereign God. Though

Daniel has a big God to contextualize the exigencies of his life, he nevertheless takes seriously his mutually interdependent relationship with God. *Ḥesed* on the part of both Daniel and God catalyzes that mutually interdependent relationship, where Daniel's spiritual infrastructure is reciprocated by God in illumination, epiphany, and revelation. Without that reciprocity, one would not do the hard work of purgation. God may not take Daniel and his people out of their existential crisis; God certainly empowers them to transcend it.

The illuminative text is Daniel 7:1–14. This text constitutes the second phase of Daniel's spiritual infrastructure. Though Daniel received illumination in earlier contexts after purgative activity in the form of kosher living, fasting, and prayer, Daniel 7:1–14 stands out as a special illumination, as it forms the centerpiece of the Book of Daniel. This text also initiates the apocalyptic section of Daniel's work. Chapter 7, then, forms an *inclusio* with chapter 2 in presenting the four empires and closing out the Aramaic section of the work. Though chapter 7 is in Aramaic like the stories, yet its content is apocalyptic like the succeeding five Hebrew chapters. Daniel 7 shares the apocalyptic genre with these five chapters, but not their language. This has left interpreters baffled, as they have sought various explanations on the diachronic level. From a postcolonial perspective, which privileges the synchronic level, the different languages are merely a function of hybridity. It is also a function of mimicry. Satire is a survival mechanism of the subalterns. The stories are loaded with satire and occasionally persecuted Jews to belittle the hubris of empire in their lived spaces away from the gaze of empire. Daniel performs the satire in the language of empire, Aramaic. In the opening verses of the text the narrator establishes the putative historical context. Then Daniel takes over, describing what he saw in his vision that is illuminative: the curtain is pulled back on empire. Empire shall be judged. Human hubris is not forever. This will be of great comfort to his audience. In their lived space, they laugh and cry, but they also hear from a sovereign God who controls history. Nothing is left to chance. There is a divine logic to the empires emerging from the chaotic sea. History is not left to its own devises. God is in control.

There is, moreover, an ideology that Daniel proffers to bolster the faithfulness of the Jews undergoing persecution during the state terror of Antiochus IV. Nebuchadnezzar's prayers in Daniel 4:34 sound like those of a pious Jew.[23] In coming out of his insanity, Nebuchadnezzar is described as having become monotheistic. This is a function of midrashism, which comports with the overall theme of the book to bolster faith in the persecuted Jews that their monotheistic religion, which is foundational to their culture, is superior to any form of polytheism, especially that of the Greeks.[24] Daniel, the hero of the Babylonian court, survived a situation comparable to what the Jews amid Antiochus IV's terror faced. He did it with the unswerving commitment to a superior *Weltanschauung* that preserved him in his trying circumstances. The people undergoing religious persecution under Antiochus IV would preserve themselves in the same way; yet, a commitment to such a worldview may lead some of them to be martyred for their faith. The first six chapters of Daniel, then, are not history, but midrashic stories to inspire a suppressed and colonized people. Bereft of their bodies and material well-being, all they have is their minds, which they will not surrender, because they are the *locus* of an edifying experience of God if they are faithful. Both sections of the work, namely the midrashic chapters 1–6 and the apocalyptic section, chapters 7–12, serve this purpose of bolstering the faith of the persecuted. One section inspires through midrashic stories and the other through an apocalyptic theology that broadens and deepens their idea of God through an overwhelming transcendentalism, dualism, and a mystical core, an experience of God that is for the colonized a *sanctum sanctorum* where the colonizers cannot tread. This mystical core is a resistant core. It empowers various forms of resistance and gives them courage in the face of death.

The four beasts that emerge from the sea have a hybrid nature. The first beast represents the Babylonian Empire; the second, the Median Empire; the third, the Persian Empire; and, the fourth, the Hellenistic Empire of Antiochus IV. They emerge out of the sea, which represents chaos. The battle between God and chaos is a long-standing one in the history of ideas and Canaanite mythology. In the Hebrew Bible the motif of God creating order out of chaos can be found in Job 26:12–13 and Psalm 89:9–11 and 74:1–17. According to John Collins, in ancient mythology creation is the imposition of order onto chaos. The four beasts emerge out of chaos. They wreak chaos. Empires tagged as animals are the source of chaos in the world, which God alone can overcome. The victory over chaos is seen in the one like the son of Adam riding on the clouds. He comes as an emissary of peace and contradicts the chaos brought on the world by empires. Daniel offers a nonviolent vision of how to deal with the chaotic times in which he and the *maskilim* live.

The motif of the four kingdoms figured in the four beasts as four successive empires is also taken over from the political propaganda of the Hellenistic world. The motif also has elements from biblical imagery, especially Hosea 13, where God brings judgment on Israel through unholy and unkosher animals (nations), namely a lion, bear, and leopard.

Moreover, Daniel's way of describing God also has an old tradition behind it, namely the Canaanite God El and Ezekiel's vision of God on the throne. Daniel is indebted to the past in the construction of his genre of apocalypticism. Yet, he adds something new. In the hybrid experience, it is not enough to reclaim the past. There is also the comparable movement to forge a new identity, to say something new about oneself given the new input from the colonizer. Daniel forges something new that will function as resistance literature against the Temple establishment and offer another trajectory in which the religion may develop. The new element the apocalypticists add to their reflection is ascent into the presence of God. This theological move polemicizes the troubled situation at the Jerusalem temple.²⁵

Daniel has a vision in the throne room of God wherein he sees the succession of empires and the ultimate demise of the fourth unnamed kingdom that is comprised of ten horns and a little one, namely Antiochus IV. Daniel does not enter the holy environs of the Temple to receive this vision. He receives it on his couch after much preparation of his body, soul, and mind as mystics are wont to do. Daniel invites his faithful followers to envision life without the Temple. God's presence is no longer there in that place. Instead, one is invited by God to observe the mysteries unfold from a heavenly perspective. The priests at Jerusalem no longer control the mysteries. They have been colonized. The mysteries are available to the ones who prepare themselves. Daniel's ascent to heaven and his living to return to tell it constitute a mystical experience, an illumination. Mysticism is a most slippery word on which to get a handle. It means many things to many people and cultures when it is understood broadly. For the apocalypticists, it is a deep study of texts and religious experience. Jewish mysticism that evolves from apocalypticism, then, is kataphatic; i.e., it is informed by images and words. Daniel the apocalypticist carves out a spiritual space where he can escape the frights of the socio-political terror foisted on the Jews in the second century BCE.

Daniel's final spiritual infrastructure is the unitive. The texts that deal with the unitive are: Daniel 11:32–35 and Daniel 12:1–4. The mystic and religionist unify with the object of their affection, desire, and longing: God. Light emanates from God. Daniel prays in Daniel 2:22c הְמֵּע [אְ][רוֹהְגְ][וּ] אֲרִיְהְגוּ אְרְשׁ "The light emanates from God." God is the source of Light and Light emanates from God and joins itself to people who seek it in a disciplined infrastructure of spirituality. The Light illumines intelligence and gives wisdom, so that Daniel and the *maskilim* become the true sages, understanding the political and social exigencies of their tragic day. Unity with the Light occurs in this life when the sage uses it as a source of clairvoyance into the mysteries of darkness propagated by empire. There is, however, always a risk of undergoing suffering when engaging the dark powers of empire. Hence, the sages are suffering servants. In their role of making people understand, they suffer. Daniel's allusion to Isaiah's suffering servant is without question. Yet, the suffering of the *maskilim* refines them, makes them white, conforms them to the Light, making them white like the Light. The Light, moreover, is the source of union with those who rise and shine like the brightness through martyrdom. They have been unified with the Light. Their martyrdom has not cut them off from God, who is Light, active amid the darkness, hidden in the darkness as light. They are resurrected into the Light. Unity with the Light, then, occurs both in this life and the next life, where resurrection occurs.

This text reveals the fate of the *maskilim* as emissaries of Light. The angel reveals the fate of those who face the darkness of corporate evil concentrated in empire. As in Daniel's time, those who teach and lead people in this present darkness are persecuted; they are martyred. Their only comfort in the process of performing their office of instruction to which they are called is that God knows darkness and God is active in the darkness disseminating light. Empire, then, is not beyond the sovereign light that is God. The angel brings light to a troubled situation.

The task of enlightening the masses may bring suffering and persecution. The *maskilim* underwent suffering and some were martyred for teaching their people to understand the hidden realities of imperial, colonial darkness. Through such teaching, the suffering servants, the *maskilim* empowered their people to prosper. All those who dare to speak against power get persecuted in some way. Enduring persecution to the point of death is proof that the political resister is animated by transcendent values for which they are willing to die. Death is the clarion call of authenticity. Enduring transformations of societies are built on the blood of the martyrs. Enlightened teaching catalyzes enduring prosperity among a people through knowledge, no matter the source. All knowledge can be repurposed for a suppressed people's milieu to catalyze prosperity. Teachers cause people to prosper through understanding. *Maskilim* derives from לכש, meaning to "to look at, to prosper, to teach." Isaiah 52:13 says, יַשְׂכִּיל עַבְדִּי הִנֵּה "Behold, my servant prospers"; "Behold, my servant teaches." Prosperity is closely tied to teaching. The *maskilim*, imitating Isaiah's suffering servant, make their people prosper through enlightened teaching. There is a risk in empowering and enlightening people: darkness reacts violently. Yet, God as Light knows darkness. Darkness cannot comprehend the Light, though emissaries of the Light get martyred.

CONCLUSION

Those who resist, those who tell the truth to power, must care for their souls. The book of Daniel proffers a viable *Seelsorge* that those who resist can follow. To the extent they do, they will keep their minds free of the degrading images of abusive power and so prepare themselves for the new thing God is about to do. For those who practice an empowering *Seelsorge* such as one finds in Daniel, no dream is absolutized; no political strategy is universalized. One does not attach oneself to human endeavors; one attaches oneself to God. Such attachment does not occasion one to ignore the world in pious flights of fancy. The Daniel figure looms large as one who is competent in all manner of science, religion, and spirituality. Adherence to pure doctrine should not ever mean ignoring the world and not siding with those who are hurt by the universalizing script of empire or neo-empire.

I shall never forget how my childhood Lutheran church reacted to the assassination of Dr. Martin Luther King Jr. There was no reaction to that seminal event. There was no mention of what had happened the previous Friday, April 4, 1968. Within the confines of the four walls of the church that housed a predominantly white congregation, it was as though that event had never happened. It was another world, a strange feeling given the harsh reality of April 4, 1968. There was no announcement of the death of King. There were no prayers on behalf of the nation. There were no prayers on behalf of King's family; not a word of comfort to some of us suffering from such a great loss. It was rather ironic that though King had expended so much energy trying to articulate a vision that all Americans shared, he was still in the end perceived as the black people's leader. Humans profoundly disappoint: another reason to practice a *Seelsorge* that affirms your humanity.

Recently, I was at a pastors' conference. Another pastor offered to us present the opportunity of doing ministry in China, all expenses paid. He noted that the Chinese government preferred Lutherans to other Christian denominations. A red flag went up in the back of my head. The number of historical examples is legendary where our doctrine of two kingdoms had made us quietistic about injustice and silent about the suppression and repression of others right under our collective nose. I suspect the two-kingdom doctrine is what caused my pastor to ignore the assassination of Dr. Martin Luther King Jr. on the Sunday after April 4, 1968. I suspect he was not an aberration throughout my Lutheran denomination. Of course, the Chinese would welcome Lutherans. Lutherans stifle their living, prophetic voice with pure doctrine. Human disappointments, accordingly, occasion one to forge a liberating *Seelsorge*. Even if every human is unfaithful, God is faithful in love. If you are doing the work of resistance, then you must foster a spiritual infrastructure where you rest in the love of God.

NOTES

1. Ralph David Abernathy, *And the Walls Came Tumbling Down: An Autobiography* (New York: Harper & Row, 1989).

2. Ahmad Bouyerdene, *Emir Abd el-Kader: Hero and Saint of Islam*, trans. and intro. Gustavo Polit (Bloomington, IN: World Wisdom, 2012), 76.

3. Anathea E. Portier-Young, *Apocalypse Against Empire: Theologies of Resistance in Early Judaism* (Grand Rapids, MI: Eerdmans, 2011), 50. At this point in the essay, I am dependent on Portier-Young's excellent treatment of the historical factors leading to the revolt against Antiochus IV.

4. Portier-Young, *Apocalypse Against Empire*, 51.
5. Portier-Young, *Apocalypse Against Empire*, 55.
6. Portier-Young, *Apocalypse Against Empire*, 73.
7. Portier-Young, *Apocalypse Against Empire*, 74.
8. Portier-Young, *Apocalypse Against Empire*, 74
9. Portier-Young, *Apocalypse Against Empire*, 77.
10. Portier-Young, *Apocalypse Against Empire*, 77.
11. Portier-Young, *Apocalypse Against Empire*, 77.
12. Portier-Young, *Apocalypse Against Empire*, 77.
13. Lester L. Grabbe and Gabriele Boccaccini, with Jason M. Zurawsky (eds.), *The Seleucid and Hasmonean Periods and the Apocalyptic Worldview* (London: Bloomsbury T&T Clark, 2016), 21.
14. Victor Tcherikover, *Hellenistic Civilization and the Jews* (Peabody, MA: Hendrickson Publishers, 1999), 154.
15. Carol A. Newsom, with Brennan W. Breed, *Daniel: A Commentary*, The Old Testament Library (Louisville, KY: Westminster John Knox Press, 2014), 24.
16. Grabbe et al. (eds.), *Seleucid and Hasmonean Periods*, 21.
17. Grabbe et al. (eds.), *Seleucid and Hasmonean Periods*, 21.
18. Grabbe et al. (eds.), *Seleucid and Hasmonean Periods*, 23.
19. Grabbe et al. (eds.), *Seleucid and Hasmonean Periods*, 24.
20. Portier-Young, *Apocalypse Against Empire*, 182.
21. Norman W. Porteous, *Daniel*, The Old Testament Library (Philadelphia, PA: Westminster Press, 1965), 29.
22. Otto Plöger, *Das Buch Daniel*, Kommentar zum Alten Testament 18 (Gütersloh: Gütersloher Verlaghaus Gerd Mohn, 1965), 9.
23. Louis F. Hartman and Alexander A. Di Lella, O.F.M., *The Book of Daniel*, The Anchor Yale Bible Commentaries (New York: Doubleday, 1978), 51.
24. Hartman and Di Lella, *The Book of Daniel*, 53.
25. Ithamar Gruenwald, *From Apocalypticism to Gnosticism: Studies in Apocalypticism, Merkavah Mysticism and Gnosticism*, Beiträge zur Erforschung des Alten Testaments und des Antiken Judentums (Frankfurt a. M.: Peter Lang, 1988), 129.

Select Bibliography

Abernathy, Ralph David. *And the Walls Came Tumbling Down: An Autobiography*. New York: Harper & Row, 1989.

Adkins, Brent and Paul R. Hinlicky. *Rethinking Philosophy and Theology with Deleuze: A New Cartography*. London and New York: Bloomsbury Academic, 2013.

Agamben, Giorgio. *Homo Sacer: Sovereign Power and Bare Life*. Translated by D. Heller-Roazen. Stanford, CA: Stanford University Press, 1998.

Alexander, Michelle. *The New Jim Crow: Mass Incarceration in the Age of Colorblindness*. New York: The New Press, 2010.

Anderson, Pamela Sue. "Feminist theology as philosophy of religion." In *The Cambridge Companion to Feminist Theology*, edited by Susan Frank Parsons, 40–59. Cambridge: Cambridge University Press, 2002.

Arendt, Hannah. *Eichmann in Jerusalem: A Report on the Banality of Evil*. Revised and Enlarged Edition. London: Penguin Books, 1994.

Aristotle. *On the Soul*. Translated by W. S. Hett. Cambridge, MA: Harvard University Press, 1995.

———. *On Memory*. Translated by Richard Sorabji. Chicago: The University of Chicago Press, 2004.

Badiou, Alain. *Saint Paul: The Foundation of Universalism*. Translated by Ray Brassier. Redwood City, CA: Stanford University Press, 2003.

Barger, Lilian Calles. *The World Come of Age: An Intellectual History of Liberation Theology*. New York: Oxford University Press, 2018.

Barnett, Victoria. *For the Soul of the People: Protestant Protest Against Hitler*. New York: Oxford University Press, 1992.

Benne, Robert. "The Two Fold Rule of God." *Journal of Lutheran Ethics* 2, no. 8 (Aug. 1, 2002). Online at https://www.elca.org/JLE/Articles/936.

Bloomquist, Karen L. "Transforming Domination Then and Now." In *Lutheran Identity and Political Theology*, edited by Carl-Henric Grenholm and Göran

Gunnar, 208–22. Church of Sweden Research Series 9. Eugene, OR: Pickwick, 2014.

Bonhoeffer, Dietrich. *Life Together/Prayerbook of the Bible*. Edited by Geffrey B. Kelly. Translated by Daniel W. Bloesch and James H. Burtness. Dietrich Bonhoeffer Works 5. Minneapolis, MN: Augsburg Fortress, 1996.

———. *Sanctorum Communio: A Theological Study of the Sociology of the Church*. Edited by Clifford J. Green. Translated by Reinhard Krauss and Nancy Lukens. Dietrich Bonhoeffer Works 1. Minneapolis, MN: Augsburg Fortress, 1998.

———. *Discipleship*. Edited by Gefferey B. Kelly and John D. Godsey. Translated by Barbara Green and Reinhard Krauss. Dietrich Bonhoeffer Works 4. Minneapolis, MN: Augsburg Fortress, 2001.

———. *Ethics*. Edited by Clifford J. Green. Translated by Reinhard Krauss, Charles C. West, and Douglas W. Stott. Dietrich Bonhoeffer Works 6. Minneapolis, MN: Augsburg Fortress, 2005.

———."Lectures on Christology." In *Berlin: 1932-1933*, edited by Larry L. Rasmussen, 299–360. Translated by Isabel Best and David Higgins. Dietrich Bonhoeffer Works 12. Minneapolis, MN: Augsburg Fortress, 2009.

———. *Letters and Papers from Prison*. Edited by John W. DeGruchy. Translated by Isabel Best, Lisa E. Dahill, Reinhard Krauss, and Nancy Lukens. Dietrich Bonhoeffer Works 8. Minneapolis, MN: Augsburg Fortress, 2009.

The Book of Concord: The Confessions of the Evangelical Lutheran Church. Edited by Robert Kolb and Timothy. J. Wengert. Minneapolis, MN: Fortress Press, 2000. Also: Edited by Theodore G. Tappert. Philadelphia, PA: Fortress Press, 1959.

Bouyerdene, Ahmad. *Emir Abd el-Kader: Hero and Saint of Islam*. Translated and Introduction by Gustavo Polit. Bloomington, IN: World Wisdom, 2012.

Boyarin, Daniel. *A Radical Jew: Paul and the Politics of Identity*. Oakland, CA: University of California Press, 1997.

Brown, Wendy. *Undoing the Demos: Neoliberalism's Stealth Revolution*. New York: Zone, 2015.

Caputo, John D. *Cross and Cosmos: A Theology of Difficult Glory*. Bloomington, IN: Indiana University Press, 2019.

Charleston, Steven. "The Old Testament of Native America." In *Native and Christian: Indigenous Voices on Religious Identity in the United States and Canada*, edited by James Treat, 68–80. New York/London: Routledge, 1996.

Christ, Carol P. and Judith Plaskow, *Goddess and God in the World: Conversations in Embodied Theology*. Minneapolis, MN: Fortress Press, 2016.

"CITY OF SHERRILL V. ONEIDA INDIAN NATION OF N. Y. (03-855) 544 U.S. 197 (2005) 337 F.3d 139, reversed and remanded." Legal Information Institute. Online at https://www.law.cornell.edu/supct/html/03-855.ZO.html (accessed September 26, 2019).

Cochrane, Arthur C. *The Church's Confession Under Hitler*. Edited by Dikran Y. Hadidian. Pittsburgh Reprint Series 4. Pittsburgh. PA: Pickwick Press, 1976.

Connolly, William E. *Capitalism and Christianity, American Style*. Durham, NC: Duke University Press, 2008.

Cornell, Deirdre. *Jesus was a Migrant*. Maryknoll, NY: Orbis Books, 2014.

Cousar, Charles B. *Galatians, Interpretation: A Bible Commentary for Teaching and Preaching*. Louisville, KY: Westminster John Knox, 2012.

Cruz, Gemma Tulud. *Toward a Theology of Migration: Social Justice and Religious Experience*. New York: Palgrave Macmillan, 2014.

Daschuck, James. *Clearing the Plains: Disease, Politics of Starvation, and the Loss of Aboriginal Life*. Regina, Sask.: University of Regina Press, 2014.

Duncan, Lenny. *Dear Church: A Love Letter from a Black Preacher to the Whitest Denomination in the U.S.* Minneapolis, MN: Augsburg Books, 2019.

Elert, Werner. *The Structure of Lutheranism: The Theology and Philosophy of Life of Lutheranism Especially in the Sixteenth and Seventeenth Centuries*. Translated by Walter A. Hanson. Concordia Classics. Saint Louis, MO: Concordia, 1962.

Ericksen, Robert P. *Theologians Under Hitler*. New Haven, CT: Yale University Press, 1985.

Everist, Norma Cook and Craig L. Nessan. *Transforming Leadership: New Vision for a Church in Mission*. Minneapolis, MN: Augsburg Fortress, 2008.

Failinger, Marie A. and Ronald W. Duty. *Lutheran Theology and Secular Law: The Work of the Modern State*. New York: Routledge, 2018.

Farley, Wendy. *Eros for the Other: Retaining Truth in a Pluralistic World*. University Park, PA: Pennsylvania State University Press, 1996.

———. *Gathering Those Driven Away: A Theology of Incarnation*. Louisville, KY: Westminster John Knox Press, 2011.

Ferreira, M. Jaime. *Love's Grateful Striving: A Commentary on Kierkegaard's Works of Love*. Oxford: Oxford University Press, 2001.

Foster, Charles R., Lisa E. Dahill, Lawrence A. Golemon, and Barbara Wang Tolentino. *Educating Clergy: Teaching Practices and Pastoral Imagination*. Stanford, CA: The Carnegie Foundation for the Advancement of Teaching, 2006.

Frankfurt, Harry. *On Bullshit*. Online at http://www2.csudh.edu/ccauthen/576f12/frankfurt__harry_-_on_bullshit.pdf.

González, Justo L. *The History of Theological Education*. Nashville, TN: Abingdon Press, 2015.

Goodman, Ronald. *Lakota Star Knowledge: Studies in Lakota Stellar Theology*. Edited by Alan Seeger. Third Edition. Mission, SD: SGU Publishing, 2017.

Gorski, Philip. *American Covenant: A History of Civil Religion from the Puritans to the Present*. Princeton, NJ: Princeton University Press, 2017.

Grabbe, Lester L. and Gabriele Boccaccini, with Jason M. Zurawsky, eds. *The Seleucid and Hasmonean Periods and the Apocalyptic Worldview*. London: Bloomsbury T&T Clark, 2016.

Gruenwald, Ithamar. *From Apocalypticism to Gnosticism: Studies in Apocalypticism, Merkavah Mysticism and Gnosticism*. Beiträge zur Erforschung des Alten Testaments und des Antiken Judentums. Frankfurt a. M.: Peter Lang, 1988.

Hall, Douglas John. *Lighten Our Darkness: Toward an Indigenous Theology of the Cross*. Philadelphia, PA: Westminster Press, 1976.

———. *Has the Church a Future?* Philadelphia, PA: Westminster Press, 1980.

———. *Thinking the Faith: Christian Theology in a North American Context*. Minneapolis, MN: Augsburg, 1989.

———. "Responses to the Humiliation of the Church." The William Porcher DuBose Lectures (Oct. 21–22, 1992). *Sewanee Theological Review* 36, no. 4 (1993): 472–81.

———. "Metamorphosis: From Christendom to Diaspora," In *Confident Witness-Changing World: Rediscovering the Gospel in North America*, edited by Craig Van Gelder, 67–79. Grand Rapids, MI: Eerdmans, 1999.

———. *Confessing the Faith: Christian Theology in a North American Context.* Minneapolis, MN: Augsburg Fortress Press, 1996.

———. *The End of Christendom and the Future of Christianity.* Christian Mission and Modern Culture Series. Valley Forge, PA: Trinity Press International, 1997; reprint: Eugene, OR: Wipf & Stock, 2002.

Hartman, Louis F. and Alexander A. Di Lella, O.F.M. *The Book of Daniel*, The Anchor Yale Bible Commentaries. New York: Doubleday, 1978.

Harvey, Jennifer. *Dear White Christians: For Those Still Longing for Racial Reconciliation.* Grand Rapids, MI: Eerdmans, 2014.

Havel, Václav. *Living in Truth.* Edited by Jan Vladislav. London and Boston: Faber and Faber, 1990.

Heidegger, Martin. *Being and Time.* Translated by John Macquarrie and Edward Robinson. San Francisco, CA: Harper and Row, 1962.

Helmer, Christine. *Theology and the End of Doctrine.* Louisville, KY: Westminster John Knox Press, 2014.

———. *How Luther Became the Reformer.* Louisville, KY: Westminster John Knox Press, 2019.

———, ed. *The Medieval Luther.* Spätmittelalter, Humanismus, Reformation 117. Tübingen: Mohr Siebeck, 2020.

Henriksen, Jan-Olav. *Christianity as Distinct Practices: A Complicated Relationship.* New York: T&T Clark, 2019.

Heschel, Susannah. *The Aryan Jesus: Christian Theologians and the Bible in Nazi Germany.* Princeton, NJ: Princeton University Press, 2008.

Hinlicky, Paul R. *Paths Not Taken: Fates of Theology from Luther through Leibniz.* Grand Rapids, MI: Eerdmans, 2009.

———. *Before Auschwitz: What Christian Theology Must Learn from the Rise of Nazism.* Eugene, OR: Cascade, 2013.

———. "Augustine, Luther and the Critique of the Sovereign Self." In *On the Apocalyptic and Human Agency: Conversations with Augustine of Hippo and Martin Luther*, edited by Kirsi Stjerna and Deanna A. Thompson, 81–92. Newcastle upon Tyne, UK: Cambridge Scholars, 2014.

———. *Beloved Community: Critical Dogmatics after Christendom.* Grand Rapids, MI: Eerdmans, 2015.

———. "Luther in Marx." In *Oxford Encyclopedia of Martin Luther.* 3 Volumes. Edited by Derek R. Nelson and Paul R. Hinlicky. New York: Oxford University Press, 2017. Volume 2: 322–41.

Horsley, Richard A. and Neil Asher Silberman. *The Message and the Kingdom: How Jesus and Paul Ignited a Revolution and Transformed the Ancient World.* Minneapolis, MN: Fortress Press, 2002.

Jorgenson, Allen G. "Empire, Eschatology and Stolen Land." *Dialogue: A Journal of Theology* 49, no. 2 (Summer 2010): 115–122.

Kant, Immanuel. "The Conflict of the Faculties." In *Religion and Rational Theology*, translated by Allen W. Wood and George Di Giovanni, 233–328. Cambridge: Cambridge University Press, 2001.

Kearney, Richard. "The Wager of Carnal Hermeneutics." In *Carnal Hermeneutics*, Edited by Richard Kearney and Brian Treanor. New York: Fordham University Press, 2015.

Keller, Catherine. *Political Theology of the Earth: Our Planetary Emergency and the Struggle for a New Public*. New York: Columbia University Press, 2018.

Kühne, Thomas. *The Rise and Fall of Comradeship: Hitler's Soldiers. Male Bonding and Mass Violence in the Twentieth Century.* Cambridge: Cambridge University Press, 2017.

Lazareth, William. "Luther's 'Two Kingdom' Ethic Reconsidered." In *Marburg Revisited: A Re-examination of Lutheran and Reformed Traditions*, edited by Paul C. Empie and James I. McCord, 165–76. Minneapolis, MN: Augsburg Publishing House, 1966.

———. "Political Responsibility as the Obedience of Faith." In *The Gospel and Human Destiny*, edited by Vilmos Vajta, 218–70. Minneapolis, MN: Augsburg Publishing House, 1971.

Lindbeck, George A. "Atonement and the Hermeneutics of Social Embodiment." *Pro Ecclesia* 5, no. 2 (1996): 144–60.

Luther, Martin. *D. Martin Luthers Werke, Kritische Gesamtausgabe*, 73 Volumes. Edited by J. K. F. Knaake et al. Weimar: Böhlau, 1883–2009.

———. *Luther's Works*. Volume 1: *Lectures on Genesis Chapters 1–5*. Edited by Jaroslav Pelikan. Translated by George V. Schick. Saint Louis, MO: Concordia Publishing House, 1958.

———. *Luther's Works*. Volume 34: "Preface to the Latin Writings (1545)." Edited by Lewis W. Spitz. Translated by Lewis W. Spitz, Sr., 327–38. Philadelphia, PA: Muhlenberg Press, 1960.

———. *Luther's Works*. Volume 24: *Sermons on the Gospel of St. John, Chapters 14–16*. Edited by Jaroslav Pelikan. Translated by Martin H. Bertram. St. Louis, MO: Concordia Publishing House, 1961.

———. *Martin Luther: Selections from His Writings*. Edited by John Dillenberger. New York: Anchor Books, 1962.

———. *Luther's Works*. Volume 26: *Lectures on Galatians (1535)*. Edited by Walter A. Hansen. Translated by Jaroslav Pelikan. St. Louis, MO: Concordia Publishing House, 1963.

———. *Luther's Works*. Volume 27: *Lectures on Galatians (1519)*. Edited by Walter A. Hansen. Translated by Jaroslav Pelikan. St. Louis, MO: Concordia Publishing House, 1964.

———. *Luther's Works*. Volume 16: *Lectures on Isaiah Chapters 1–39*. Edited by Jaroslav Pelikan. Translated by Herbert J. A. Bouman. St. Louis, MO: Concordia Publishing House, 1969.

Mahn, Jason A. "What are Churches for? Toward an Ecclesiology of the Cross after Christendom." *Dialog: A Journal of Theology* 51, no. 1 (2012): 14–23.

Manne, Kate. *Down Girl: The Logic of Misogyny*. Oxford: Oxford University Press, 2017.

McBride, Jennifer. *The Church for the World: A Theology of Public Witness*. Oxford and New York: Oxford University Press, 2012.

———. "White Protestants aren't Aliens: Resident Aliens at 25." *Christian Century* (Sept. 16, 2016). Online at https://www.christiancentury.org/article/2014-09/white-protestants-arent-aliens.

McIntyre, Lee. *Post-Truth*. Cambridge, MA: MIT Press, 2018.

Mirowski, Philip and Nik-Khah. *The Knowledge We Have Lost in Information: The History of Information in Modern Economics*. Oxford: Oxford University Press, 2017.

Mitchell, Timothy. *Rule of Experts: Egypt, Tecno-Politics, Modernity*. Berkeley, CA: University of California Press, 2002.

Mjaaland, Marius Timmann, ed. *The Reformation of Philosophy: The Philosophical Legacy of the Reformation Reconsidered*. Religion in Philosophy and Theology 102. Tübingen: Mohr Siebeck, 2020.

Moe-Lobeda, Cynthia D. *Public Church: For the Life of the World*. Lutheran Voices Series. Minneapolis, MN: Augsburg Fortress, 2004.

———. "The Holy Spirit: Power for Confessing Faith in the Midst of Empire." In *Being the Church in the Midst of Empire—Trinitarian Reflections*, edited by Karen L. Bloomquist, 125–46. Theology in the Life of the Church Series. Minneapolis, MN: Lutheran University Press, 2010.

Moon, Hellena. "Immigrant Mothers of Color, Pastoral Theology, and the Law." *Pastoral Psychology* 61, no. 3 (2012): 343–58.

Nelson, E. Clifford. Editor. *The Lutherans in North America*. Revised Edition. Philadelphia, PA: Fortress Press, 1980.

Newsom, Carol A., with Brennan W. Breed. *Daniel: A Commentary*. The Old Testament Library. Louisville, KY: Westminster John Knox Press, 2014.

Padilla, Elaine. "Expanding Space: A Possibility of a Cavernous Mode of Dwelling." In *Contemporary Issues of Migration and Theology*, edited by Elaine Padilla and Peter C. Phan, 53–72. Christianities of the World. New York: Palgrave Macmillan, 2013.

Pahl, Jon. "An Economic Reading of Martin Luther's Catechisms in Long Context." In *The Forgotten Luther: Reclaiming the Social-Economic Dimension of the Reformation*. Volume 1, edited by Carter Lindberg and Paul Wee, 55–66. Minneapolis, MN: Lutheran University Press, 2016.

Parsons, Keith M. and Paris N. Donahoo. *Polarized: The Collapse of Truth, Civility, and Community in Divided Times and How We Can Find Common Ground*. New York: Prometheus, 2019.

Pelikan, Jaroslav. *The Christian Tradition: A History of the Development of Doctrine*. 5 Volumes. Chicago, IL: The University of Chicago Press, 1973–1990.

Phan, Peter C. *Vietnamese-American Catholics*. Ethnic-American Pastoral Spirituality. Mahwah, NJ: Paulist Press, 2005.

Philip, M. SourbeSe. *Zong!* Middletown, CT: Wesleyan University Press, 2008.
Plöger, Otto. *Das Buch Daniel*. Kommentar zum Alten Testament 18. Gütersloh: Gütersloher Verlaghaus Gerd Mohn, 1965.
Põder, Christine Svinth-Værge. "Die Römerbriefvorlesung bei Karl Holl und Rudolf Hermann." In *Lutherrenaissance: Past and Present*, edited by Christine Helmer and Bo Kristian Holm, 52–73. Forschungen zur Kirchen- und Dogmengeschichte 106. Göttingen: Vandenhoeck & Ruprecht, 2015.
Porteous, Norman W. *Daniel*. The Old Testament Library. Philadelphia, PA: Westminster Press, 1965.
Portier-Young, Anathea E. *Apocalypse Against Empire: Theologies of Resistance in Early Judaism*. Grand Rapids, MI: Eerdmans, 2011.
Raheb, Mitri. *Faith in the Face of Empire: The Bible through Palestinian Eyes*. Maryknoll, NY: Orbis Books, 2014.
Reid, Jennifer. "The Doctrine of Discovery and Canadian Law." *The Canadian Journal of Native Studies* 30, no. 2 (2010): 335–59.
Ritschl, Albrecht. *The Christian Doctrine of Justification and Reconciliation: The Positive Development of the Doctrine*. Translated by H. R. Mackintosh and A. B. Macaulay. Edinburgh: T&T Clark, 1902.
Sanders, James A. "Torah and Paul." In *God's Christ and His People*, edited by Jacob Jervell and Wayne A. Meeks, 132–40. Oslo: Universitetsforlaget, 1977.
Scheub, Ute. *Heldendämmerung: Die Krise der Männer und warum sie auch für Frauen gefährlich ist*. New York: Pantheon Verlag, 2010.
Schleiermacher, Friedrich. *The Christian Faith*. Edited by H. R. Mackintosh and J. S. Stewart. Translated by D. M. Baillie et al. Edinburgh: T&T Clark, 1999.
Schlink, Edmund. "The Witness of the German Lutheran Church Struggle." In *Man's Disorder and God's Design*. Volume 1. Edited by W. A. Visser't Hooft, 97–206. New York: Harper & Brothers, 1948.
Schmid, Heinrich. Editor. *The Doctrinal Theology of the Evangelical Lutheran Church. Translation of Sixth German Edition*. Translated by Charles A. Hay and Henry E. Jacobs. Second Edition. Philadelphia, PA: Lutheran Publication Society, 1889.
Sheldrake, Philip. *Spaces for the Sacred: Place, Memory and Identity*. Baltimore, MD: The Johns Hopkins University Press, 2001.
Schneider, Laurel C. and Stephen G. Ray Jr., eds. *Awake to the Moment: An Introduction to Theology*. Louisville, KY: Westminster John Knox Press, 2016.
Schreiter, Robert J. *Reconciliation: Mission and Ministry in a Changing Social Order*. The Boston Theological Institute Series 3. New York: Orbis Books, 1992.
Simpson, Audra. *Mohawk Interruptus: Political Life across the Borders of Settler State*. Durham, NC: Duke University Press, 2014.
Sirvent, Roberto and Danny Haiphong. *American Exceptionalism and American Innocence: A People's History of Fake News—From the Revolutionary War to the War on Terror*. New York: Skyhorse, 2019.
Six Nations Land and Resources. "The Haldimand Treaty of 1784." Online at http://www.sixnations.ca/LandsResources/HaldProc.htm (accessed March 19, 2018).

Snyder, Timothy. *On Tyranny: Twenty Lessons from the Twentieth Century*. New York: Tim Duggan Books, 2017.

———. *The Road to Unfreedom: Russia, Europe, America*. New York: Penguin Random House, 2018.

Solberg, Mary M. *Compelling Knowledge: A Feminist Proposal for an Epistemology of the Cross*. Albany, NY: SUNY Press, 1997.

Stout, Jeffrey. *Democracy and Tradition*. New Forum Books. Princeton, NJ: Princeton University Press, 2004.

Tanner, Kathryn. *Politics of God: Christian Theologies and Social Justice*. Minneapolis, MN: Fortress Press, 1992.

Tcherikover, Victor. *Hellenistic Civilization and the Jews*. Peabody, MA: Hendrickson Publishers, 1999.

"The Theological Declaration of Barmen." *Confessions of the Presbyterian Church U.S.A.* Online at http://www.westpresa2.org/docs/adulted/Barmen.pdf.

Thompson, Deanna. "Calling a Thing What It Is: A Lutheran Approach to Whiteness." *Dialog: A Journal of Theology* 53, no. 1 (2014): 49–57.

Trelstad, Marit. "~~Charity~~ Terror Begins at Home: Luther and the 'Terrifying and Killing' Law." In *Lutherrenaissance: Past and Present*, edited by Christine Helmer and Bo Kristian Holm, 209–23. Forschungen zur Kirchen- und Dogmengeschichte 106. Göttingen: Vandenhoeck & Ruprecht, 2015.

Truth and Reconciliation Commission of Canada. Online at http://www.trc.ca/websites/trcinstitution/index.php?p=905 (accessed March 19, 2018).

Tveit, Olav Fykse. *Truth We Owe Each Other*. Geneva: World Council of Churches, 2016.

Walther, C. F. W. *The Proper Distinction Between Law and Gospel*. St. Louis, MO: Concordia Publishing House, 1929.

Westhelle, Vítor. *Transfiguring Luther: The Planetary Promise of Luther's Theology*. Foreword by David Tracy. Cambridge: James Clark, 2017.

White, Lewis Beck. *Early German Philosophy: Kant and His Predecessors*. Bristol, UK: Thoemmes Press, 1996.

Williams, Reggie L. *Bonhoeffer's Black Jesus: Harlem Renaissance Theology and an Ethic of Resistance*. Waco, TX: Baylor University Press, 2014.

Index of Biblical Passages

Ex 3:14, 25
Lev 19:33–34, 113
Deut 6:4, 105
Deut 10:17–19, 113
1 Kgs 19, 153
Job 26:12–13, 157
Psalms, 136
Ps 74:1–17, 157
Ps 89:9–11, 157
Ps 97, 136
Ps 110:2, 84
Is 52:13, 158
Dan 1–6, 157
Dan 1:8–21, 152
Dan 1:18–21, 151, 154
Dan 2:17–23, 151, 154
Dan 2:22c, 158
Dan 6:10, 154
Dan 7–12, 157
Dan 7, 156
Dan 7:1–14, 156
Dan 9, 155
Dan 9:1–3, 151–52
Dan 9:4–19, 151, 154–55
Dan 10:1–5, 151–53
Dan 11:32–35, 158
Dan 12:1–4, 158
Hos 1:10, 82
Hos 2:23, 92

Hos 13, 157
Amos 5:18, 67
Matthew, 118
Matt 5:9, 136
Matt 5:38–39, 136
Matt 5:43–45, 136
Matt 6, 100–101
Matt 6:9–10, 135
Matt 6:25–34, 134
Matt 7:29, 135
Matt 10:16, 140
Matt 12:28, 136
Matt 14:14, 135
Matt 14:16, 134
Matt 16:3, 3
Matt 18:5, 88
Matt 20:1–16, 134
Matt 21:12–17, 136
Matt 22:15–22, 136
Matt 22:21, 130, 135
Matt 22:32–35, 136
Matt 22:37–39, 135
Matt 25:31–46, 134
Matt 25:35–46, 113
Mk 1:15, 135
Mk 3:27, 52
Lk 5:29–32, 134
Lk 6:30, 134
Lk 6:39, 90

Lk 10:9, 135
Lk 10:25–37, 135
Lk 10:27, 105
Lk 13:31, 135
Lk 19:42, 136
Lk 22:14–20, 134
Lk 23:34, 136
Jn 3:19–21, 57
Jn 3:21, 25
Jn 8:11, 39
Jn 8:31–32, 24
Jn 8:32, 13
Jn 14–16, 69
Jn 14:6, 25
Jn 14:17, 69
Jn 14:26, 69
Jn 15:1–11, 69–70
Jn 15:5, 70
Jn 15:12–17, 70
Jn 15:26, 69
Jn 15:26–27, 69
Jn 16:8, 69
Jn 16:13, 69
Jn 18:37, 13
Jn 19:1, 135
Jn 20:22–23, 69
Acts 2:43–47, 134
Acts 2:46–47, 104
Acts 6:1–6, 134
Acts 14:8–10, 135
Acts 15:1–21, 134
Rom 1:17, 39
Rom 7, 47
Rom 7:12, 86

Rom 7:24–25, 86
Rom 8, 47
Rom 9–11, 83
Rom 9:3–4, 83
Rom 9:25, 82, 92
Rom 12:1–2, 87
Rom 14:13–23, 90
1 Cor 8, 95
1 Cor 12:27, 86
2 Cor 8–9, 83
Galatians, 77
Gal 1:2, 84
Gal 1:9, 82
Gal 2:1–10, 83
Gal 2:11–14, 83
Gal 3:6–29, 83
Gal 3:28, 82
Gal 5:6, 33
Gal 5:12, 82
Gal 5:13–14, 82
Gal 2:20, 41
Gal 11:2, 83
Gal 11:26, 83
Gal 11:34, 83
Gal 11:28–29, 83
Eph 1:22–23, 121
Eph 4:4–6, 23
Col 1:15–29, 86
Col 1:15, 86
Col 1:17, 86
Col 1:18, 121
Col 1:18–20, 121
2 Thess 2:4, 84

Index of Names

Abernathy, Ralph, 143
Abraham, 82
Abyssinian Baptist Church, 131
Achtemeier, Paul, 101
Adam (biblical), 87; son of, 157
Africa, 92
Agamben, Giorgio, 56
Alabama, 143
Alexander, Michelle, 70–71
Alexander the Great (king), 146, 149
Anderson, Pamela Sue, 32
Anishinaabe (people). *See* Ojibwe
Antioch, 149
Antiochus III, 147–48
Antiochus IV, 145, 148–50, 152, 156–58
Aquinas, Thomas, 29
Arendt, Hannah, 49
Arioch (biblical), 154
Aristotle, 26, 37, 101
Asia, 77
Asia Minor, 146, 148
Augustine, 51

Baal (god), 153
Babylon, 151
Babylonian Empire, 157
Badiou, Alain, 51
Baraga County, 80
Barnabas (biblical), 135

Barth, Karl, 1, 30, 130
Beck, Lewis White, 51
Begay, Eugene, 102
Benne, Robert, 63
Berry, Wendell, 138
Bertram, Robert W., 35
Birmingham, 154
Bloomquist, Karen, 67–68
Bonhoeffer, Dietrich, 63, 76, 130–32
Boston University, 144
Brown, Wendy, 48, 51, 56
Burns, Ken, 127
Bush, George W., 57
Butler, Jennifer, 71

Caledonia (place), 22
Canada, 21–22, 103
Carleton College, 78
Carter, J. Kameron, 89
Cassander (king), 146
Charleston, Steven, 98, 103
China, 160
Chippewa (people), 103
Choctaw (people), 98
Christ, Carol P., 29–31, 34
Cilicia (region), 146
Clinton, Hillary, 37–38, 81–82, 85, 88
Cochrane, Arthur C., 64
Collins, John J., 157

Connolly, William, 132
Constantine (emperor), 129
Cornell, Dierdre, 120
Crow, Jim, 143
Cruz, Gemma Tulud, 117, 119
Cypress, 146
Czechoslovakia, 50, 52, 56–57

Daniel (biblical), 145–46, 151–53, 154–59; book of, 145, 154, 159
David (king), 153
Davis, Angela, 89
Davis, Jewelnel, 78
the Deuteronomist, 155
Dionysius (god), 150
Douglas, Kelly Brown, 70
DuBois, W. E. B., 89

Eckhart, Meister, 89
Egypt, 118, 146, 150
Eichmann, Adolf, 49
Elam, 148
Elert, Werner, 30, 33–35
Elijah (prophet), 153
Emir Abd el-Kader, 144
England, 99
Erlangen, 30, 35
Europe, 57, 114, 148
Evangelical Lutheran Church in American (ELCA), 65–66, 75, 91, 107, 123, 137
Eve (biblical), 87
Ezekiel (prophet), 153, 157

Facebook, 91
Farley, Wendy, 11, 13, 15
Finkenwalde (town), 131
Finland, 91
Forde, Gerhard, 35
Foucault, Michel, 47, 52

Gabriel (angel), 152
Galatia (region), 84
Galatians, 84
Gandhi, Mahatma, 154

Gekko, Gordon, 58
Germany, 30–31, 33
Gerousia (leaders), 149
Gomez, Medardo (bishop), 79
González, Justo, 105
Goodman, Ronald, 98
Guatemala, 79
Gyori, Grace, 79

Hall, Douglas John, 64–67
Han, 98
Harlem, 131
Hartshorne, Charles, 107
Harvard University, 57
Harvey, Jennifer, 68
Haudenosaunee (people), 22
Hauerwas, Stanley, 66
Havel, Václav, 47–56, 60
Heidelberg, 30
Heliodorus, 148
Hellenistic Empire, 157
Henriksen, Jan-Olav, 21, 23–25, 27
Herod (king), 118, 135
Hiroshima, 60
Hitler, Adolf, 60, 63, 88, 131
Holl, Karl, 6
Hong Kong, 111

Illinois, 92
India, 92
Inuit (people), 22
Inyan, The Rock, 98
Isaiah (prophet), 158
Israel, 83, 157

Jacob (biblical), 153
Jason (brother of Onias), 149–50
Jeremiah (prophet), 153
Jerome, (saint), 84
Jerusalem, 83, 133, 136, 147, 149–50, 152–54, 158
Jesus, 2, 13, 16–17, 25, 41, 118–21, 123–25, 133–38, 140
Jezebel (queen), 153
Joel (prophet), 153

Index of Names

John (evangelist), 69
Johnson, Lyndon B., 127
Jorgenson, Allen, 90–91
Joseph (biblical), 153
Joseph (saint), 118
Joseph Tobiad, 149
Josephus, 101, 147
Judea, 146, 150

Kahlo, Frida, 122
Kant, Immanuel, 33, 50–51, 99
Kearney, Richard, 26
Keller, Catherine, 132, 139
Kennedy, John F., Jr, 127
Kierkegaard, Søren, 34
King, Martin Luther, Jr., 78, 143–44, 153, 160
King, Michael, 145. *See also* King, Martin Luther, Jr.
Klemperer, Victor, 88

Lac Courtes Oreilles (nation), 102
Lake Superior, 77
Lakota (Nakota, Dakota), 98–102
Lasserre, Jean, 131
Lazareth, William, 63
the Levant, 146, 149
Lilla, Mark, 51
Lincoln, Abraham, 127
Lincoln Memorial, 143–44
Los Angeles, 143
Luther, Martin, 1–5, 7–8, 27, 30–31, 39, 48, 51–52, 56, 63–64, 66, 69–70, 77, 81, 84, 86–90, 101, 139, 145–46
Luther Works: *Heidelberg Disputation*, 77, 87; *Large Catechism*, 77, 88; *Lectures on Genesis*, 27; *Preface to Latin Writings*, 39; *Sermons on John's Gospel*, 64, 69–70; *Small Catechism*, 77, 87–88
Luther Northwestern Theological Seminary, 98
Luther Renaissance, 31
Lutheran Church in America (LCA), 75

Lutheran Church Missouri Synod (LCMS), 29
Lutheran School of Theology at Chicago (LSTC), 106
Lysimachus (king), 146

Macedonia, 146
Macomb, Illinois, 79
Magnesia (battle), 148
Mahn, Jason, 67
Maka (Earth), 98
Manne, Kate, 36–38
Marcion, 77
Mariña, Jacqueline, 44n13
Marx, Karl, 50, 53
Mary (saint), 118
Massachusett (people), 21
McBride, Jennifer, 66–67
McIlwain, David, 117
Median Empire, 157
Mesopotamia, 146
Midwest, 82, 92
Milwaukee, 123
Minnesota, 78, 97, 100
Moe-Lobeda, Cynthia, 64, 70
Moon, Hellena, 114
Moses (prophet), 56, 84
Mount Carmel, 153
Mount Horeb, 153
Muhammad (prophet), 144

Nashville, Tennessee, 79
Navajo (people), 22
Nebuchadnezzar (king), 143, 156
Nelson, E. Clifford, 65
Netflix, 104
New York, 131
Niemöller, Martin, 64
Nik-Khah, Edward, 51
Nixon, Richard B., 127
North Africa, 144
North America, 21, 65

Obama, Barack, 81
Obama, Michelle, 59

Ojibwe (people), 91
Oka (place), 22
Oklahoma, 98
Oniad (family), 149
Onias III, 149
Ortega, Daniel, 79
Orwell, George, 12
Osage (people), 22

Padilla, Elaine, 111, 122–24
Pahl, Jon, 67
Palestine, 146–47
Paul (apostle), 26, 48, 77, 81–84, 86–88, 90, 135, 145
Pawtucket (people), 21
Pelikan, Jaroslav, 29
Persian Empire, 157
Petra (city), 146
Phan, Peter, 119–20
Philip, M. NourbSe, 89
Philip II of Macedon, 146
Philo, 101
Phoenicia, 147
Pietists, 40
Pilate, 13, 16, 54–55
Pinochet, Auguste, 63
Plaskow, Judith, 29, 34
Plato, 32, 101
Pokantoket (people), 21
Pollan, Michael, 104
Porete, Marguerite, 89
Portier-Young, Anathea E., 148
Potočka, Jan, 55
Proust, Marcel, 26
Ptolomies, 150
Ptolemy I, 146–47
Ptolemy V, 148

Raj (British), 154
Reid, Jennifer, 21
Rich, Adrienne, 29
Ritschl, Albrecht, 33, 40
Rohr, Richard, 129
Rome, 84, 133, 148
Roosevelt, Franklin D., 78, 127

Salomonsen, Jone, 9n1
Sanballats (family), 149
Schleiermacher, Friedrich, 3, 41
Schlink, Edmund, 30
Schreiter, Robert, 68
Seleucus I, 146–47
Seleucus IV, 149
Seleucus V, 148
Sheldrake, Philip, 99–100, 102–3
Simpson, Audra, 12
Six Nation of the Grand River Nation, 24
Snyder, Timothy, 88
Sodom and Gomorrah, 84
Solberg, Mary, 67
Solomon, Eva, 103
Solzhenitsyn, Alexandr, 48, 51, 56–60
South (U.S.), 92
South Korea, 92
Sri Lanka, 77
Stalin, Joseph, 60, 63
Standing Rock (place), 22
Star Trek, 99
Stout, Jeffrey, 15
Syria, 148
Syria-Palestine, 146

Tanner, Kathryn, 81
Theodosius (emperor), 129
Thompson, Deanna, 67, 89
Thrace (region), 146
Thurman, Howard, 78, 144
Tobiad (family), 149; Lysimachus, 149; Menelaus, 149–50; Simon, 149
Trelstad, Marit, 5, 35
Transjordan, 149
Truman, Harry S., 127
Trump, Donald J., 12, 50, 71, 77, 81–82, 89, 111, 115, 123
Truth and Reconciliation Commission, 23
Twin Cities, 79

Uganda, 92
Union Theological Seminary, 70

United States of America, 21–22, 57, 65, 82, 85, 89, 91–92, 111, 114–18, 123, 125
University of Berlin, 131
University of Cambridge, 99
U.S.S.R., 56–57

Vanderbilt Divinity School, 79
Vietnam, 127
Vorster, John, 63

Wakan Tanka, 98, 101–2
Walther, C. F. W., 35
Washington, D.C., 71
Wellstone, Paul, 78–79
West Bank, 92
Westhelle, Vítor, 48–49, 60
Willimon, William, 6
Wisconsin, 102
Wittenberg Castle Church, 31
World War I, 30

Yale University, 29–31

Zeus, 150
Zingst (town), 131

Index of Subjects

abuse, 23, 34, 36, 112; domestic, 5
accountability, 12–14
action, collective, 79
activism, 48, 71, 78, 131, 145
activist, 77–79
Adam, old, 31
admonish, 88
adults, 104
African American Progressive National Baptist, 78
African Americans, 68, 143
agency, divine, 34
agony, 118
agriculture, 117
alien, 113; resident, 66
alienation, 50
America, 21, 66, 82, 116, 132; Central, 87; North, 91
American Academy of Religion, 70
American Indian, 97
Americans, 118; Vietnamese, 119; white, 117
antipoverty, 79
anti-racism, 106
anti-Semitism, 1, 64
anti-war, 79
apocalyptic, 155–58
Aramaic, 156
army, 146, 150; Egyptian, 146

Aryan Paragraph (1933), 35, 64
assassination, 160
assimilation, 114, 116–17
atonement, 133
authoritarianism, 1, 81, 85, 88
autonomy, 58–59, 147
awakening, 70

baby, unborn, 81
Babylonian Exile, 147
balance, 101–2
baptism, 6, 23, 82, 87, 92, 97
Baptist, 78
Barmen Declaration, 52, 130
battle, 157
beasts: four, 157
belief, 117; traditional, 102
belonging, 79, 82–84, 91
Beloved Community, 47
bias, implicit, 114
Bible, Christian, 77, 113, 132; Hebrew, 136, 153, 157; Septuagint, 101
bigotry, 71, 107
bi-racial, 100
birth, new, 71
bishop, 105
blackness, 89
blessings, 104
blood, 98; of martyrs, 159

body, 26–27, 36, 98, 104, 118, 129, 151, 157; of Christ, 26–27, 31, 40, 42, 75, 86, 91, 107, 112, 114, 121–24, 130, 138; of church, 39; of death, 86; and mind, 32, 98; mystical, 8, 32, 36, 38, 42; politic, 26–27, 39, 82; and soul, 42, 158; women's, 39
bondage, 24
border, 122–25
border-crosser, 119
born-again, 76
boundaries, 83, 121, 134
Buddhists, 77
bull, papal, 21, 91

calling, 132
campaign, presidential, 82
cancer, 39
canon, 77
capitalism, 49–50, 52, 59, 90, 132
care, 14, 117, 134, 138–39; of souls, 145, 159
caregiving, 36–37
carnal, 26
Carnegie Foundation for the Advancement of Teaching, 105
castration, 82
catechesis, 60
catechism, Luther's, 67
Catholic, 75–76, 91
ceremony, 102
change, 139; radical, 55; social, 77, 79
chaos, 157
Chicago Religious Leadership Network on Central America, 79
children, 104, 134; of God, 136
Christ, 12, 14, 17, 41–43, 54, 60, 66, 69–70, 75, 82–84, 86, 103, 105, 130–32, 138, 140; benefits of, 128; blood of, 39; body and blood of, 128; body of, 8, 31, 36, 38–39, 42–43, 75, 77, 86, 91, 107, 112, 114, 121–24, 130, 138; as center, 131; character of, 133; conformed to, 131; congregation of, 56; crucified, 67, 82; crucified and risen, 51; crucifixion, 130, 133; death, 119–20; death and resurrection, 6, 67, 91–92, 119–20, 129, 133; firstborn from dead, 121; followers of, 127, 129; as head of body, 121; image of, 25; immigrant experience, 119; incarnation, 119; life of, 68, 129, 134; as person for me, 131; the physician, 42; presence of, 8; reality of, 128; resurrection, 119, 128; risen, 82; as Savior, 133; substitutionary death of, 133; suffering of, 68, 119; teachings of, 129, 134; Way of, 139
Christians, 83, 91, 113, 129, 133; American Indian, 97–98; conservative, 82; early, 104; German, 131; Lutheran, 107; progressive, 81, 132; second century, 77; white evangelical, 89
Christianity: American, 43, 117; Aryan, 131; Constantinian, 130; history of, 29, 120; and immigration, 114
Christology, 129–31, 133–34, 136
church, 6–8, 12, 14–15, 18, 23, 26–27, 41, 64–66, 69, 77, 84, 114, 118–19, 121–24; black, 130; Catholic, 84; -community, 131; in community, 25; Confessing, 130; divisions of, 83; early, 130, 134, 137; and empire, 130; failure of, 70; historians, 30; history, 105, 136, 138; immigrant, 23, 117; invisible, 6; in Jerusalem, 83; Jewish, 84; life of, 119; Lutheran, 65, 160; mission of, 133; one, 83; and politics, 17; reforming, 83; of Rome, 84; secular, 80; /state, 64, 76, 135; suffering, 67; Upper Michigan Lutheran, 80; whitest, 65;
churchicality, black, 89
citizen, 88, 123
civil rights, 78–79, 130
civilization, 152; mass, 43; technological, 51
classism, 47, 114, 138
clergy, female, 38; queer, 38

Index of Subjects

climate change, 15, 128, 133
collaborators, 54
colonialism, 21–23, 27, 51, 91; French, 144
colonization, 57
comfort, 69, 159–60
commandment: eighth, 87–88, 90; of love, 70; seventh, 145
Committees of Correspondence, 80
commitment, 117–18; social, 80
common good, 57–58, 64, 78, 81, 128, 138–39
communion, 75–76, 92; as *communio*, 101. *See also* Eucharist
communism, 50, 52
communists, 80
Communist Manifesto, 53
Communist Party, 80
community, 4, 6–8, 11, 14, 17, 18, 23, 41–43, 98, 104, 107, 138–39; American Indian, 97; Christian, 130; of color, 68; covenantal, 83; Norwegian, 100; sustainable, 138; of truth, 14; vulnerable, 112, 115, 117
compassion, 117
complicity, 47–48, 68, 70, 76
Confessing Church, 64
confession (of sin), 75, 85, 145, 152
confinement, solitary, 111–12
conflict, 119, 127, 139
congregation, 56; African American Lutheran, 143; Midwestern Lutheran, 76; religious, 139; white, 160
conquest, 146
consciousness, 41; false, 53; immediate, 41; self-, 41; sensible, 41
consolation, 87
construction, 99
consumerism, 51–52, 54
consumption, 154
contemplation, 144
conversion, 85–86
conviction, 69
coram deo, 40, 47, 49
coram hominibus, 40, 49

coram mundo, 47
Council of Trent, 105
courage, 57, 69, 71
covenant, 102, 155
creation, 3, 5, 43, 47, 91, 98–99, 102, 104, 138, 157; new, 52, 85–86, 129; old and new, 86; orders of, 65; Scandinavian theology, 5
Creator, 98–99, 102, 104–5, 108
creature, 99
creed, 85
crisis, 128, 156; ecological, 27, 63
critical theory, 43
cross, 17, 133, 136, 139; blood of, 121; ecclesiology of, 66; suffering on, 121; theology of, 66, 87, 89
crypto-theology, 50, 52, 54–55
culture, 43, 56, 100, 125, 138; dominant, 65; Greek, 146; Hellenistic, 145; Norwegian American Haugean, 100; western, 58

darkness, 67, 98, 158–59
Dawes Act, 91
death, 159; of Martin Luther King, Jr., 160
deceit, 17
deception, 14
decolonize, 103
defenseless, 56
Deferred Action for Childhood Arrivals (DACA), 115
deity, Jewish, 77
deliberation, 137–38
deliverance, 51
democracy, 49, 51–52, 56–57
Democrats, 81
deplorables, 82
depression, 57; Great, 127
desire, 48–49, 57, 158
despair, 48, 77, 88, 108, 140; of self, 52; political, 56
despotism, 12, 15
destiny, manifest, 132
devil, 69

devotion, 105
dialogue, interreligious, 78
diaspora, 66
dictatorship, 52–53
dignity, 50, 123
Ding-an-sich, 99
direction, spiritual, 129
disciples, 66, 135–36
discipleship, 25, 127, 129, 139; costly, 130
disciplines, 144
discord, 15
discrimination, 143
disease, 39
disgust, 36–39
distrust, 112
diversity, 81, 100, 107, 114, 138
divisions, 18, 92, 127; of church, 84
divisiveness, 15
dream, 143–44, 154
doctrine, 29–30, 38–39; disembodied, 34, 36; and gender, 31; of original sin, 80; pure, 160; of salvation by works, 80; truth of, 36; of two kingdoms, 63, 160
Doctrine of Discovery, 21–22, 91
duty, 49

earth, 27; as mother, 27; new, 139
East, totalitarian, 59
Easter, 133
eating, 104–5
ecclesiology, 5–7, 75–91; of entitlement, 24; Lutheran, 6, 80; of resistance, 4, 6, 23; of subsistence, 27
economy, 117
ecumenism, 29
education, 144; higher, 97; theological, 105
election, 83; presidential, 37, 79
embodiment/disembodiment, 26–27, 31, 33–40, 43
emperor, 147; Hellenistic, 148

empire, 22, 27, 67, 89, 130, 146, 148, 152, 155–60; and church, 130; four, 157; Syrian, 148
employment, 144
energy, 98; transformative, 129
enjoyment, 104
enlightenment, 99, 159
enslavement, 22
entitlement, 91
envy, 48, 58
epistemology, 32
equality, 116
ethic: exceptional, 35; work, 132
ethos, modern, 35
Eucharist, 67, 134–35, 145
evangelism, 113
evil, 48, 59, 159; banality, 49
exception, state of, 56
exceptionalism, 132
exile, 120
Exodus, 120
experience, 16, 29, 99–100, 106–7, 114, 118, 120; of God, 144, 157; illuminative, 145; immigrant, 123–25; Jesus' immigrant, 120–21, 124; mystical, 158; personal, 138; religious, 158; spiritual, 155; Vietnamese-American, 119
exploitation, 147
expropriation, 24

faces, 90
facts, 14; alternative, 11–12, 14, 88–89; empirical, 88
faith, 17, 23, 64–65, 97, 117, 119, 130, 138–39, 151, 157; weak, 85
faithfulness, 151–52, 155–57
fake news, 12, 22
falsehood, 14
family, 54, 102, 104, 132; heterosexual, 81; Martin Luther King, Jr.'s, 160; rival, 149; separation, 123
fanatics, 84
fascism, 3, 49, 130, 132
fasting, 151–56

Father, in heaven, 100, 135
fear, 14–16, 18, 112, 118, 122, 128, 144; of death, 27; of deportation, 125
feeding, 153; the hungry, 134–35, 138
feeling, 38, 40
feminism, 29
feminist, 6, 36, 77; perspectives, 32; scholars, 32
Finndians, 76, 91
Finnish-Americans, 76
flesh, 27
flood, 102
flourishing, 14, 17
followers, of Christ, 127, 129
forgiveness, 128, 130
form criticism, 30
formation, 97–108, 129–30
freedom, 24–25, 32, 59, 82, 88, 121, 154; personal, 58; of the press, 58
friends, 104
friendship, 91
future, 26–27, 86, 102

gender, 31–32, 114, 134, 138
generosity, 134, 138
Gentiles, 82–83, 134
geography, spiritual, 102
geopolitics, 111, 122
German Christians, 64–65
German Church Struggle, 64–65
gift, 3, 87, 100, 104, 117, 124–25
glass ceiling, 37
globalization, 57
glory, theology of, 66, 87–89
God, 2, 4–5, 14, 17, 31, 40, 42–44, 50, 65, 67, 84, 90, 97–98, 101–2, 104–5, 113, 121, 128–29, 132, 135, 145, 148, 151–56, 158–59; Canaanite, El, 157; children of, 136; the creator, 8; dwelling place of, 121; essence of, 39; experience of, 144, 157; faithfulness to, 151; favor of, 27; feast of, 76; grace of, 69; the healer, 4; hidden, 87; idea of, 157; identity of, 133; image of, 18, 27, 60; the judge, 4; justice of, 39, 120; as king, 136, 148; law of, 63; is light, 158; likeness of, 60; love of, 69, 113, 160; mercy of, 121; mystery of, 97–98; people of, 121, 138; presence of, 158; promise of, 108; the Redeemer, 4; reign of, 12, 14, 75, 78–79, 86, 133–35; response from, 154; revelation of, 132; righteousness of, 39–40; rule of, 136; salvation of, 121; sovereignty of, 155; Spirit of, 136; throne room of, 158; Triune, 119; twofold rule of, 63–64; vision of, 157; word of, 38, 56, 63, 131, 138, 153
good news, 129–30
goodness, 80
gospel, 3–5, 17, 31 38, 41, 43, 70–71, 76, 78, 83–84, 91, 128–29
government, 127; branches of, 127; tyrannical, 63
grace, 3, 5, 7, 69, 84, 92, 129; stories of, 91
gratitude, 104, 134
Great Commandment, 70, 105, 135
greed, 58
Greek, 82, 156
ground, 27, 41, 48
guilt, 47, 49
Gulf War, 79
guns, 81, 90

habituation, 37–38
haggadah, 82–83
halakha, 82
hamartiology, 3
hand, 37–38
happiness, 57, 59
harmony, 102, 119; spiritual, 101
healer, Jesus the, 135
healing, 135, 138
healthcare, 15
the hearts, 104, 144, 153; hardening of, 83
Hellenization, 149–50

heterosexism, 80, 85
hierarchy, 49, 85
historicism, 50
history, 68, 81, 102, 131–32, 156; American, 118, 127, 143; of Christianity, 120, 129, 134; of the church, 105, 137, 138; elitist, 103; of the second century, 146
Holocaust, 49
holy, 84, 147
Holy Spirit, 42, 64, 68–71, 76, 87, 90; of truth, 69; power of, 130; the Comforter, 69
homeless, 16
hope, 3, 17, 67–68, 108, 128, 130, 139, 130
hospitality, 122, 124, 134, 138
hostage, 148
hostility, 112, 116, 122
housing, 144
human, 3, 8, 27; being, 25
humanism, 59
humanity, 18, 50, 54–55, 122, 124–25, 145, 160; destruction of, 145; failings of, 155; renewal of, 144; shared, 112, 114, 121, 124–25
humility, 66–67
hungry, 134–35
hybridity, 151, 156, 157
hymn, 143
hypocrisy, 17, 71

identification, 80, 91
identity, 31, 68, 82, 99–100, 102–3, 118, 120, 143, 148, 150, 155; Canadian, 91; in Christ, 114; Christian, 78; collective, 85; corporate, 84; crisis of, 152; Finnish-American, 76; German-American, 76; intersectional, 91; Jewish, 82, 148; Judean, 147; national, 84; Native American, 91; new, 157; performed, 89; personal, 85; political, 80; public, 77; Swedish-American, 76; U.S., 91; universalizing, 83; white, 76, 89

ideology, 11, 53, 70, 90–91; fascist, 90; Hellenistic, 146; socialist, 80
idolatry, 67, 71
idols, 85
illumination, 153–56, 158
illuminative (mystical), 145, 151, 156
image, of Christ, 25; of God, 18, 27, 70, 79
imagination, 112, 148; pastoral, 105
immigrants, 81, 111–15, 117–19, 122–25; care of, 114; hatred of, 123; Jesus the, 120; Latin American, 68; love of, 114
immigration, 111–12, 121–22, 138; and Christianity, 114; policy, 128, 132
Immigration and Customs Enforcement (ICE), 111–12
Imperium Romanum, 145
incarcerated, 17
incarceration, mass, 70
inclusion, 83, 122
Indigenous people, 22, 24. *See also* Native Americans
individual, 58–59, 101
indulgence, papal, 31
industrialization, 104
indwelling, 40–43, 122–23
infant, 102
injustice, 13, 23, 36, 40, 47, 49, 64, 68, 71, 76–78, 85–86, 88, 92, 114
Institute for the Study and Eradication of Jewish Influence on German Religious Life (1939), 131
integrity, 50–51
interpretation, 99; of dream, 154
Islam, land of, 144
Israel, people of, 82

Jesus Christ (*see* Christ)
Jews, 49, 79, 82–84, 147–48, 153, 155–56, 158; persecuted, 156; pious, 156
journey, 98–99; spiritual, 97
joy, 43, 122
Judaism, 83; practice of, 151
judge, 87

judgment, 36, 38, 86, 157
justice, 13, 17, 30, 39–40, 42–44, 70, 86, 89–90, 101, 113, 131; of God, 121; immigrant, 112; procedural, 58; social, 77, 92, 128
justification, 82; doctrine of, 3, 6, 30–36, 38–44; toxic doctrine of, 35;

Keweenaw Bay Indian Community, 91
kindness, 80
king: Babylonian, 151; food of, 152
kingdom, of God, 69, 135–36, 157; unnamed, 158. *See also* reign, of God
knowing, 26
knowledge, 32, 102, 138, 152, 159
kosher, 151, 154, 156

labor, 117
land(s), 21, 27, 102; foreign, 118; Indigenous, 23
landscape, 100, 117
language, 131, 156; of empire, 156; of worship, 76
law, 4, 48, 64, 84, 86; accusing, 35; ancestral, 147, 150; of God, 63–64; international, 132; Jewish ritual, 82; kosher, 147; preaching of, 35; prophetic, 64; rule of, 137; works of, 82
law and gospel, 4–5, 34–35, 63, 86, 92
leader(s)hip, 88–89, 105–7, 113, 129, 137, 147, 151; African American, 130; female, 36–38; Jewish, 147; pastoral, 131; religious, 135
legalism, 58
liberals, 81–82
liberation, 50, 80; theology, 16
lie(s), 14, 68, 71, 88. *See also* mendacity
life, 40, 42, 55, 90–91, 98, 100, 104, 105, 154; abundant, 108, 120; active, 144; black social, 89; common, 92; communal, 89; and death, 131, 153; -destroying, 99; economic, 138; -giving, 99; in God, 79; of Jesus, 120; new, 107, 114; public, 138; religious, 117; spiritual, 99
light, 57, 67, 158–59
linguistic turn, 26
liturgy, 85, 145; Lutheran, 91–92
livelihood, 138
local, 99, 139
Lord, day of, 67
Lord's Supper. *See* Eucharist
love, 3, 17, 69, 128; commandment, 70, 105, 135; of enemies, 92, 136; exceptional ethic of, 35; of God, 105, 113, 135, 160; Jesus', 120; of neighbor, 35, 82, 86, 92, 135; radical egalitarian, 17; of self, 82; of truth, 16
Lutheran Volunteer Corps, 79
Lutherans, 65, 103, 160

march, 71
March for Our Guns, 81
March for Our Lives, 81, 90
marginalized, 18, 67, 71, 89, 119–20, 137
martyrdom, 145, 151, 157–59
Marxism, 90
Marxism-Leninism, 49, 53, 59
Marxist, 79
masculinity, 30–31; German, 34; toxic, 36; #toxicLutheran, 30
maskilim, 151, 153, 158–59
materialism, 57
materiality, 99
meal: home-made, 104; sacred, 104
meat, 85
memory, 26, 99, 103, 118
men: arrogant, 30; Lutheran, 30
mendacity, 51–52, 54, 60. *See also* lies
mentor, 98
mercy, of God, 121
metaphysics, 40
midrash, 82, 156, 157
migration, 115, 117, 120
military, 79
mind, 26, 98; and body, 32, 98

ministry, 105, 107, 119, 134, 160
minorities, 112
misogyny, 30, 36, 39, 71
mission, 66, 79
mobility, human, 120, 122
modernity, 51, 59
monasticism, 130
Montgomery Bus Boycott, 144
mother, 37; earth, 103
movement, 122, 139; civil rights, 143; reform, 137; social justice, 80
murder, 149–50, 153
Muslims, 81, 132
mystery, 97, 101–2
mystic, 153–54; Sufi, 144
mysticism, 40, 89, 145, 157–58; Jewish, 158
mythology, Canaanite, 157

nakedness, 27
narrative, 103; of immigrants, 112, 120; of the lie, 68; of migration, 120
nation, 65, 77, 87, 102, 131–32, 157, 160
National Socialism, 1, 36, 49, 63–64, 76, 130–31
nationalism, 14, 132
Native Americans, 76, 97, 102–3; perspectives, 91, 101; political theorists, 91. *See also* Indigenous people
nature, 50, 99, 139; corruption of, 52
neighbor, 68, 71, 77, 85, 87–88, 90–92, 130, 134–35, 137, 139, 146; love of, 82, 86; politics, 137–38
neoliberalism, 48–49, 57–58
New Israel, 132
New Monasticism, 67
New Testament, 103, 113, 138
nonviolence, 136

obedience, 53
obligation, 113
Old Testament, 103, 113
omnipresence, 41

oppression, 67–68, 80, 87, 118, 155
order, unjust social, 80
orphan, 113

Palm Sunday, 133
panentheism, 102
pantheism, 102
parable, 90, 134; of the good Samaritan, 135
paradox, 34
particle theory, 99
passport, 22
past, 26–27, 102
pastors, 105; women, 92
patriarchy, 36–38
patriotism, 132
peace, 136, 138, 157; -making, 136, 138
Peasant uprising (1525), 64
pedagogy, 105
penance, 85
people, 82, 100, 155–56, 158–59; colonized, 157; covenanted, 155; of God, 101, 121, 138; Jewish, 155; persecuted, 155; under stress, 121
perpetrator, 49
persecution, 115, 157, 159
person: new in Christ, 5–6
pessimism, 52, 80
Pew Research Center, 115
philosophy: neo-Kantian, 40; present-moment, 102
physics, 99
Pietism, 130
piety, 155; creation, 98–108
place, 99–100, 102–3; theology of, 102
plague, 130
pneumatology, 68–69
polarization, 76–77, 80–83, 92
police, 53
policy: public, 137; social, 137
politician, female, 36–37
politics, 43, 54–56, 77; American, 12, 15; and church, 17, 43; identity, 137; neighbor, 137–38; sectarian, 80
polycrisis, 1

poor, 16–17, 64, 115, 118, 134
pope, 88
postcolonial, 156
postmodern, 89, 128
post-totalitarian, 52
post-truth, 88, 128
power, 12–13, 16, 23, 43, 47, 49, 52–54, 71, 88, 98, 119; abusers of, 153; abusive, 159; authoritarian, 85; colonizing, 148; cultural, 66; of empire, 158; foreign, 147; of forgiveness, 69; of God, 153; Jesus' healing, 135; of life, 98; of love, 69; male, 34; over body, 154; political, 56, 128, 155; speak against, 159; of truth, 18; truth to, 13, 23–24, 144–45, 159; of word, 65
powerless, 49, 52
practice(s), 37, 130–31, 136, 138, 155; Christian, 129–30; devotional, 130; of Jesus, 136–38; Jewish, 148; of Judaism, 151; spiritual, 97, 99, 102, 104–6, 129, 145–46, 151–54
praise, 104, 154
prayer, 129–31, 135, 144, 151, 153–56, 158, 160; Deuteronomistic, 155; doxological, 154; liturgical, 155; Lord's, 135–36; of repentance, 155; of thanksgiving, 155; triumphant, 155
prejudice, 107, 114
presence, 106; divine, 42; of Christ, 8, 42
the press: freedom of, 58
presumption, 77, 81, 85–86, 90, 112
priest(s), 92, 158; high, 149
priesthood: high, 149–50, 152; of all believers, 64
principle, legislative, 101
privilege, 65–67, 89, 116, 121, 137, 147–48, 150; class, 69; gender, 71; racial, 69, 71; white, 89
proclamation, 40, 60, 63, 131, 145
production, of food, 104

professor(s): female, 36; Lutheran, 30, 34; male, 31; of church history, 29; of theology, 29
progress, 49, 59
progressives, 89
promise(s), 83, 119; of God, 108
property, 21; private, 146
prophets, 153
prophetic, 65–66, 78
Protestant(s), white, 66
Protestantism, 65
protester, 79
providence, 65, 78, 90
public, 81, 106, 129, 140; new, 139
pure and impure, 147
purgative (mystical), 145, 151, 154, 156

quietism, 51–52

race, 114, 131, 138
racism, 3, 14, 47, 68, 78, 80, 85, 87, 89, 106, 128, 132
rapture, 133
rationality, 32, 37, 47–48, 57, 89; western, 32
rationalization, 50–51
reality, 3, 43, 88, 99, 102, 106, 154; of God, 44; harsh, 115, 160; hidden, 159; objective, 99;
reason, 52, 138, 144; pure, 32
rebirth, 70
reciprocity, 43, 156
reconciliation, 24, 68–69, 83, 119, 121, 136
redemption, 47, 75, 90, 92, 121
reform, 80, 134; immigrant, 113
reformation, Protestant, 130
refugee(s), 68, 119, 123
reign, of God, 12, 14, 75, 78–79, 86, 133–36
relation(s), 100–103, 105, 108; blood, 98; right, 99, 101–2, 107–8; spiritual, 98, 100
relationship(s), 31–32, 98, 101–2, 104, 155

religion, 158–59; American civil, 132; monotheistic, 156; secularized, 53; study of, 2
remembrance, 118
reparation, 68
repentance, 24, 67, 86; prayer of, 155
Republican(s), 79, 81–82, 91
reservation, 100
residential schools, 23
resignation, 48
resilience, 124
responsibility, 12–16, 49, 53–56, 59, 65, 112, 130, 155
resurrection, 84, 158
revelation, 131–32, 153, 155
revolution: Islamic, 59; spiritual, 70–71
rewards, spiritual, 104
righteous, 101, 133
righteousness, 40, 42, 100–101, 108, 134; essential, 41; liberal, 81; of God, 39–40
right(s), 58, 81, 128; civil, 127–28; human, 17, 71, 132; immigrant, 123; legal, 101; religious, 132–33, 137; women's, 71
ritual, 6–7, 102
Roman Empire, 129
Romans, 136
rule: Christian, 22; covenantal, 101; of law, 137; Seleucid, 147
ruler(s), 146

Sabbath, 129
sacrament(s), 40; and word, 76, 78, 81, 84, 86, 88, 91–92, 128
sacred, 101–2
sacrifice, 54, 150
sages, 158; Babylonian, 154–55
saints, 32
salvation, 40, 82, 121, 133; eternal, 81; political, 81
sanctification, 34
sanctuary, 123
scapegoating, 115
scarcity, 25, 135

schools, residential, 23
scripture(s), 113, 131, 138, 153; Jewish, 77
Second Temple, 155
sectarian, 80
Seelsorge, 144, 146, 151, 159–60
self, 154; -deception, 14; determination, 154; -righteousness, 122; technology of, 34
seminary, 70, 105–7
senator, 97
sermon(s), 78; Ash Wednesday, 100; on the Mount, 133
sexism, 3, 37, 45, 80, 85
share, 104
shooter, white supremacist, 89
sick, 16–17, 130, 135
signifier(s), 38, 43
simony, 149
simul iustus et peccator, 34, 75, 128
sin, 49, 51, 68–69, 86, 89–90; doctrine of, 48, 51; liberal of presumption, 81; original, 51–52, 80; original of racism, 68; public, 88; structural, 89; systemic, 85; universal, 47
Sinhalese Buddhists, 77
sinner(s), 31, 35, 40, 134
site, sacred, 102
skin, 27, 97, 112, 115
slave, 82; trade, 25
slavery, 127, 143, 150; opposition to, 128
Social Gospel, 130
social media, 127
social statements, 137–38
socialism, 53, 58
society, 5, 14–15, 55, 79, 112, 114, 116, 137; American, 114; capitalist, 80; contemporary, 138; subjugated, 146; transformation of, 159
solidarity, 67–69, 71, 118, 139
soul(s), 31, 40–43, 144; /body, 42, 158; care of, 145. See also *Seelsorge*
sovereignty, 21–22, 51; Native, 91

space, 99–100, 111, 122–25; lived, 156; sacred, 150; spiritual, 158
spirit, 98, 102, 144; troubled, 152
spirituality, 4, 99–100, 158–59; Benedictine, 100; Franciscan, 100; Ignatian, 100; immigrant, 117
standard, ethical, 101
Star of David, 78
state: and church, 76, 135; of exception, 56
stereotype, 116, 118
sterilization, forced, 91
stewardship, 25
story(ies), 91–92, 105
stranger(s), 113, 118–20
structure(s), 89, 121; hierarchical, 121
struggle, 97–98, 107
subalterns, 155–56
subject, 48; modern, 51; revolutionary, 50; theological, 50
subjectivity, 40–42
sublimation, 128–29
suffering, 67–68, 113, 130, 139, 145, 158–60; of Isaiah, 158; of *maskilim*, 158; servant, 158–59
supremacy, white, 85, 89–90
survival, 54
suspicion, 37–38
synecdoche, 84
Syrians, 148
system(s), 47–55, 58, 85, 125; of domination, 68; immigration, 118; oppressive, 66–67; post-totalitarian, 50–54; unjust, 70

table: dinner, 104; of Lord, 104
Tamil Hindus, 77
tellings, oral, 98
temple, 136, 147, 150, 152–53, 157–58; Baalzeus, 148; heavenly, 153; holy environs of, 158; Jerusalem, 148, 158; plunder of, 150; sacred items of, 150, 152; of Solomon, 153
Terra Nullius, 21

terror, 69, 122, 150, 152, 158; religious, 145; state, 156
terrorism, 128
theologian(s), 3, 7–8, 43; American, male, 34; Catholic, 81; constructive, 18; female, 30; feminist, 26; German, 63; German Lutheran, 35; German male, 34; Jewish feminist, 29; Lutheran, 1–2, 4, 30; Lutheran female, 30; Lutheran feminist, 67; Lutheran Orthodox, 40–41; male, 30, 33; mujerista, 26; systematic, 30; womanist, 26
theology, 2, 32, 42, 102, 105, 132; apocalyptic, 157; christocentric, 132; constructive, 4; of the cross, 66, 70, 89, 107; Deuteronomistic, 155; as engaged practice, 4; of glory, 66, 89; of liberation, 16, 130; liberation-minded, 85; Lutheran, 75, 91–92; of markets, 48; Native, 101; natural, 65; of place, 102; postliberal, 34
theory: cultural, 81; post-colonial, 106
theosis, 59
thinking, 40; false, 39; magical, 88
time, 100
Torah, 82, 147
totalitarianism, 88, 90
trade, 21
tradition, 151–52, 155; ancient Jewish, 147; authoritative, 148; biblical prophetic, 43; church, 121; German Lutheran, 5; Lutheran, 1–2, 6, 34, 43, 64; Lutheran theological, 63; monological, 155; old, 157; Scandinavian Lutheran, 4–5, 7; scriptural, 148; spiritual, 106
transcendental, 35–36, 38; -ism, 157
transformation, 123, 140, 151, 159
trauma, 36, 43
treaties, 22
tribe, 102
trust, 14, 151
truth, 7–8, 11–19, 23–25, 32, 47, 51, 54–55, 70, 88, 90, 131, 137;

anti-realist, 34; biblical, 137; of Christ, 71; as coherence, 34; embodied, 26; empirical, 89; factual, 88; oracular, 88; to power, 13, 23–24, 144–45, 159; prophetic, 85
Turks, 84. *See also* Muslims
two kingdoms doctrine, 63
tyranny, 81, 88, 130
tyrant, 84

union, with Christ, 78
unitive (mystical), 145, 151, 158
unity, 83, 87, 107; Christian, 129; ecclesial, 82–84; in Christ, 87; with light, 158
universal, 99
universe: moral, 89, 99; spiritual, 102
universities, 30, 105

value(s), 14, 38–39, 85, 133
veterans, Native, 91
victim, 49, 54
Vietnamese, 119
violation, 87
violence, 55, 68, 115, 118, 125, 146–47, 151; moral, 58; racial, 70; sexual, 35
virtue, 101–2; civil, 101
vision, 84, 92, 154, 156, 158, 160; eschatological, 83, 92; of God, 157; of identity, 79; new, 86; proleptic, 75; of redemption, 78; sacramental, 79, 84–85
vocation, 43, 50, 55, 60 107, 129, 139; baptismal, 130
voice, 37, 155; prophetic, 66
voting, 80

war(s), 34, 115; American Civil, 127; civil, 150; Fifth Syrian, 147–48; holy, 144; Syrian, 146; U.S., 91; First World, 127; Second World, 127

way: good, 102; the, 66, 129–30, 136, 139; traditional, 102
wealth, 15–17
web, 98
well-being, 26, 139, 157
west, 57, 59
white, 65, 97
widow, 113
will, 43, 90; good, 104
wisdom, 158
witness, 14–15, 17, 67; false, 87–88; Lutheran, 97; Protestant Christian, 76
woke, 86
women, 29–30, 36–37, 39, 128, 134; immigrant, 114, 116–17; Native American, 91; pastors, 91; rape of, 147; transgressive, 37–38; white, 37, 114
Women's March, 71
word, 158; divine, 92; of God, 38, 56, 63, 85–86, 131, 138, 153; pastoral, 87; preached, 78; preaching of, 40; prophetic, 85, 87, 92; reconciling, 85; and sacrament(s), 76, 78, 81, 84, 86, 88, 91–92, 128
work(s), 32; good, 31, 114; of love, 32; righteousness, 68, 78, 80; spiritual, 128, 140
worker: domestic, 116; undocumented, 117
world, 8, 11, 44, 66, 119, 121, 133, 138, 160; beginning of, 98; come of age, 131; multipower, 57; violent, 112
worldview, 11, 34, 66, 81, 117, 119, 157; apocalyptic, 133; dualist, 80, 132; self-righteous, 86; totalitarian, 89
worship, 106, 114, 129, 131
writing, 148, 151

xenophobia, 14, 112, 116, 121–25

About the Editor and Contributors

Christine Helmer is the Peter B. Ritzma Chair of Humanities and Professor of German and Religious Studies at Northwestern University, Evanston, Illinois. She is the recipient of an honorary doctorate in theology from the University of Helsinki (2017). She is the author of numerous publications in the many areas of her theological interests, including biblical theology, German intellectual history, and philosophical theology, most recently in her edited volume *The Medieval Luther* (Mohr Siebeck, 2020). Helmer's most recent book, *How Luther Became the Reformer* (Westminster John Knox Press, 2019) was awarded a gold medal in theology in the Illuminations Book Awards 2020 Competition.

* * *

Amy Carr is Professor of Religious Studies in the Liberal Arts and Sciences department at Western Illinois University, Macomb, Illinois. She is the author of numerous essays and presentations on Lutheran theology, Simone Weil, and feminist theology, especially on trauma-related experiences of God. She is a lay leader at Trinity Lutheran Church of Macomb and has held leadership positions in the Midwest American Academy of Religion.

Jan-Olav Henriksen is Professor of Philosophy of Religion at MF Norwegian School of Theology, Religion and Society, Oslo. Henriksen has written numerous books, recently *Religion as Orientation and Transformation* (Mohr Siebeck, 2017); *Christianity as Distinct Practices—A Complicated Relationship* (Bloomsbury, 2019); and *Religious Pluralism* *and Pragmatist Theology* (Brill, 2019). He is especially interested in the interface of religion and culture/society, in the critique of religion, and in theological anthropology.

Allen G. Jorgenson is Professor of Systematic Theology and Assistant Dean at Martin Luther University College at Wilfrid Laurier University, Waterloo, Ontario, where he holds the William D. Huras Chair in Ecclesiology and Church History. In addition to his work on the thought of Martin Luther and Friedrich Schleiermacher, he has published in the areas of immigration and religion, especially as it relates to Indigenous peoples and settlers in North America. Jorgenson co-edited *Strangers in this World: Multireligious Reflections on Immigration* (Fortress Press, 2015) and co-translated (with Iain G. Nicol) a collection of sermons by Schleiermacher: *Jesus's Life in Dying: Friedrich Schleiermacher's Pre-Easter Reflections to the Community of the Redeemer* (Cascade, forthcoming). He is also author of *Indigenous and Christian Perspectives in Dialogue: Kairotic Place and Borders* (Lexington Books, forthcoming).

Paul R. Hinlicky is Tise Professor of Lutheran Studies at Roanoke College in Roanoke, Virginia, and a docent of the Protestant Theological Faculty of Comenius University in Bratislava, Slovakia. He is the author of numerous books in the areas of historical, doctrinal, systematic, and constructive theology, recently *Before Auschwitz: What Christian Theology Must Learn from the Rise of Nazism* (Cascade, 2013), which was also featured in a review on Syndicate Network in 2015 (https://syndicate.network/symposia/theology/before-auschwitz/); *Beloved Community: Critical Dogmatics After Christendom* (Eerdmans, 2015); *Divine Simplicity: Christ the Crisis of Metaphysics* (Baker Academic, 2016); *Luther versus Pope Leo* (Abingdon, 2017); *Between Humanist Philosophy and Apocalyptic Theology* (T&T Clark, 2018); *Luther for Evangelicals: A Reintroduction* (Baker Academic, 2018); *Lutheran Theology: A Critical Introduction* (Cascade, 2020); and *Joshua* in the Brazos Theological Commentaries on the Bible series (Brazos, 2021). In addition to other collaborative publications, Hinlicky is senior co-editor of the three-volume *Oxford Research Encyclopedia of Martin Luther* (Oxford University Press, 2017).

Craig L. Nessan is Professor of Contextual Theology and Ethics and Academic Dean at Wartburg Theological Seminary, in Dubuque, Iowa, where he holds the William D. Streng Professor for the Education and Renewal of the Church. He has published extensively in the areas of contextual theology, pastoral theology, and theological ethics and collaboratively, most recently *Liberating Lutheran Theology: Freedom for Justice and Solidarity in a*

Global Context (Fortress Press, 2011) with Paul Chung and Ulrich Duchrow. He is the author of *Shalom Church: The Body of Christ as Ministering Community* (Fortress Press, 2010); *Beyond Maintenance to Mission: A Theology of the Congregation* (rev. edn., Fortress Press, 2010); and a guide to Dietrich Bonhoeffer's *Life Together* titled "Intentionally Christian" which is intended for group study by pastors and deacons (www.wartburgseminary.edu/wp-content/uploads/2019/03/Bonhoeffer_Intentionally-Christian_Study-Guide.pdf).

Cheryl M. Peterson holds the Trinity Endowed Chair in Mission and Ministry at Trinity Lutheran Seminary at Capital University, in Columbus, Ohio, where she serves as Professor of Systematic Theology and Associate Dean for Academics. Peterson is the author of *Who is the Church? An Ecclesiology for the Twenty-First Century* (Fortress Press, 2013) and numerous articles and books chapters. Her current research focuses on the person and work of the Holy Spirit in dialogue with Wesleyan, Pentecostal, and charismatic theologies.

Timothy L. Seals has been a Lutheran (LCMS) pastor for thirty-six years. After ordination in 1984, he pastored Hope Memorial Lutheran Church in Los Angeles for ten years before becoming a campus pastor at the University Lutheran Chapel at UCLA, which he led for ten years. In 2003 he was installed as pastor of St. Luke Lutheran Church, Claremont, California, where he is presently active. He earned both an MA and a PhD from the Claremont School of Theology. He is currently completing a book on the Book of Daniel. His research interests are apocalypticism, mysticism, and postcolonial thought.

Gordon J. Straw was a member of the Brothertown Indian Nation, who brought this identity as a gift into every relationship and endeavor. He was a scholar of Native American thought with specialization in the work of Vine Deloria Jr. He was ordained on July 13, 1986 and served as a Lutheran pastor for thirty-two years. He is a graduate of Luther Seminary, Saint Paul, Minnesota. On May 20, 2018, he received an honorary degree of Doctor of Divinity from Wartburg Theological Seminary, Dubuque, Iowa. He engaged in multifaceted ministry within the ELCA, serving as interim minister for the Metropolitan Chicago Synod, Program Director for American Indian and Alaska Native Ministries, and Program Director for Lay Schools for Ministry and Missional Leadership. The Rev. Gordon J. Straw was called to his position as professor and Cornelsen Chair for Spiritual Formation and Coordinator for Candidacy at the Lutheran School of Theology at Chicago on July 1, 2017.

Man Hei Yip is Assistant Professor of Systematic Theology at Wartburg Theological Seminary in Dubuque, Iowa. Her appointments have included Visiting Researcher at Boston University School of Theology in connection with the Center for Global Christianity and Mission, and work for the offices of the Lutheran World Federation (LWF) in Geneva, Switzerland, and Phnom Penh, Cambodia. She is a contributor to *Global Lutheranism: Vitality and Challenges* (Lutheran University Press, 2018) and *Luther's Small Catechism: An Exposition of the Christian Faith in Asian Contexts and Cultures* (Christian World Imprints, 2019).

www.ingramcontent.com/pod-product-compliance
Lightning Source LLC
Chambersburg PA
CBHW050906300426
44111CB00010B/1403